FIRST CANADIAN ARMY
NORTH-WEST EUROPE
1944-1945

LIBERATION
The Canadians in Europe

BILL McANDREW
BILL RAWLING
MICHAEL WHITBY

LIBERATION
The Canadians in Europe

ART GLOBAL

Canadian Cataloguing in Publication Data

McAndrew, Bill, 1934-

    Liberation: The Canadians in Europe
    Issued also in French under title: La Libération.
    Includes bibliographical references.
    ISBN 2-920718-59-2

1. World War, 1939-1945 - Canada.
2. Canada. Canadian Armed Forces - History - World War, 1939-1945.
I. Rawling, Bill, 1959-. II. Whitby, Michael J. (Michael Jeffrey), 1954-. III. Title.

D768.15.M32 1995   940.53'71   C-95-900098-4

Project coordinator: Serge Bernier

Publisher: Ara Kermoyan

Editing: Jane Broderick

Photographs of war art for Canadian War Museum by William Kent

Jacket illustration by Stéphane Geoffrion
inspired by Alex Colville's painting
Infantry near Nijmegen, Holland

Printed and bound in Canada

Cet ouvrage a été publié simultanément en français sous le titre de:
La Libération. Les Canadiens en Europe
ISBN 2-920718-58-4

Published by Éditions Art Global Inc.
384 Laurier Avenue West
Montreal, Quebec
Canada H2V 2K7
in cooperation with the Department of National Defence
and under licence from the
Canada Communication Group - Publishing, Supply and Services Canada.

ISBN (Art Global) 2-920718-59-2

TABLE OF CONTENTS

ACKNOWLEDGEMENTS

The publication of Liberation: The Canadians in Europe *would not be possible without the continuing support of the Minister of National Defence, the Deputy Minister, and the Chief of the Defence Staff. It differs from the others in the series of commemorative books* — Canada and the Battle of Vimy Ridge, Dieppe, Dieppe, *and* Normandy 1944: The Canadian Summer — *because of the broader scope and scale of its coverage, from the end of the battle for Normandy to the last days of the war in Europe eight months later. In such a span of time, involving so many Canadians, it was impracticable to include as many details of individual actions and unit operations as the authors would have liked. Limited space dictates cruel selectivity, and we are very conscious of what we have left out. We have tried to identify events that might be typical, or illustrative, or that have not been documented elsewhere, and regret that so many stories which deserve telling are not here. We ask veterans, particularly, for their forbearance. Wherever practicable, excerpts from first-hand accounts are distinguished by italic type.*

The authors would like to acknowledge the generous assistance given them, directly and indirectly, by many individuals. They include David O'Keefe and the family of Private R. E. Bradley; Brigadier General S.V. Radley-Walters; Lieutenant Colonels J.C. Stewart and L.R. Fulton; and David Bryce Wilson, Ab Saunders, and Gordon Olmstead. We would like to thank Victor Suthern, Laura Brandon, and Bill Kent of the Canadian War Museum, and Serge Bernier, Roger Sarty, and our colleagues at the Directorate of History. Lieutenant Commander Doug McLean graciously shared his extensive knowledge of the inshore naval campaign, and Pieter de Houck his intimate association with wartime in the Scheldt. We are grateful for all their many kindnesses and, of course, absolve them from any errors, which remain our prerogative.

ABOUT THE AUTHORS

Dr. Bill McAndrew is an infantryman turned historian whose books include *Battle Exhaustion: Soldiers and Psychiatrists in the Canadian Army, 1939-1945* (with Terry Copp) and *Normandy 1944: The Canadian Summer* (with Donald Graves and Michael Whitby).

Dr. Bill Rawling, a graduate of the University of Toronto, is the author of *Surviving Trench Warfare: Technology and the Canadian Corps, 1914-1918.* He is currently preparing a history of field engineers from ancient times to the present.

Michael Whitby, a naval historian, is co-author of *Normandy 1944: The Canadian Summer.* He has published widely in naval journals on twentieth-century sea warfare.

PREFACE

We are pleased to introduce Liberation: The Canadians in Europe, *the latest in a series of books produced by the Department of National Defence to commemorate Canada's military heritage.*

In a rapidly changing society like Canada's, it is difficult for most people to conceive of the scale of this country's commitment to the liberation of Europe during the Second World War. More than a million men and women of a population of scarcely 11 million wore uniforms, and others served in the Merchant Marine and in support services. Recruiting, organizing, and training the Royal Canadian Navy, the Canadian Army, and the Royal Canadian Air Force to fight a modern war was a remarkable undertaking. As late as 1938, militiamen were still in the habit of riding their own horses to cavalry camps; yet just six years later they were acquitting themselves admirably against one of the most proficient professional armies in the world, while airmen had moved from open cockpits to Typhoons and sailors from coastal patrols to the high seas. It was an extraordinary transformation, and these Canadians, from all regions and all walks of life, who were barely out of the Great Depression, helped significantly to free Europe.

It is ironic that the story of the part played by Canadian soldiers, sailors, and airmen in the liberation of France, Belgium, and Holland is better known there than in Canada itself. As any visitor soon learns, a great many Europeans freely express their sincere gratitude for the sacrifices that young Canadians made to free their villages, cities, and countries from the tyranny of occupation. Their schools keep the memory alive, and those Canadians fortunate enough to see the care with which they tend Canadian graves in the many cemeteries that dot the landscape experience a moving legacy that demands preservation.

We are glad to make this record of the achievements of those Canadians available to the general public on the 50th anniversary of the ending of the Second World War. It was the sacrifices of their generation that made possible the emergence of modern Canada — both the development of its civil society and its constructive international role in the United Nations. The thread connecting Vimy Ridge, Normandy, the Scheldt, the Rhineland, and Arctic convoys with Bosnia and Rwanda is unbroken.

Jean Chrétien
Prime Minister

David Collenette
Minister of National Defence

(PA 173416)

CHAPTER I

PURSUIT

It's really quite the thing to go through these towns; we are always the first troops in the town, and the French people go mad with joy when they see us. No sooner do we enter a town, than every house has flags of the Allies and France, and they just plaster the tanks with flowers. I had quite an experience of my own a few days ago. We had been travelling all day and about 8 o'clock we stopped just outside of a town by the name of Béthoncourt-sur-Mer. We were to stop for the night, but we had to find out if there were any enemy there or not. So our platoon officer, sergeant, and myself were told to take a jeep and to recce the town; we put a machine gun on the front of the jeep and I got the radio set. The idea was to go like the devil right to the centre of town and if nobody fired on us, OK, but if we were fired on to come back. We set off across the open field on to the road and right in to town without no trouble. We stopped at the town centre, got out and did not see a soul; we did not know what to do; we could not go back with a report like that, and yet there was not enough of us to look through

all the houses. I then remembered the old Canadian hockey team's song, so I roared as loud as I could "Les Canadiens sont là." Well, it worked swell; in five minutes the streets were jammed tight with French people. All I did for the next hour was kiss beautiful girls and drink wine.[1]

Once the cork popped from the bitter bottle that was the Falaise Gap, in late August 1944, the campaign in northwest Europe changed irrevocably.

Throughout the summer, following the massive assault landing on 6 June, Canadians, Britons, and Americans fought grimly to break out of their confined bridgehead against an enemy determined to drive them back into the English Channel. Early in August the Germans mounted a fatal offensive to split the Allied lodgement, but the Americans strung a noose around them by sending tanks and infantry in a wide sweep towards the Loire and the Seine.

---

[1] D Hist, Private R.E.C. Bradley to his mother, 6 September 1944.

The Canadians and British then attacked south from Caen to meet the Americans and trap the Germans in the Falaise Gap. While fighter-bombers attacked relentlessly from the air, the Allied breakout was transformed into a spectacular pursuit. Even before the trap was sealed, General Omar Bradley's tanks and infantry had reached Orléans, Chartres, and Dreux, and on 25 August General Leclerc's 2nd French Armoured Division entered Paris. Others swept up the Seine towards Rouen to meet the lead units of General H.D.G. Crerar's First Canadian Army.

Athough decisively beaten in Normandy, the Germans had exacted a severe price. The three Allied Armies together suffered more than 200,000 casualties, and the vicious holding attacks that Canadians conducted around Caen ensured that their costs were cruelly high. Normandy repeatedly demonstrated how a well trained and finely tuned unit could be shattered within minutes by a few shrewdly placed enemy machine guns or mortars. Infantry battalions lost more than half their original riflemen, and at least that many non-commissioned officers and platoon and company commanders. In the first week after the invasion alone, the assault units of 3rd Division and 2nd Armoured Brigade had taken almost 3000 casualties, one third of them killed, and 2nd Infantry and 4th Armoured divisions had comparable losses in July and August. By early autumn, 3rd Canadian Infantry Division had the highest casualty rate of any in General Bernard Montgomery's 21st Army Group, and 2nd Division was just behind.

In all, 18,444 Canadians were killed or wounded, most of them riflemen in the small fighting point of the army. Through wounds or unsuitability, two of three divisions had new commanders, as had most brigades, while almost all infantry and tank units had had at least one new commanding officer, and some three or four. Several battalions reorganized themselves into three rather than four rifle companies, and 4th Division's armoured regiments were operating with just two under-strength squadrons. By the end of August, units badly needed time to integrate replacements into cohesive platoons, troops, and batteries before they had to fight again.

There was no time, however, for Canadians to mourn their dead or savour and reflect upon their victory. They had to switch roles immediately. Instead of grinding set-piece assaults for limited objectives, they now had to fight a highly mobile pursuit against what appeared to be a beaten enemy. Speed was the vital factor. General Montgomery, still the commander of the Allied armies, declared that they had to first,

> block the withdrawal of the enemy survivors across the Seine, and second, ... to drive quickly across the Pas de Calais to capture ports to facilitate our maintenance requirements, and the flying bomb sites in order to diminish the effect that the "V" weapons were having on the United Kingdom.[2]

Canadians were on the left flank of the charge through France. Next to them was General M.C. Dempsey's Second British Army, and on its right were General Courtney Hodges' First and General George Patton's Third United States armies, both in General Bradley's 12th Army Group. On the far right flank was General Alexander Patch's Seventh US Army, which had landed on the Mediterranean coast of France in mid-August and was moving up the Rhône River Valley.

The Canadians' immediate task was to clear any Germans remaining south of the Seine; its next was to cross that river, isolate the Le Havre peninsula, and push across northern France into Belgium. General Crerar directed I British Corps, on the Army's left flank, to clear the coastal sector. On its right, Lieutenant General G.G. Simonds drove the three divisions of his II Corps to the Seine on separate axes: Major General Charles Foulkes' 2nd Infantry on the left towards Bourgtheroulde and Rouen, Major General Daniel Spry's 3rd Infantry in the centre towards Elbeuf, and Major General Harry Foster's 4th Armoured on the right towards Pont de l'Arche.

Reconnaissance regiments were finally in their element to lead the breakout from Normandy. Squadrons of the 12th Manitoba Dragoons fanned out like probing fingers on a spread hand several kilometres in front of infantry and tanks,

---

[2] D Hist, CMHQ Report 183.

hunting out enemy rearguards, locating intact bridges or fords across rivers and streams, and gathering the vital information that commanders needed to deploy their units. It was a heady time. Troopers in the 7th and 8th Canadian Reconnaissance regiments exulted:

> This was reconnaissance as we had learned it in England...the Scout Troops pushing on, closely followed by the infantry, chasing a badly beaten and retreating enemy.[3]

Just beyond Bernay, early on 25 August, scout cars met Americans who had reached the Seine up-river and swept downstream along its left bank. After paying mutual respects, and sharing information about stray Germans in the area, one Dragoon squadron made for crossing sites at Elbeuf, and another to Louviers and Pont de l'Arche. While engineers moved their bridging equipment to the river, the scout platoon and D Company of the Lincoln and Welland Regiment scrounged boats near the village of Criquebeuf and paddled across the Seine to form a small bridgehead for the other battalions of 10 Brigade, the Algonquin Regiment, and the Argyll and Sutherland Highlanders of Canada. A few kilometres downstream, at Elbeuf, 7 Brigade's Regina Rifles and the Canadian Scottish crossed during the morning of the 27th, followed by the Royal Winnipeg Rifles. Sappers ferried tanks across that afternoon. By next morning they had completed two bridges over which poured the rest of 3rd and 4th divisions.

The experiences of units flowing along paths of least resistance in this fluid advance defy easy generalization. Those fortunate enough to have vehicles rode, others marched, with companies leap-frogging one another when they could find scarce transport. Supply trucks and reconnaissance parties of artillery regiments looking for suitable gun positions often found themselves liberating towns well in front of the advance. Unlucky groups met Germans who were attempting to slow the Canadian advance until they could escape across the Seine. One rearguard caught 4th Field Regiment in the open near Orbec, and other Germans bushwhacked nine British Columbia Regiment tanks (in 4 Armoured Brigade with the Governor General's Foot Guards and the Canadian Grenadier Guards). Prisoners streamed to the rear in the hundreds, many simply making their own way because few guards could be spared.

Private Charlie Bradley, who had joined the Highland Light Infantry as a replacement shortly after D-Day, wrote faithfully to his mother during the last months of the war. In one letter he described how, in freebooting fashion,

> Our unit took about 5000 prisoners; our platoon went into a town and took 864 in one haul, and there was another 600 wounded in the town, which we picked up later. All in all it was a pretty busy day. I got myself a gold wrist watch that would cost at least $150 back home; it's really a smart watch. I also got a revolver, a candid camera, a pen and pencil set, also gold. I also got French money worth about $700; the only trouble is that it can only be spent in France, and there is not a thing to buy here, and can't be sent out of the country, so it's not much use to me, but I think I done OK. I am going to try and send the watch and pen and pencil set home if I can; it's really expensive stuff. I don't doubt the German looted it in some country they've overrun. It might not sound right taking all that stuff, but that's what is called booty, and really is legal as long as it is taken off an enemy in uniform.[4]

Above them, squadrons of fighter-bombers wreaked havoc on retreating Germans. Royal Canadian Air Force fighter pilots in Nos 83 and 84 groups were among those who, in two days alone in late August, delivered a normal month's worth of bombs, rockets, and cannon shells. One of them, Flying Officer W. Warfield, a Spitfire pilot with 403 Squadron, kept a diary that preserves a rare picture of the episodic rhythm of an airman's day-to-day life in those hectic times.

> August 23rd. Found a Hun convoy near Bolbec (Rouen area) carrying guns and ammo. Left the whole thing a mass of flames and exploding ammo. What damn fools they can be at times — the superior race!
> August 24th. A recce but not eventful as it was raining like hell and a low cloud base.
> August 25th. Up at 5. A.M. for early readiness. Patrols all day long in

3   D Hist, unit reports.
4   D Hist, Bradley letters.

Lisieux-Bernay and Dreux areas, breaking in several new pilots that arrived....

August 26th. I was giving top cover to "A" Flight E. of Rouen when we ran into 20 Focke Wulf 190s. All the flight were very green and had never been in a scrap before but despite the fact that we were 2,000 feet below the Hun three of them at least had a shot at them though they didn't get any kills. Six of us against 20 odd!!!! I nearly got two of the bastards but they had the advantage of height on me and managed to run away home — yellow curs that won't fight! I finally got pretty mad at the whole bunch and got on the ass of one remaining one and rode him to the ground where I straddled him and forced him right into the ground at 400 m.p.h. where he exploded after ploughing up three fields! I didn't even fire a shot at the yellow guy — another destroyed that all he could think of was running!!! In the afternoon I covered Typhoons who rocketed a bridge across the Seine south of Rouen after beating up the flak positions. Bags of flak {information about} which I turned into ops and three hours later {it} was wiped out by the Royal Artillery advancing from Lisieux. Hard luck! ...

August 30th. Still raining so I took a small truck and four of the boys to Paris. What a reception. We were the second batch of pilots to go. Stayed at the Plaza Hotel and weren't charged a penny for a marvellous accommodation comparable to the Ritz in London!! Went to the most elite bars and cafés. The people clapped when we entered and the drinks were all on the house. In some ways it was a very embarrassing time especially when we went to see the Eiffel Tower where we were surrounded by 200-odd people who just wanted to shake hands.

August 31st. Returned and did two armed recces strafing Hun columns pulling out of the Amiens district.[5]

Warfield and his British, French, Dutch, Norwegian, Polish, Czech, Australian, and New Zealand mates in the Second Tactical Air Force left such devastation and *"debris that a bulldozer had to clear {it} before the column could pass."*

The treatment meted to the fleeing remnants was the work of the air force alone. Tightly packed columns of lorries, staff cars, tanks, guns and carts had been caught in the deadly rain of destruction that dropped from the skies... Engineers with rags tied around their faces struggled to drag the rotting horses out of the way. Bulldozers attacked the broken, battered, burnt-out rubble that once was the materiel of war, and cleared a narrow track through which the armour of 4th Division could pass. As the sun grew warm the smell of smouldering vehicles and decaying flesh, both horse and human, became unbearable.[6]

Another, more pleasant, factor that delayed them was the outpouring of heartfelt gratitude from villagers being freed from years of occupation, emotion that touched the most battle-hardened soldiers. The reactions of French citizens, many of whose families had been killed and whose homes had been destroyed by their liberators' awesome firepower, were as complex as the range of human emotions allows. John Morgan Gray, a Canadian intelligence officer, described in his memoir how he struck up a conversation with a couple while sitting in his jeep waiting to get through Rouen. They pointed out to him *"an elderly woman standing back and quite alone."*

Her lined face was heavy with sadness, and they told me that all her family had been killed when their house was destroyed by our bombs; she had no one left. When they moved on she looked across at me and, making the only gesture I could, I saluted her. After a little hesitation she came forward and stood beside the jeep, stroking my arm while I patted her hand. With her head covered by a black shawl she was the personification of a sorrowing world; and yet in her lined face there was both indestructible courage and peace. We had not spoken, when suddenly she burst out, "Contente, monsieur, je suis contente." I could not respond except to nod and go on with the patting of the old brown hand. The convoy began to move and she stood back. I threw her a kiss and, just before we moved out of sight, a wave. She raised her arm. For a precious moment we had shut out the war.[7]

Defeat in Normandy shattered German campaign plans. Initially confident that they

---

5   D Hist, Warfield biographical file.

6   D Hist, CMHQ Report 183.

7   J.M. Gray, *Fun Tomorrow* (Toronto: Macmillan, 1978), 286-287.

The many faces of liberation. A Perspective of Rouen Cathedral that Claude Monet did not paint... (PA 131346)

would readily defeat the Normandy invasion, and then be free to reinforce their increasingly beleaguered armies on the Eastern Front, they had instead lost almost half a million men while their Fifth Panzer and Seventh armies were being destroyed. They could spare little to face the overwhelming onslaught of the Red Army, and fresh divisions sent south of the Seine could only delay, not stop, the Allied advance. German commanders had planned to defend three river lines — the Dives, Touques, and Risle — but were continually outflanked before they could stabilize a front. As they withdrew to the Seine, the three divisions in the way of the Canadian advance were so badly hit that remnants were concentrated as one to guard their escape route over the Seine at Rouen. Command and control faltered badly, one German commander later reporting that the

> greatest difficulties grew from the fact that each corps and division was trying to operate only in its own interest at the ferry embarkation points. In fact, the SS divisions and I Panzer Corps had the few embarkation points well in hand, ruled them with brutal force, and would let no one else use them. Only by a comrade-like contact with the 2 SS Panzer Division commander could 116 Panzer Division secure crossings for its units. The troops, trying to go everywhere and defend only their own interests, met with little success because of the lack of roads and materiel. They stole boats and other equipment from each other.... Shootings, threats, and violent measures occurred. Corps and Army troops, and columns and trains of every kind both completely without command, were forced back, driven into inextricable confusion, and became victims of the continuous and heavy enemy air attacks.[8]

Still, as was its habit, the German Army managed to salvage something out of apparent disaster. On the immediate Canadian front it deployed two battle groups in the great bend of the Seine immediately south of Rouen, where the rugged terrain of the Forêt de la Londe is located. While many soldiers may have recalled their pursuit to the Seine fondly, the Forêt de la Londe reminded 2nd Division units too much of Verrières Ridge, near Caen. Their headquarters interpreted contradictory intelligence reports

about enemy defences in the most optimistic way. Expecting no opposition, therefore, infantrymen climbed into Royal Canadian Army Service Corps trucks for a welcome drive. While boarding the vehicles in Brionne in the early hours of 26 August, flares lit up the town for Luftwaffe bomb-aimers whose loads killed 15 Calgary Highlanders and wounded 72 more, along with several others in Le Régiment de Maisonneuve. The Black Watch replaced the mauled Calgarys and set out, once more in unprotected three-ton trucks, with a squadron of Sherbrooke Regiment tanks. When the leading troops reached Bourgtheroulde, a German rearguard sprung an ambush, and a confused mêlée ensued in the darkness. Caught in its midst were the RCASC drivers who were not customarily exposed to infantry fighting, but they pitched in to control vehicle movement, evacuate wounded, and help infantrymen clear Germans from the town.

Belying communiqués trumpeting a happy pursuit, this ugly encounter with a supposedly beaten enemy brought down a weight of continuous fire as bad as any that 2nd Division had taken before. It was just the beginning. Bourgtheroulde was to be the firm base from which 2nd Division advanced to the Seine at Rouen on either side of the deep pocket formed by the wide Seine loop. Along the base of the pocket, the rugged, forested terrain is cut by a valley through which ran a road and railway line. Two German battalions with tanks and antitank weapons occupied a formidable defensive position on the high ground north of the draw and watched the Canadians approach.

On the night of 26/27 August, 4 Brigade (the Royal Regiment of Canada, the Royal Hamilton Light Infantry, and the Essex Scottish Regiment) moved out of Bourgtheroulde on the right to the eastern base of the Seine loop, while 6 Brigade (Les Fusiliers Mont-Royal, the Queen's Own Cameron Highlanders of Canada, and the South Saskatchewan Regiment) advanced to Moulineaux and Grand-Couronne on the western flank. Again, both units drove in unprotected troop-carrying trucks presuming that the enemy had gone. After taking a wrong left turn as it

---

8   D Hist, German interrogation reports.

neared Elbeuf, the RHLI came under severe shelling, which forced them, and the Essex Scottish behind them, to pull back. The brigade commander then sent the Royal Regiment on a wide flanking march through the woods, but they too were pinned down among the trees. At the same time 6 Brigade was also brought up short in the woods at the western side of the pocket. When the commander of 6 Brigade, two of his battalion commanders, and several company commanders were killed or wounded, and communications broke down, control of the battle faltered.

The encounter in the Forêt de la Londe offers a classic example of how easy it was to get trapped, and how hard it was to get out when things turned bad. In retrospect, it is difficult to understand why senior commanders did not simply mask the Forêt loop — the Germans were hardly interested in breaking out in the opposite direction — and send 2nd Division across the Seine at Elbeuf and Pont de l'Arche. Over-optimism, and contradictory intelligence reports of German strength and intentions, played a part; the inability of commanders to regain control, and their unwillingness to modify an inappropriate plan, made it worse. Instead of responding flexibly to altered circumstances, 2nd Division lurched into a forest that the Germans, unexpectedly, had no immediate intention of leaving; this was their last position south of the Seine, and it protected the remaining ferries that were still transporting men and equipment to safety. Apparently some thought was given to bypassing the position after the initial clash, and sending 2nd Division across the river by way of 3rd Division's uncontested crossing points, but for reasons that were not recorded Generals Simonds and Foulkes decided to persist. On three successive days — the 27th, the 28th, and the 29th — understrength battalions were flung in succession against strong German defensive positions that they were unable to overwhelm, outflank, or avoid.

When they withdrew, none of the Royal Regiment's rifle companies had more than a platoon's worth of men, and they debated whether to retain four skeleton companies or to consolidate the survivors into one or two weak ones. The South Saskatchewan's diarist reported at the end that they had

reformed four rifle companies — 3 men in A Company, 21 in B Company, nine in C Company and 12 in D Company.[9]

In all, the division took 791 casualties in four days, for no gain. On the 29th, the Germans began withdrawing to their last ferry site, where they crossed the river and marched north, while 3rd Division patrols entered Rouen.

There is nothing pleasant to be said about the Forêt de la Londe débâcle. Soldier-poets often encapsulate irreverent truths better than most, and it was such encounters that inspired ditties like:

Let's throw in another battalion,
They cried with glee.
Let's throw in another battalion
Or maybe we'll throw two or three.
We've got the men, and we've got the time,
Another battalion won't cost a dime,
So throw in another battalion
Or maybe the old L.A.D.
[Light Aid Detachment]

* * *

After a short pause at the Seine until 3rd and 4th divisions secured the bridgehead, the pursuit resumed on the last day of August. General Crerar gave I British Corps the task of sealing the Le Havre peninsula and opening the city's port, while II Canadian Corps cleared the Channel coast to Holland. Second Division moved on the left towards Dieppe, 3rd Division in the centre towards Le Tréport and Boulogne, and 4th Armoured Division on the right to Buchy, where it was to rest and refit while 1st Polish Armoured Division took the lead. As units got under way there was unbounded optimism that the Germans were finished. Moving forward with his battalion, Private Bradley wrote his mother at the end of August:

The way the war is going these days, a fellow starts thinking of getting settled down when he gets back; ... well, I've been doing my share... if you've seen the new grants for returned soldiers, I think it's pretty good. I figure when I get my discharge I'll have about $1000 at the least,

---

9   Unit and personal war diaries cited in the text are in the National Archives of Canada, RG 24 series.

besides what I have in my pay book; I got $107 there now. So even when the war is over we'll still be here for awhile. If I'm here another year I'll have $450 and I won't need to draw any of that while I'm here. I don't know what I'll do as soon as I get home, but I'm not going to waste any time; I think I'll get a job right away, through the government if necessary, and go to night school at the expense of the government... I'll start off cleaning streets if I have to, but I'm going to work as soon as I get civilian clothes on.[10]

Post-war planning was still premature, for it was a long march to Berlin; and while German forces north of the Seine were reeling they were not beaten. Still deployed in the Pas-de-Calais, looking seaward for a phantom invasion that never came, Fifteenth Army had sent units to Normandy, but its divisions remained intact as organized formations, and those in the north and west had not been involved in the fighting. After leaving a garrison to defend Le Havre, General Gustav Von Zangen, the army commander, began a controlled withdrawal from the Seine to the Somme, where he planned to establish a new defensive line with the remnants of Seventh Army that had escaped from Normandy.

On 31 August, however, rapidly moving British tanks got to the Somme first near Amiens, where they captured General Heinrich Eberbach at the planned junction of his Seventh and Von Zangen's Fifteenth armies. Roaring through the Somme defences, the British continued right on to Brussels and Antwerp, leaving Von Zangen little choice but to continue withdrawing north along the coast to avoid being trapped. Autonomous garrisons remained isolated in Boulogne, Calais, and Dunkirk, but the bulk of Fifteenth Army marched back to Belgium on foot, at a rate of 25-50 kilometres a day, trying to avoid aircraft while fighting rearguard actions at river lines and other obstacles to delay the Allies' advance.

None of this was readily apparent to 2nd Division units as they set out on their long-anticipated liberation of Dieppe; *"a triumphal procession,"* the reconnaissance troopers called it. On the move at first light on the last day of August, squadrons advanced so quickly that they were soon out of radio range and fighting their own detached war against scattered German rearguards. At Totes, midway between Rouen and Dieppe, the leading troop ran into a retreating German vehicle convoy, which they promptly shot up, *"one car {driving} through the enemy while the crew threw grenades right and left."* As others came up to join in, *"it was a weird scene."*

The inhabitants of the town, undeterred by the fact that a battle was raging, were plying troops with champagne, vin rouge, vin blanc, etc. The battle was viewed by Major D. S. F. Bult-Francis, the squadron commander and his headquarters staff from the top story of the Cygne Hotel, famous historical inn, while M and Mme Richard, the kind-hearted propriétaires, kept a steady flow of champagne into glasses. Fortunately the troop leaders were too busy to avail themselves of this generosity and the battle progressed favourably.[11]

Squadrons harboured overnight at Totes before beginning a hectic race, next morning, to Dieppe. A Squadron won at 0930 on 1 September, and its leading troop commander, Lieutenant L.A. MacKenzie, described the drive.

We moved cautiously at first, noting the fact that the ground was fairly open with the odd copse here and there. There were also quite a number of houses along the roadside which might have afforded concealment for the enemy. At the town of Belmesnil two civvies climbed aboard the lead car, commanded by Corporal Samuels, waving home-made flags. One of them told us that he had just come from Dieppe and that the enemy had left. On hearing this we stepped on the accelerators and with the two civvies still aboard took off. The French civilians now began lining both sides of the road shouting, cheering, waving flags and throwing flowers as though they had gone wild. Any vehicle that halted was at once mobbed... As we came to the top of the big hill outside Dieppe we got our first view of the city and dipping down into the valley we came upon an anti-tank ditch which was dug across the road. The civilians

---

10 D Hist, Bradley letters.

11 D Hist, unit reports.

were already building a bridge with planks and the whole thing had been completed before the following troop reached the position. We rolled on and were the first troops to enter the city. Thousands of wildly cheering people climbed aboard the vehicles, covering the crews with flowers and plying them with liquor...
Meanwhile the FFI had been running around picking up collaborators. Rough treatment was meted out in many cases. The women's heads were shaved and then they were stripped and beaten in the main streets. This to the accompaniment of cheers and clapping of hands from the gathered populace. One male collaborator was dragged past us with his right eye hanging out and subsequently had his throat cut. However this was an exceptional case, for in the main, the cheering and unbounded joy was such as we have never seen, before or since.

Two days later, on 3 September, 2nd Division marked its return to Dieppe with a ceremonial march to commemorate the more than 3000 casualties it had suffered in the disastrous raid on the port city in August 1942.

As 2nd Division savoured Dieppe and absorbed badly needed reinforcements, 3rd Division moved around them to Boulogne, and 4th Armoured approached the Somme — while the local German commander *"personally listened to the B.B.C. broadcasts in order to advise his troops as to their next move."* General Simonds ordered the Poles to force a crossing of the Somme at Abbeville before the Germans had time to prepare its defences, and they then led the advance to Hesdin, St. Omer, Ypres, and Ghent. After their brief respite, having received a supply of 30 different map sheets *"that took the better part of the night to fold,"*[12] 4th Division moved out on the morning of 6 September to St. Omer, where units fanned out to the left of the Poles and drove towards Eecloo and Bruges. After Normandy it was an exhilarating experience to move through countryside untouched by battle. The Argyll and Sutherland's diarist described it:

The rival armies were passing through so rapidly that the even tenor of existence was hardly ruffled. The Germans had gone as they had arrived in 1940, swiftly and unexpectedly. In 1944 as four years before this part of

France, so cruelly ravaged in 1914-1918, practically escaped damage. It was by way of being a negative recompense for that earlier war...it was always onward, onward, past the little French towns, travelling by day and by night; signs reading "Abbeville 15 km," "St Omer 6 km," and then no longer the white French road signs but the blue of Belgium: "Bruges 10 km."[13]

Keeping tanks fuelled, weapons loaded, and men fed during the pursuit placed great demands on quartermasters, as supply points were also continually on the move. Fourth Division's chief administrative staff officer explained that

whenever the tanks begin shooting, my ammo trucks drop their loads and head to the rear for more supplies. If we have a breakout, then they drop their ammo and go back for petrol.[14]

The commander of the divisional Royal Canadian Army Service Corps supply columns, Lieutenant Colonel M.L. Brennan, told his corps historian that no matter how carefully laid, plans sometimes went awry. After moving several days, tank units were outdistancing their supply points, forcing truck drivers to make 400-kilometre round trips to keep them fuelled. Supplies of gas were sometimes down to a few litres, and everyone was exhausted. When Brennan reached his own headquarters one particularly tiring day, his Senior Supply Officer told him that the tanks were stopping and that, after the evening delivery, they would have a reserve of about 30,000 gallons (125,000 litres). Reassured, Brennan had just gone for a much-needed sleep when his adjutant came to tell him that a couple of Polish officers had arrived in a jeep and a van and needed gas. Brennan continued:

Well, I was very tired. I looked out the window at them and said to myself, "There are the vehicles they want petrol for," so I instructed the Adjutant to give them a chit to the Petrol Point, and to tell them to draw what they needed.

---

[12] G.L. Cassidy, *Warpath: The Story of the Algonquin Regiment, 1939-1945* (Toronto: Ryerson, 1948), 128.

[13] H.M. Jackson (ed.), *The Argyll and Sutherland Highlanders of Canada (Princess Louise's), 1928-1953* (Montreal: The Regiment, 1953), 107-108.

[14] Tony Foster, *Meeting of Generals* (Toronto: Methuen, 1986), 384.

I went to bed and I slept — oh, I guess I slept fifteen or sixteen hours. Next morning I got up feeling good. The sun was shining. I dressed, had a shave, went outside, and there stood my Senior Supply Officer. He was pretty nearly in tears. He said, "Do you know what happened, sir?" I said, "No, for Christ's sake, don't tell me something happened last night."

"It certainly did," he said. "Some stupid son-of-a-bitch in this Headquarters gave the Poles a chit to the Petrol Point and they refuelled the Armoured Brigade — 28,000 gallons."[15]

Improvisation overcame difficulties as they arose, for instance in carrying ammunition. The 65th Tank Transporter Company had 100 large, 40-ton Diamond-T tractor-trailers whose primary function was to move tanks in order to save wear on their treads. Someone got the idea to rig racks on their trailers to carry supplies, especially

heavy, low centre of gravity loads like ammunition. The trailer could take twenty tons, and by off-loading the ballast, the prime mover could carry another ten tons.

One company alone could carry 2700 tons of ammunition, the equivalent load of 10 transport companies. Overall, the head of the Army Supplies and Transport Branch had to deliver 7000 tons of commodities daily to Army Roadheads which replenished divisions. Once in Belgium, this meant columns of vehicles shuttling to and from Channel ports, or making a seven-day, 1600-kilometre round trip to Normandy. Routes were signed, and a system of radio-equipped checkpoints along them helped, but road maps were confusing at best, and light aircraft were used to intercept convoys when priorities changed unexpectedly.

The logistics network was the base of a broad Corps triangle, at the point of which were the reconnaissance scout cars. On the extreme left flank, when Manitoba Dragoon cars took fire from the outer defences of Dunkirk, they hooked inland to enter Belgium, the leading squadron heading for Ostend. Obtaining valuable assistance from the underground Belgian White Brigade, they secured the city, blocked off the roads south to Dunkirk, and drove north along the coast until coming under heavy fire near Zeebrugge. On the Corps right flank, the Poles were stopped on 9 September when they tried to force a crossing of the Ghent Canal west of that city. Next day they relieved British troops in Ghent and began to clear Germans from the sector of the ship canal that runs north to Terneuzen.

Alongside the Poles, 4th Division approached the southern outskirts of Bruges where, on 7 September, a member of the underground gave them information about a weak point in the German defences at Moerbrugge, on the Ghent Canal, a few kilometres east of the city. General Foster ordered 10 Brigade to cross the canal, and the Argylls moved that afternoon with tanks of the South Alberta Regiment. The Bruges sector was at the junction of the German 245th and 64th divisions, the former having bounced in front of the Canadians all the way from the Seine, its engineers and rearguards blowing bridges, setting demolitions, and causing delays all along the Canadian route. On the night of 5/6 September its units had marched back through Poperinghe to Ypres, and were continuing north to Bruges on the 7th when the divisional commander, Lieutenant General Erwin Sander, saw a task force of 15 tanks speed past him making for Ostend. He told his interrogators after the war:

Had that force turned east and discovered there was nothing protecting the right flank of 245 Division and that in fact the way was open to Breskens, the position would have looked gloomy indeed.[16]

In view of later developments, the implications of that near miss were monumental. That evening Sander deployed his division along the Ghent Canal to cover the continuing withdrawal and was in position to meet the Argylls.

David Marshall was a young trooper who had just joined the South Albertas (4th Division's Armoured Reconnaissance Regiment) as a replacement. He was made a gunner-operator in No 2 Troop of C Squadron, which was still commanded by Major David Currie, who was awaiting the Victoria Cross he had earned for his

---

[15] A. Warren, *Wait for the Waggon: The Story of the Royal Canadian Army Service Corps* (Toronto: McClelland and Stewart, 1961), 308-309.

[16] D Hist, German interrogation reports.

... a dispatch rider escorts prisoners with members of the underground, an old man sweeps his street, somebody is wearing a new pair of German boots... (PA11 5861)

... while others settle personal scores. (PA 190010)

gallantry in the Falaise Gap. Many years later Marshall described his experience:

We passed through Oostcamp and on to Moerbrugge, on the Ghent Canal, towards the bridge in the town. We moved along a street parallel to the canal and separated from it by a row of houses that provided us with some cover. The enemy were a few yards away on the other side of the canal listening to our progress. We found the bridge intact. The sergeant edged his tank, with me tucked inside, towards the bridge and out in the open away from the protection of the buildings while discussing the situation with Lt Roberts who was somewhat behind us and out of sight. Roberts gave his troop the order to cross and with our driver rapidly increasing speed we headed toward it and with only a few yards to go a deafening explosion hit us as the German engineers blew up the bridge. We were sitting out in the open with pieces of bridge falling all over when the enemy started firing with a barrage of anti-tank and small arms fire. The Argylls, who were walking beside us, ran for cover and we started backing up hoping that the tank behind us would get the same idea, no time for a fender-bender, and simultaneously we opened fire with our 75mm gun and our two machine guns.[17]

Temporarily stalled, the Argylls found two boats in the town, which a company manhandled to the canal and crossed in the late afternoon, followed soon after by the rest of the battalion. Opposition intensified and casualties increased as riflemen cleared streets in the town. The Lincoln and Wellands got over on the 9th, but counterattacks all day continually threatened their precarious hold. One rifle company was down to 46 men by the time sappers bridged the canal and South Alberta tanks got over. Meanwhile, fortunately for the city of Bruges and civilization generally, the city was spared. After blowing its bridges, the Germans withdrew to their next defensive position, on the Leopold Canal.

This vigorous German opposition gave fighting soldiers their first indication that the pursuit was over, and they could readily see that the terrain was admirably suited for defence. Circling the Breskens enclave were two concentric rings of permanent concrete and stone

canals, each as effective an obstacle as a steep-banked river. The outer ran from Zeebrugge on the coast to Bruges and Ghent. On the inner ring, about 12 kilometres north, the Leopold Canal connected the North Sea just above Zeebrugge with the West Scheldt near Terneuzen. Between the two, the Canal de Derivation de la Lys paralleled the Leopold for about 20 kilometres from Zeebrugge before turning south just above the village of Maldegem to cross the Ghent Canal 15 kilometres west of Ghent. These water barriers, along with others between Ghent and Antwerp, formed an interconnected antitank ditch. General Von Zangen used the outer ring as a covering position to shield his withdrawal; when Ghent and Bruges fell, he withdrew to his main defensive line on the inner ring of the Leopold Canal.

The Algonquins had hardly an inkling of German intentions when they entered the Argylls' bridgehead and moved northeast to the town of Sysseele, where they paused to scout the five-kilometre route to Moerkerke on the Leopold. Intelligence reports that the Germans were not interested in defending the Canal led the Algonquins to expect nothing more than token resistance as they prepared to win a bridgehead on the night of the 13th. Ominously, the unit historian remarked,

Promised reinforcements arrived late, and it was barely possible to take down their names, assign them to companies, give them the briefest of briefings, and show them what an assault boat looked like, and then it was time to move off.

A last-minute change of plan delayed the companies, causing them to lose their supporting artillery fire, and the Germans soon began their own shelling and mortaring. At the crossing the men had to paddle across the Lys Canal, manhandle the boats across an intervening dyke, launch them again in the Leopold Canal, paddle across it, then fight for their objectives. Extraordinarily, most made it and the enemy fire slackened.

The silence was deceptive. General Sander, whose division had withdrawn to the Leopold from Moerbrugge, recorded that the Algonquin intrusion caused him the gravest concern. If exploited, the attack would threaten the

---

[17] D Hist, D. Marshall, "Me and George."

24

open German withdrawal route through Breskens, and Sander was told to drive the Canadians back at all costs. By that time the Algonquins were short of ammunition, and they had no communications still working except their artillery observer's radio, so at noon General Foster ordered all available guns to cover the battalion's withdrawal. One battery command post was startled to receive the unusual order to *"fire until ammunition is expended,"*[18] but the gunfire isolated the bridgehead and allowed the troops to evacuate their wounded and paddle or swim back. Sander was at first alarmed by the heavy concentration of artillery fire, the worst he had encountered, and feared that it signalled another, stronger attack. He was pleasantly surprised to realize that the artillery was shielding the Canadian withdrawal. Soon after, he turned the defence of the Leopold over to others and continued his withdrawal to Breskens, across the Scheldt, and along the Beveland Peninsula to the mainland north of Antwerp.

* * *

Just before the Canadians and Poles reached Bruges and Ghent, a young Dutch boy living a few kilometres away in Oostburg, in the centre of the Breskens enclave, watched Sander's troops march through.

On Monday 4 September, the first day after the summer-holidays, the headmaster suddenly sent us home. He warned us that the Germans were stealing bikes everywhere. On the way home we heard that the English had liberated Antwerp. The next day, later called "Mad Tuesday," people thought Holland was on the threshold of liberty. Nobody went to work, the Allied forces might arrive any moment. The Germans were retreating everywhere. They blew up their cars and trucks with hand grenades and left also behind soldier's kits, canned foods, bottles of French wine and radio sets. After a few days that picture changed. Anti-aircraft guns were placed in and around the village and units marched in again in a well-disciplined way under the command of officers and NCOs on their way to the harbour of Breskens. For days on end soldiers of the 15th German Army passed through the village streets and we, young and old, watched them. They looked very tired, they

had marched hundreds of kilometres from the Pas de Calais, constantly attacked in France and Belgium by fighter-bombers. In single file, close to the houses, always on the alert for the enemy in the sky, they went on to the Scheldt. On the other side of the river was the main escape route to the "Heimat." Before 1944 was over many soldiers of the 15th German Army were to kill or be killed elsewhere.[19]

Pieter de Houck could not have been aware of it at the time, but he was observing the tangible results of another, most remarkable change in the campaign. Apparently abjectly defeated, the Germans were recovering. Instead of ending quickly in 1944, the war dragged on for another eight months, claiming countless lives. Like most great events that combine tragedy and farce, this story of missed opportunity still engages biographers and historians, and although the controversy has stacked enough shelves to fill a good-sized library, a brief summary can place Canadian operations in context.

The spectacular breakout from Normandy had revealed Allied operational possibilities that were comparable to the German blitzkrieg that swept through France in the other direction in 1940. Commanders were confident that they could end the war quickly; how could it be otherwise? After crashing through France the British 11th Armoured Division reached a tumultuous Brussels on 3 September, and next day an equally ecstatic Antwerp. Near Mons, Major General J. Lawton Collins' VII US Corps ambushed a large number of retreating Germans and took more than 25,000 prisoners, and a week later his lead divisions were on the German border not far from Aachen. South of the Ardennes, General Patton's Third Army crossed the Meuse River and linked up with US Seventh Army near Nancy. In days, the Allied armies had strung a line around Western Europe like a tightly drawn bow: north along the Channel coast from Le Havre to Ostend; east from Bruges to Aachen; south along the Siegfried Line by way of the Ardennes and the Saar to the Swiss border. It seemed that it remained only to fix an arrow, or

[18] R.A. Spencer, *History of the Fifteenth Field Regiment* (Amsterdam: The Regiment, 1945), 154-155.

[19] Personal, Pieter de Houck letters.

25

arrows, to the bow to finish the war in a few weeks.

Tragically, however, at this key point in the campaign senior Allied commanders could not agree on where to aim the killing bolt. The very success of the rapid advance across France in the first week of September had jarred the premises on which the Allies had planned their campaign. Well before the invasion of Normandy, SHAEF (Supreme Headquarters Allied Expeditionary Forces) planners had selected the German industrial heartland, the Ruhr and the Saar, as their principal objectives, with Berlin to follow. They marked the passage to Germany in several discrete phases: the assault landings, the bridgehead battle, a regrouping before breaking out, an advance on a broad front to the German border by about D+360, another regrouping to draw in a massive logistics tail, and then the final battle in Germany at an undetermined time. Apprehensive that the Germans would be able to block a restricted single thrust to the Ruhr, planners proposed advancing on two axes within a broad front, one on either side of the Ardennes. The sea would protect the left flank, and Seventh Army's advance up the Rhône to Alsace covered the right.

After the war, the British Chief Planner at SHAEF, Major General Kenneth McLean, spoke to Professor Forrest Pogue, who was researching the story of General Eisenhower's command in Europe:

In April we had worked up a paper on the advance into Germany. Gave it to Ike in April or May. I outlined it to Ike. We said there were four routes — Aachen, Verdun (Moselle Valley, Mainz or Frankfurt), Mulhouse, Ardennes. Mulhouse ruled out. Then Moselle out. Then Ardennes out, although it was recognized as good enough for Germans to come through. Decided we must go north or by Frankfurt. Argued for considerable time. Decided on northern advance. Shortest LOC {lines of communication}; quickest to Ruhr. Might swing around Aachen. Siegfried Line {West Wall} more of a bogey then than later. The southern route was longer; LOC more difficult. We considered doing the advance on both sides of Ardennes. Thought it might divide forces too much. Yet we needed surprise, so we said let's go on both routes. Main route to north;
southern route in nature of bluff. Keep enemy there. If we couldn't advance in north, switch to south. No doubt about the southern route. I presented this to Ike and he accepted it. Favorably impressed. The plan did not come from 21 Army Group. Ike discussed it with Monty who agreed.[20]

From this early draft the matured appreciation that guided the campaign plan reasoned that:

Our main chance of success would appear to lie in advancing astride the Ardennes with two mutually supporting forces, extending the enemy forces and, by surprise and deception, achieving superiority of forces in one or the other of the groups and defeating the enemy in detail. Such a course of action would enable us to exploit the flexibility of our superior air power by concentrating air support in one sector or another in accordance with need.[21]

When the breakout placed the Allies on the German border nine months earlier than had been foreseen, it seemed that earlier planning assumptions had been overtaken by events. The primary operational need was to identify the vital objective that would paralyze Germany's capacity and will to fight, and then follow the most direct path to it.

This was not as straightforward as it may seem: the primary objective might be the German army itself, or a key command and control headquarters, or significant industrial regions like the Ruhr and the Saar, or Berlin. Destroying or neutralizing any one of them might turn the key of early victory. While acknowledging that the Ruhr and the Saar fuelled Germany's military capability, General Eisenhower emphasized that destroying the German Army remained his primary aim, and it was thus essential to keep it from establishing new defences on interior lines along the Rhine. If prevented from linking up, the separate German withdrawing armies could be defeated in turn. Junctions between them — Antwerp, Aachen, and Trier — were particularly vulnerable. SHAEF planners had identified

---

[20] United States Military History Institute, Carlisle Barracks, Pennsylvania.

[21] Quoted in Carlo D'Este, *Decision in Normandy* (London: Collins, 1983), 464.

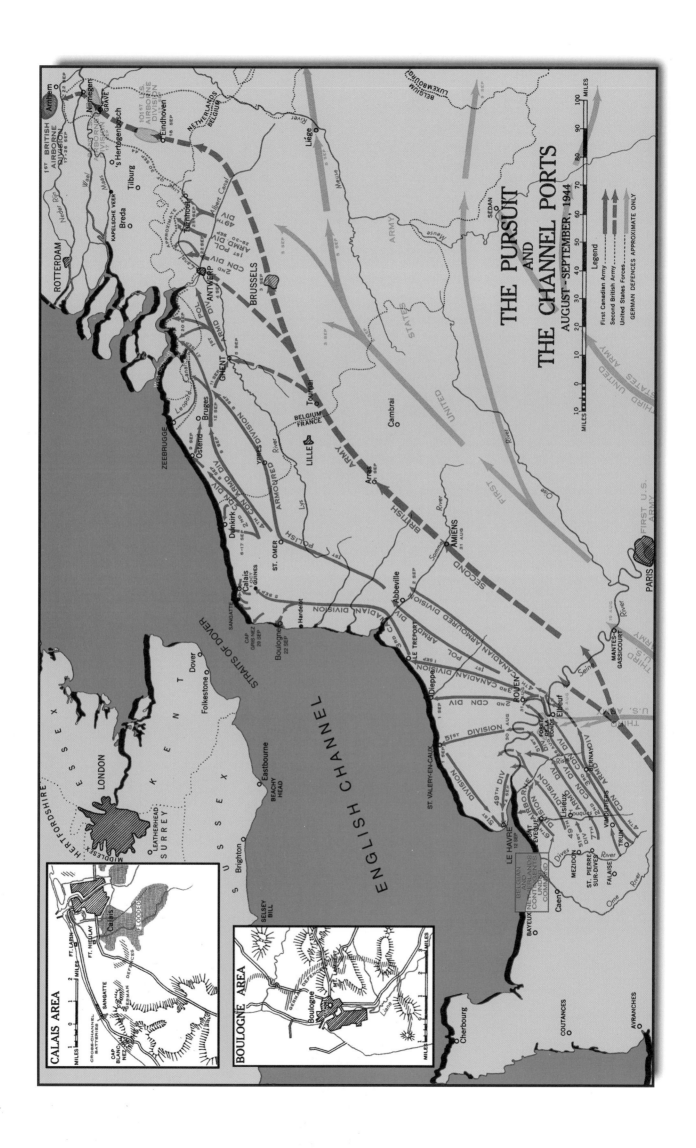

THE PURSUIT
AND
THE CHANNEL PORTS
AUGUST–SEPTEMBER, 1944

Legend

First Canadian Army
Second British Army
United States Forces
GERMAN DEFENCES APPROXIMATE ONLY

MILES

ENGLISH CHANNEL

STRAITS OF DOVER

LONDON

HERTFORDSHIRE
ESSEX
MIDDLESEX
SURREY
LEATHERHEAD
KENT
SUSSEX
Dover
Folkestone
Eastbourne
BEACHY HEAD
Brighton
SELSEY BILL

CALAIS AREA

CROSS-CHANNEL BATTERIES
CAP BLANC NEZ
SANGATTE
FT. LAPIN
Calais
FLOODED
GERMAN DEFENCES
FT. NIEULAY
MILES

BOULOGNE AREA

MT. LAMBERT
Boulogne
GERMAN DEFENCES
MILES

ROTTERDAM
Nijmegen
Arnhem
1ST BRITISH AIRBORNE DIVISION
17-26 SEP
GRAVE
's Hertogenbosch
Tilburg
Breda
KAPELSCHE VEER
Eindhoven
101ST U.S. AIRBORNE DIVISION
NETHERLANDS
BELGIUM
Liège
ANTWERP
BRUSSELS
GHENT
Tournai
LILLE
BELGIUM
FRANCE
Cambrai
SEDAN
LUXEMBOURG
BELGIUM
Meuse River

ZEEBRUGGE
Ostend
Bruges
Dunkirk
ST. OMER
GUINES
Calais
CAP GRIS NEZ
Boulogne
Hardelot
Arras
Amiens
Abbeville
Le Tréport
Dieppe
ST. VALERY-EN-CAUX
Le Havre
PONT L'EVEQUE
Lisieux
ROUEN
Elbeuf
MANTES
GASSICOURT
PARIS
FIRST U.S. ARMY
THIRD U.S. ARMY

49TH DIV
51ST DIVISION
2ND CDN DIV
3RD CDN DIV
VIMOUTIERS
TRUN
FALAISE
ST. PIERRE SUR-DIVES
MEZIDON
BERNAY
Caen
BAYEUX
Coutances
Cherbourg
AVRANCHES

BELGIAN AND NETHERLANDS UNITS UNDER COMMAND

UNITED STATES ARMY
FIRST ARMY
BRITISH SECOND ARMY

Seine River
Somme River
Oise River
Meuse River

Aachen and Trier as main gates to Germany. Antwerp, one of Europe's largest ports, was the logistical base needed to sustain any major operation to reach them. The SHAEF concept of operations, which, it must be stressed, was the blueprint for all the complex logistical planning required to move a massive mechanized army across vast distances, designated the primary thrust from Normandy along the Amiens-Maubeuge-Liège-Aachen-Ruhr route, with a secondary thrust to Frankfurt through Verdun, Metz, and the Saar. General Montgomery's 21st Army Group had the northern axis and General Bradley's 12th Army Group the southern. The concept, in other words, entailed a systematic advance on two strong axes to press the Germans back to the Rhine, where both thrusts would pause to regroup before crossing.

As the breakout began to take shape in mid-August, questions were naturally raised about whether the original planning assumptions remained relevant. At that time, General Montgomery, who was shortly due to relinquish his position as Allied ground force commander to General Eisenhower, proposed to General Bradley that their two army groups mount a single, powerful thrust to the Ruhr. Side by side, he urged, they could drive through France and Belgium to secure the Channel ports, open up Antwerp's facilities, gain forward airfields, and overrun V-bomb sites. Then they would cross the Rhine to gain the good tank country of the northern German plains, isolate the Ruhr, and possibly even reach Berlin. He emphasized that, in order to supply their combined 40 divisions on the northern route, they would have to halt any major move along the southern axis.

Assuming from Bradley's lack of open objections that he concurred, and that he would be left in overall command, Montgomery took his single-arrow proposal to Eisenhower the following week. Eisenhower's biographer possibly had this meeting in mind when he wrote that "Montgomery tended to hear what he wanted to hear, read what he wanted to read; Eisenhower tended to seek out words and phrases that would appease. There was, consequently, a consistent misunderstanding between the two men."[22] While the nuances of their discussion will never

be fully recaptured, it is apparent that these were sufficiently ambiguous to mask serious differences between Montgomery and Eisenhower, and their differing command and personal styles produced a monumental miscommunication. Montgomery assumed that he had at least tacit approval to proceed along his narrow front, while Eisenhower assumed that his British commander would abide by the previously agreed broad-front SHAEF campaign plan.

As Eisenhower's immediate objective was to open the port of Antwerp, he gave 21st Army Group priority, but not exclusive claim to scarce supplies. Eisenhower also went part way to meet Montgomery's other demands but, declining to abdicate his overall responsibility, made clear that he would assume direct command of the campaign as scheduled on 1 September. That was the very day, it may be observed, that Montgomery was promoted to the rank of Field Marshal. Refusing to subordinate General Bradley's 12th Army Group entirely to the Field Marshal, Eisenhower agreed that Montgomery could coordinate operational movements between his own Army Group and General Hodges' First Army, but he also authorized Bradley to keep Patton's Third Army moving towards the Saar. Several factors underlay Eisenhower's decision to stick to his campaign plan, one being the unanimous advice of his British-American staff. Major General Kenneth Strong, SHAEF's intelligence chief, has written that the senior staff

> strongly opposed this {the narrow front}. The final meeting on the matter took place in Bedell Smith's {Eisenhower's Chief of Staff} caravan. Present were the senior American and British staff officers of Supreme Headquarters in almost equal numbers, perhaps ten of us all told. Each was closely questioned by Bedell Smith in order that he might be able to present a considered staff opinion to General Eisenhower.[23]

Supply was the main concern, and if the campaign plan was possibly predicated on "the

---

[22] Stephen Ambrose, "Eisenhower's Generalship," *Parameters* (June 1990).

[23] K. Strong, *Intelligence at the Top* (London: Cassell, 1968), 146-147.

tyranny of logistics," it was understandable; more than two million soldiers had to be fed and clothed, their weapons ammunitioned, their vehicles fuelled, their airfields built, and their aircraft serviced. Tactical phase lines and movement schedules were inseparably correlated, if not governed, by logistics. One of the major considerations that had landed the Allies in Normandy rather than the Pas-de-Calais was that they had had no need to seize a working port immediately, because they brought their own prefabricated floating harbours with them. However, Mulberries and over-the-beach unloading had to be supplemented eventually by ports that could accommodate the vast amounts of supplies and reinforcements that poured into France. Cherbourg and Marseilles, as well as the smaller Channel ports — Le Havre, Dieppe, Boulogne, and Calais — could fill some needs, but by far the best was Antwerp. Besides its 50 kilometres of docks that annually handled more than a thousand vessels, it had hundreds of cranes, warehouses, fuel storage tanks, and railway facilities that could hold and distribute the materiel the Allies would need to advance deep into Germany.

Antwerp remained paramount in the minds of SHAEF planners, and Montgomery's plan to head straight for the Rhine and Germany concerned them. Recent studies have suggested that Montgomery may have been able to push his 40 divisions across the Rhine, if all others had been stopped and their supply systems cannibalized to support him — but barely, and with precious little room for the unanticipated difficulties that the Germans were wont to produce. Extending the metaphor, there were serious doubts that Montgomery's single arrow could be driven with sufficient killing force.

Another inescapable reality was that Eisenhower was managing an unbalanced coalition. Although the British Commonwealth had borne the war much longer than the Americans, by 1944 there was no question about which was the dominant partner. The ratio of American to British and Canadian troops was three to one and growing. Under these circumstances it was inconceivable that a British commander, no matter how competent, would be given the dominant role in the campaign at the expense of Americans with equally credible professional views about how to win the war quickly. Neither Eisenhower's superiors nor American public opinion, especially with congressional elections looming, would have accepted it.

Montgomery's narrow-front proposal also raised, inevitably, the character of his generalship, a topic about which, it seems, it is almost impossible to be dispassionate. In his felicitous essays on President Roosevelt's military commanders, Eric Larrabee perhaps came closest to putting interpretative differences about Montgomery in perspective:

> For an American to write about the military Montgomery is an awkward exercise, since there is a wrenching disproportion between the legend and the reality as Americans perceive it.... British discussion of his leadership accordingly tends to begin with an assumption of his "greatness" and go on to admit certain deplorable faults, while the American begins with an assumption of unproven merit and goes on to admit certain strengths.[24]

While Montgomery was arguably the outstanding British commander of the Second World War — his superior, Lord Alanbrooke, thought him the best tactical commander since Wellington — there is no gainsaying the corrosive legacy of his command presence in Normandy. Montgomery's conduct of the lodgement battle raised doubts about his competence not only among Americans but also among many senior British officers in SHAEF Headquarters as well as most air commanders. His reputation had been established by masterfully staging set-piece, or deliberate, attacks, with El Alamein as the epitome. Although the British breakout from Normandy was every bit as spectacular as General Patton's more heralded charge, Montgomery's record raised legitimate doubts about his ability to command a mobile battle effectively. When, therefore, he proposed to command the Allies' sole thrust to Germany in a gigantic manoeuvre

[24] Eric Larrabee, *Commander in Chief: Franklin Delano Roosevelt, His Lieutenants and Their War* (New York: Harper and Row, 1987), 471.

battle, there were serious misgivings about whether he was the type of commander who could make the most of that opportunity. Field Marshal Alexander suggested to Professor Pogue that in urging a deep, decisive stroke Montgomery might have been trying to prove his critics wrong:

> *Monty accused of caution; this time he wanted to go faster. Says every time commanders have a big race, there is a point where they stop. If they stop too soon everyone says "Why didn't they go on?" They could have won.*[25]

The unfortunate result of these different views is that commanders went their separate ways, particularly Montgomery in the north and Patton in the south, while Eisenhower failed to exert his full authority to control them. The situation is especially difficult to understand, or accept, considering that all the while, as Ralph Bennett demonstrated persuasively in his important work, *Ultra in the West,* the Allies knew what the Germans were doing, and knew where they considered themselves to be most vulnerable.[26] It was a particularly fruitful season for Ultra. Because the rapid advance from the Seine had disrupted their landlines and telephone network, the Germans had to communicate more than usual by radio. Ultra decrypts described how their High Command was particularly concerned about Antwerp, Aachen, and Trier.

Aachen and Trier were both on main routes into Germany, and the Siegfried Line fortifications in both sectors were inadequate and unmanned. Aachen, on the Belgian border, was the first enemy city immediately threatened by the Allies, and the Germans hurriedly undertook strenuous efforts to defend it. Ultra also revealed that the Germans worried even more about defending the sector extending south from Trier, where they were more vulnerable. This was the corridor from Metz through the Saar and the Moselle valley that was the sole escape route to Germany for the tens of thousands of Germans withdrawing from southwest France. It was also the junction of their northern and southern army groups, and where General Patton's Third Army was heading when his tanks stopped for lack of gasoline.

Antwerp's significance was as evident to the Germans as it was to the Allies. They knew from their own experience that the rapid advance across France was bound to lose momentum as fighting units distanced themselves from their supplies. No other port had the capacity to support the country-wide pursuit, and Hitler ordered that those along the Channel — Le Havre, Boulogne, Calais, and Dunkirk — be defended to the last man. As the British entered Antwerp, Ultra revealed that the Germans accorded the same priority to its lengthy sea approaches, and that they had ordered that a new defence line be established immediately north of the city. Before the Germans could defend Antwerp, tanks of 11th Armoured Division arrived, their crews so overwhelmed by a joyous populace that they could hardly move through the city. Their mission was to secure the docks, and in the early afternoon a troop of tanks with a company of infantry reached the sprawling maze of wharves and machinery. By then a gallant underground band, led by a remarkable ship's captain named Eugene Colson, had already neutralized the Germans' prepared demolitions and seized many of Antwerp's vital points: the power station, the sluice gates controlling water levels, and the lift gates over the Albert Canal, which bisects the city. On meeting Colson's men, and having secured the docks intact as ordered, the British stopped. Colson urged them to cross the captured lift locks over the Albert Canal and to occupy the northern shore, but in vain: their orders were to stop at the docks and so they did.

As indispensable as they were in themselves, Antwerp's port facilities were very much hostage to their geographical surroundings. The city is located near the mouth of the Scheldt River, about 15 kilometres from where the river empties into the broad West Scheldt. The 40-kilometre-long and four- to eight-kilometre-wide West Scheldt is bounded on the north by the South Beveland Peninsula and Walcheren Island and on the south by the mainland Dutch enclave of Breskens. The Germans garrisoned both shores with large coastal gun batteries, and so long as they held them they controlled Antwerp's vital approaches.

---

[25] Pogue interview, USMHI.

[26] R. Bennett, *Ultra in the West: The Normandy Campaign of 1944-45* (New York: Charles Scribner's Sons, 1979), 129-163.

Second Division's delicious pleasure of returning to Dieppe. (PA 167564)

Overlooking Dieppe's main beach. (PA 131232)

The decision to stop in Antwerp, rather than seal off the Beveland Peninsula, haunted both the divisional and corps commanders, Generals Philip Roberts and Brian Horrocks, in later years. Roberts lamented that he had not been properly briefed, otherwise he

> would have crossed the Albert Canal with tanks to the east of Antwerp and closed the Germans' route into Beveland and Walcheren.[27]

Horrocks explained that in his preoccupation with going east to the Rhine he neglected the importance of the sector north of Antwerp that not only controlled movement in and out of the port but was key to the German defences in Holland. By either bypassing Antwerp or moving across the Albert Canal bridges in the dock area, which the underground had taken for them, his troops likely could have advanced the 25 kilometres to Woensdrecht to seal off the Beveland Isthmus and trap the German Fifteenth Army.

> At the time this {Antwerp} seemed the obvious objective, but I realise now that it was a serious mistake. My excuse is that my eyes were fixed entirely on the Rhine, and everything else seemed of subsidiary importance. It never entered my head that the Scheldt would be mined, and that we would not be able to use Antwerp port until the channel had been swept and the Germans cleared from the coastline on either side. Nor did I realise that the Germans would be able to evacuate a large number of the troops trapped in the coastal areas across the mouth of the Scheldt estuary from Breskens to Flushing.[28]

The withdrawing Germans were among those who had escaped the Normandy débâcle. While losing heavily between 20 and 24 August, a period coinciding with bad weather that grounded attack aircraft, they had also managed to ferry upwards of 300,000 men and 25,000 vehicles north of the Seine. Just as important, most of their vital command and control centres escaped. Of two army, four corps, and 13 divisional headquarters, only one corps and three divisional staffs had been destroyed, and four corps and 12 divisional commanders got away to command again. Now they set about devising a new defence based on their remarkable capacity to delay, regroup, and counterattack. By early September tens of thousands of workers were already fortifying the neglected Siegfried Line or West Wall, an 800-kilometre reverse Maginot Line stretching along the Rhine and the German border from Holland to Switzerland.

On the day the Allies reached Antwerp, as Ultra had warned, Hitler ordered the newly formed First Parachute Army to establish a defensive line along the Albert Canal from Antwerp to Maastricht. Its commander, General Kurt Student, received the order:

> I had been at the Fuehrer's Headquarters on 2 September, and on 4 September I was in my office at Berlin-Wannsee with a small staff. Unexpectedly received a telephone call: I was ordered to form a new defence line along the Albert Canal immediately. Its right wing was to extend to the mouth of the Scheldt, where this river flows into the West Scheldt.[29]

Student assumed command the next day, most of his soldiers coming from the Fifteenth Army divisions that withdrew systematically from France through Belgium to Holland. Throughout September, behind the barriers of the Ghent and Leopold canals that were being contested by the Canadians, the Germans pulled out their supply troops first, then their fighting units. From central headquarters in Breskens retreating units were told where to assemble and when to cross the Scheldt, in two civilian vessels, three large rafts, a ferry, and 16 smaller boats. Together they took out the remnants of eight divisions — almost 70,000 men, as well as 12 heavy guns, 215 medium and field guns, 750 trucks and wagons, and 1000 horses. It was a remarkable organizational feat, accomplished in the face of air attack the relentlessness of which was moderated only by the vagaries of weather. Once across the Scheldt to Walcheren, units marched along the Beveland Peninsula to the mainland where they were integrated into Student's defences.[30]

Despite the quality of Ultra's regular intercepts, the Allies failed to exploit the opportunity open to them. Having given

---

[27] Richard Lamb, *Montgomery in Europe, 1939-45* (London: Buchan and Enright, 1983), 201.

[28] B. Horrocks, *A Full Life* (London: Collins, 1960), 204.

[29] D Hist, AHQ Report 69.

[30] D Hist, German interrogation reports.

Montgomery's northern axis priority, and a generous allocation of limited supplies to keep it going, Eisenhower reasonably assumed that Montgomery had agreed on the overriding importance of quickly opening Antwerp's port. In fact Montgomery had not, determining instead that with one reasonable Channel port and a daily airlift of 1000 tons he would be able to get to the Ruhr without Antwerp. Clearing Antwerp's approaches was the last of the tasks he allocated to First Canadian Army. While Von Zangen's Fifteenth Army slipped into its new positions in front of him, Montgomery spoke less of of Antwerp and became fixated with gaining a bridgehead over the Rhine — instead of using Antwerp as a base to get across the river, he now wanted to get across the Rhine to free up Antwerp. Consequently, instead of forestalling Student, 11th Armoured and the rest of Horrocks' XXX Corps paused for three days and moved east; Second British Army towards Venlo, Wesel, and the northern edge of the Ruhr parallel with the First American Army, which was advancing on Liège and Aachen.

With the Germans still in disorder during this first week of September, there seemed to be a possibility of bouncing the unmanned Siegfried Line and the Rhine, but that would have required the British and Americans to mount a closely coordinated and concerted drive on a single axis. It could have been at Wesel — the Germans thought the British *"could have cycled to Wesel"*[31] — or at Aachen, which was also undefended at the time. Montgomery decided instead to turn north and head for Arnhem. He had at his disposal I Airborne Corps, an elite formation whose three divisions had been waiting for months in Britain for operations that never came. Now they were committed to an audacious gamble. The American 101st and 82nd Airborne divisions would capture the many river and canal crossings between Eindhoven and Nijmegen to enable General Horrocks' XXX Corps to reach the Rhine at Arnhem, which the 1st British Airborne Division would have secured. Arnhem apparently had not been Montgomery's first choice. General Bradley recalled that during their earlier meeting

Montgomery's August plan didn't envisage the Holland push. At that time Monty had in mind going north of Aachen. Changes this later; instead of advancing parallel with us, he turned north.... In September Monty got up Arnhem plan. Seems definitely to believe that if he could get around there he might be able to go on to Berlin.[32]

Several explanations have been suggested for his change. One is that air commanders preferred Arnhem because its anti-aircraft defences were lighter. Another is that an Arnhem bridgehead would have brought Montgomery closer to the V2 bomb sites in Holland, which had just begun launching their deadly missiles to London. Yet another explanation is that an Arnhem crossing would have allowed Second Army to both outflank the Siegfried Line and move quickly north to the Ijsselmeer where it could trap the German forces in western Holland. There was also the general euphoria that enveloped the Allied camp when quick victory seemed to be at hand. Montgomery wrote early in September that he expected to be in Berlin in a few weeks, and on 11 September his staff signalled that

if Germany should not surrender when Second Army reaches Osnabruck I suggest Arnhem is the most suitable location for our HQ after Brussels provided not destroyed in battle. If damaged, I recommend we should move to either Munster or Bonn.[33]

This was forward planning at its most optimistic, but it ran strangely counter to the intelligence that Ultra was providing as it tracked the Germans' laborious but steady recovery.

Arnhem had several serious disadvantages, about which Montgomery was aware but strangely unconcerned. Both the Dutch underground and Ultra had indicated that German armoured forces, which could wreak havoc on lightly armed paratroopers, were deployed around the British drop zone. Moreover, the low, flooded Dutch countryside restricted XXX Corps to a single, easily obstructed road in its drive to the Arnhem bridge. Horrocks' superior, General Dempsey,

---

31 Lamb, *Montgomery in Europe, 1939-45*, 215.
32 Pogue interview, USMHI.
33 Lamb, *Montgomery in Europe, 1939-45*, 196-227.

apparently told Montgomery that he doubted Horrocks' tanks would be able to relieve the under-gunned paratroopers quickly. Dempsey also pointed out that turning north would expose his Second Army's flank as his axis of advance diverged from the American First Army on his right. Dempsey, as well as Montgomery's own planning staff, preferred to attack east in conjunction with the Americans rather than north and risk getting bogged down in the Dutch lowlands.

Others had more fundamental objections, reasoning that employing the Airborne Army at all was a waste of scarce aerial resources. Air Marshal Coningham, the commander of Second Tactical Air Force, told Professor Pogue that

We could have gone to the Rhine if we had done one thing. If we had released the airborne lift in England which was being held for airborne attack after airborne attack which never came off, we could have taken the gasoline to Georgie Patton — not Monty...If we had used the 2000 ton lift (could have made two trips a day — giving him 2000 tons daily) he could have done it.[34]

Montgomery declined the advice. Arnhem it would be, and there is a certain irony in his decision to switch his advance from east to north. Having argued strenuously the merits of a concentrated narrow front, he now chose to spread his own forces — in a campaign within a campaign — over a sector that was too broad for their numbers. Gaps between the Canadian, British, and American armies widened. In the west, First Canadian Army lacked the resources to take the Channel ports and secure the Scheldt, and their operations inevitably diverged from Second British Army's as the latter drove to Arnhem. In the east, the advance on two weakened parallel thrusts, towards Aachen and Wesel, was further diluted when Montgomery changed direction and gambled on gaining the last bridge, at Arnhem.

Together, Antwerp and Arnhem largely decided the course of the last eight months of the war. Brigadier Edgar Williams, Montgomery's chief intelligence officer, told Richard Lamb that, in retrospect, the chain of decisions was calamitous.

It was an appalling decision to go for an airborne operation instead of clearing the banks of the Scheldt to open up Antwerp. Monty impulsively decided to go for Arnhem, not Wesel, and I was shocked by the sheer wilfulness of the decision. At that time Monty had the psychology of pursuit with the elation of the advance, and I had it too, and found it difficult to keep my intelligence reports and judgements completely free from the heady feeling that we had won the war. During these few days it was difficult to be dispassionate. If Ike had preferred the Scheldt option he should have imposed his will on Monty. But you must remember at that time Ike was in no position to contradict Monty, because the incredible victory in Normandy had established Monty as a brilliantly successful commander in the field.[35]

The Allied campaign ground to a halt. In the south, Patton's Third Army stalled short of the Saar. In the centre, Hodges' First Army's front was split dangerously by the Ardennes, and his forces north of that barrier were too widely dispersed to get through the Siegfried Line at Aachen while it was unmanned and vulnerable. First Army also failed to appreciate the vital operational importance of the nearby Roer River dams that controlled the flow of water in the lower Rhineland, which it might have secured had it not entangled itself in the inhospitable environs of the Huertgen Forest. The oversight deplorably affected Canadians when they fought in the Rhineland a few months later.

In the north, Arnhem was a bridge too far for General Dempsey's Second Army, and on the coast First Canadian Army was left with the unpalatable task of clearing the Germans out of Breskens, Walcheren, and Beveland to open up the port of Antwerp. Although what might have happened is never certain, it is quite likely that the decisions taken, or not taken, in the first week of September made another eight months of fighting inevitable.

---

[34] Pogue interview, USMHI.

[35] Lamb, *Montgomery in Europe, 1939-45,* 215-216.

CHAPTER II

SCHELDT

We meet with two jerries with white flags in their rifles, they also advise us to look for safety in the bunker, for the tanks may begin to shoot at any moment now. We went to fetch the women and the suitcases. After we had been 10 minutes in the bunker a terrific gunnery bombardment set in. The bunker rocked, the shells flew overhead in the direction of Zuizande. Yet I was very calm and all the others as well, we felt safe and knew it would soon be over. Strange, but it was like that. When it was quiet Luteyn crept outside and at a short distance he saw a Canadian on the dyke. A Canadian, a Canadian, a Canadian!

A flagpole doesn't go well with ruins. Those who are not here now cannot visualize the disconsolate spectacle our town offers on the liberation day. A chaos of completely or partly destroyed houses. Streets with ruins, broken glass and shell holes. BUT WE ARE FREE.[36]

The battle to free the approaches to Antwerp was lengthy, disagreeable, and costly. When 4th Division withdrew from its precarious bridgehead on the Albert Canal in mid-September, it was evident that the pursuit had given way to a new, as yet uncertain phase, but few could foresee that those operations would occupy the Canadians until Walcheren Island fell six weeks later. High-level command differences over narrow and broad fronts, which took American and British armies towards Germany on diverging routes, had left the First Canadian Army stranded along the Channel with unfocused priorities. The result, as Major General J.L. Moulton pointed out in *Battle for Antwerp*, was that Montgomery's instructions to the Canadians "show[ed] uncharacteristic signs of vacillation between the Channel ports and Antwerp."[37] Not until mid-September did Montgomery begin to give Antwerp hesitant priority, and it was another month after that before he gave the Canadians sufficient resources

---

[36] Personal, Pieter de Houck letters.

[37] J.L. Moulton, *Battle for Antwerp* (London: Ian Allan, 1978), 94-101.

to clear the vital Scheldt approaches. In the meantime they were fully absorbed in reducing the fortresses of Boulogne, Cap Gris Nez, Calais, and Dunkirk.

As integral bastions of the Atlantic Wall, these fortress-ports had been developed by the Germans early in the war to defeat landings in the Pas-de-Calais. Their huge naval guns could also fire on ships moving in the narrowest sector of the Channel, and regularly shelled the Dover coast, which, on a clear day, seems a mere stone's throw away. Mutually supporting and buried in deep steel and concrete bunkers, the coastal guns were virtually impregnable to anything but a direct hit through their firing apertures. They did have two weaknesses, however. Not until the Normandy front collapsed in August did German commanders fortify the land approaches to the positions and, therefore, their usual array of antitank ditches, wire obstacles, and minefields were incomplete. The other weakness was with the defenders themselves. Germans who were told to deny the use of the Channel ports by standing fast to their last round of ammunition were a mixed lot, one of their commanders describing them as *"fortress troops, sailors, home guards, harbour technicians and stragglers."*[38] With few exceptions, they were there not because they wanted to sacrifice their lives for Hitler and the Third Reich, but because they were unfortunate enough to be caught up in events beyond their control.

The 3rd Division, whose task it was to take Boulogne and Calais, had moved quickly once clear of Rouen, despite bad roads and little room to manoeuvre. The North Novas covered 120 kilometres in three days before coming under fire on arriving at the outskirts of Boulogne on the morning of 5 September, and other units reached Calais and Dunkirk soon after. It was clear that the Germans intended to fight for them, as well as the batteries on the windswept headlands of Cap Gris Nez. While the topography and defences of each position differed — for example, Boulogne's landward approaches were protected by a ring of high ground, while those at Calais were channelled by flooded land — reducing them presented the attackers with similar tactical problems. Although indifferently garrisoned, each of these entrenched fortresses was strong enough to defeat anything but a well-prepared, deliberate assault. Consequently each had to be reduced in turn, as one battalion commander remarked, in *"a strange drama of medieval siege mingled with modern warfare."*[39]

Modern siege technology had several components. First, waves of heavy and medium bombers saturated the defences, followed by massive artillery barrages. Flail tanks then pounded paths through minefields for armoured infantry carriers and modified tanks mounting heavy bunker-busting guns and flame-throwers. In a different category was a morale weapon that turned out to be effective as well. Leaflets showered upon the defenders, many of whom were either ethnic Germans from other countries or foreign volunteers, induced considerable numbers to conclude that a prisoner-of-war cage was a better place to be than a cemetery. When low-morale defenders saw unexpected weapons at short range, especially terrifying flame-throwers, many surrendered.

Because siege weapons were in short supply, each fortress had to be reduced in turn. Hence 3rd Division had to wait for two weeks, until Le Havre had been captured, before tackling Boulogne, and the division prepared well. Boulogne's German commander remarked to his interrogators after capture that he had had virtually no intelligence about the strength of the Canadians who were about to attack him, and three Canadian prisoners had given no information. He knew, however,

> that when the attack did come it would be thoroughly prepared to the last weapon, and that the Canadians would attempt to take the port with as few losses as possible.

(General Spry, commander of 3rd Division, wrote opposite the comment on his copy of the interrogation report just one word: "Thanks.")

As the assault neared, a Civil Affairs officer went into the city to negotiate arrangements for evacuating civilians, and Captain Jack Martin, 3rd Division's Historical Officer, watched as several thousand of them trudged to an uncertain fate. He wrote in his war diary that he

---

[38] D Hist, German interrogation reports.

[39] D Hist, unit reports.

Halifax bombers of No 6 Group RCAF relentlessly attacked German V Bomb sites before Canadian soldiers overran them. (PL 30780)

... while bomb and rocket Typhoons flew close support missions. (PA 192001)

saw a part of the extraordinary procession of refugees streaming out of the city. Moving slowly, their brightly coloured clothes in sharp contrast to their unhappy expressions, these people all have enormous burdens; some said nothing and looked almost sullen though a few appeared exhuberant and made confident gestures of violence concerning "Les Boches." Small dogs, some in baskets and some peeping from brief cases, and others straining at leashes, were plentiful. Few if any of these people realized that food, shelter and transport were to be provided for them. To most it seemed only that the besieging forces were indirectly responsible for their eviction and flight into the countryside.

Boulogne was surrounded by high ground, dominated by Mont Lambert, on which the Germans had developed a connected ring of defended strong points. General Spry deployed 8 Brigade on the right of the main approach road and 9 Brigade on the left. In a planned one-day operation — that turned out to last six — 8 Brigade was to attack west through to the Liane River that bisects the city and then turn north, and 9 Brigade was to cross the river to secure the southern sector. While units awaited their special equipment, bombers made 49 separate attacks on selected targets and, on the evening before the ground assault, others dropped 3000 more tons of bombs. An air force officer with Brigadier John Rockingham, commanding 9 Brigade, had direct radio contact with the master bomber and was able to ensure that his target markers were correctly placed. In a shrewd ruse to keep the defenders in their bunkers while infantrymen crossed open ground to their objectives, a wave of empty aircraft flew a last pass with their bomb bay doors open. Then, 328 field, medium, heavy, and anti-aircraft guns led rifle companies moving towards their objectives in armoured personnel carriers, or Kangaroos. The only fire support lacking was that from the navy, whose ships were out-matched by the coastal guns. As a unique touch, two 14-inch and two 15-inch guns sited 40 kilometres across the Channel in England fired on the Calais batteries. Helped by air observers, one 15-incher scored a direct hit on a German 16-incher, and troopers of the First

Hussars, in positions just behind Calais, had a ringside seat.

It was an odd feeling to be sitting behind some Huns who were about to be shelled by the Dover guns...a great blue line on the map told us where the danger zone was. Every few minutes one would hear a terrific din — and it was almost impossible to tell whether they were "comers" or "goers." Here is about the only time when our shells were a bit unwelcome — mainly because at 21 miles we were uncertain as to the beaten zone and we could just visualize what a Sherman would look like after an encounter with an allied "freight train."[40]

Although the bombing struck comparatively few of the targeted guns, the commander of one position told his interrogators it *"had had a shattering effect on the nerves of the garrison,"* adding that

some of the bunkers had been severely damaged, but this was to be expected, as the TODT organization which had built them was out to make money like everyone else, and had probably skimped on the cement and put in too much sand.[41]

Captain Martin had earlier been instructed *"to discover what supporting arms are most effective and in what quantity,"* in such an attack and, questionable construction practices aside, he could not help but compare this siege to others in earlier times. While it took six days, Martin wrote,

the swiftness of this operation forms a striking contrast with medieval sieges. Centuries ago Calais was besieged for 11 months. Today even the comparatively brief stand of the Brest fortress seems overlong {five to six weeks}. All leisure has gone out of war. It is no longer possible to stand before the gates of a fortress and enquire, like Shakespeare's Henry V,

> *How yet resolves the Governor of the town?*
> *This is the latest parle we will admit*

They were six punishing days, however, and despite the massive bombardment, and the questionable morale of the defenders, enough of the 10,000-strong garrison manned their weapons long enough to kill or wound 634 Canadians.

---

[40] D Hist, unit reports.
[41] D Hist, German interrogation reports.

With Boulogne battered but secured, 3rd Division moved up the coast to take on the batteries at Cap Gris Nez and Calais, the latter surrounded by a combination of natural and man-made defences — flooded land interspersed with connected strong points — all linked by wire and minefields and defended by a garrison of 7500. Once again, Bomber Command attacked on three successive days preceding the assault, and returned during the siege. Artillery fire drenched each position in turn, and the armoured zoo, especially flame-throwing Crocodile tanks, were devastatingly effective. Cap Gris Nez, located between Boulogne and Calais, differed in some respects; for instance, infantry platoons had to go in on foot rather than in armoured personnel carriers. Nonetheless, 9 Brigade's deliberate attack went so smoothly that at the end the North Novas' Commanding Officer observed,

> The scene now indeed resembled the conclusion of a scheme in England, for the troops were plainly aware that they had only to await the order to stand down. North NS Highlanders, leaving one company to guard the area, soon marched back to Ambleteuse to their quarters in time for dinner and were met at the outskirts by the battalion's pipe band.[42]

Meanwhile, Brigade Headquarters informed 3rd Division to "tell Dover they can start their celebration at any moment now."

While 3rd Division was preparing its operations at Boulogne, Cap Gris Nez, and Calais, 2nd Division left Dieppe for Dunkirk after having enjoyed a much-needed break to absorb reinforcements. Protected by flooded land and ringed by several defended villages, Dunkirk was also a fortress that had to be reduced by siege tactics; but until the others had been taken, and heavy weapons became available, all the division could do was secure the surrounding hamlets and invest the city. By the time Calais was taken, priorities had changed, and 2nd Division turned Dunkirk over to British troops and moved to Antwerp. The British, in turn, were relieved by the 1st Czechoslovak Independent Armoured Brigade, which invested Dunkirk until May 1945 when its commander accepted the German surrender.

Having cleared the Channel ports, planning staffs turned to the task of opening the sea approaches to Antwerp — keeping very much in mind the historical precedent of an unsuccessful British attempt in 1809 to clear the same ground. It was a most challenging problem. By the end of September, 4th Canadian and 1st Polish Armoured divisions had cleared the enemy from the sectors south of the Leopold Canal, east of the tidal flats in Braakman Inlet, and from Terneuzen to Antwerp. That left three key objectives controlling the West Scheldt water route to the port — Breskens Pocket, South Beveland Peninsula, and the island of Walcheren — whose shores controlled the lengthy approaches. Tactically, the defences formed an interconnected puzzle. Before cargo and troop ships could reach Antwerp, the Scheldt waterway had to be cleared of mines; but minesweepers could not operate until the large coastal guns covering them — at Zeebrugge, Heyst, Knocke, and Cadzand on the mainland, and Flushing and Westkapelle on Walcheren — were silenced. Before the heavy guns could be neutralized, infantrymen had to remove the defenders who protected them. General Simonds gave Breskens Pocket to 3rd Division, Beveland Peninsula to 2nd Division, and Walcheren to British Commandos.

The terrain was the worst imaginable for military operations. Breskens was a rough 35-by-15-kilometre rectangle, bounded on the north by the West Scheldt River and on the south by the 15-metre-wide Leopold Canal. It was, as one contemporary report noted,

> completely flat with a network of minor canals and ditches, and numerous areas which are permanently flooded. It is criss-crossed by dykes which mostly carry roads or tracks. The fields, or "polders," are open and afford little or no cover. Church towers and buildings are the only view-points.[43]

There were just three approaches beyond the Leopold Canal that did not have to negotiate a deep-water obstacle. The first was at the Isabella Polder south of Braakman Inlet on the Dutch-Belgian border, the second along the main

---

42 D Hist, unit reports.
43 D Hist, CMHQ Report 188.

Ghent-Breskens road through Watervliet, and the third along the road running north from Maldegem to Aardenburg and thence to Breskens and Knocke. On the northern side of the West Scheldt, Walcheren Island and Beveland were similarly protected by natural obstacles. Walcheren was saucer-shaped, its below-sea-level interior surrounded by a high-earth dyke. The only land approach was along a narrow causeway linking the island with South Beveland Peninsula. Beveland, in turn, joined the mainland north of Antwerp across a slim isthmus. Any attack along the Beveland corridor had first to secure the sector near the town of Woensdrecht that controlled the entrance to the isthmus, then move along the narrow roadway to reach Walcheren.

By the end of September the Germans had had time to strengthen their defences. While the battle for Arnhem was under way, General Von Zangen's Fifteenth Army Headquarters left Breskens and Walcheren for the mainland, leaving a garrison, 70th Division, on Walcheren, and another, 64th Division, in the Breskens enclave. The 70th, the White Bread or Stomach Division, as it was nicknamed, was composed of men who had been medically downgraded for a variety of ailments, and were on special diets that required Walcheren's abundance of fresh vegetables, eggs, milk, and white bread. They were not the highest quality troops but their commander later acknowledged that *"behind concrete these men could probably pull a trigger as well as another."*[44]

The 64th was a much higher quality formation, its officers and NCOs being combat veterans of the Eastern and Italian fronts. Including coastal gunners and others, the division had around 11,000 men, its six infantry battalions and other units being abundantly armed and munitioned with weapons of all descriptions. Ordered to deny the Allies access to Antwerp's port facilities, and to tie down as many of them as they could for as long as possible, the Walcheren and Breskens fortresses were expected to hold out for between three and four weeks after the start of a serious attack.

In the midst of preparations, General Crerar was sent to England because of illness and was replaced by General Simonds whose command of

II Corps, in turn, was taken over by 2nd Division's General Foulkes. Because the terrain was unsuitable for tanks, or vehicle movement of any kind, Simonds first ordered a major redeployment. First Polish Armoured Division moved east of Antwerp towards Bergen, where it came under the command of I British Corps; 4th Armoured Division sent its armoured brigade to the same area, while its 10 Infantry Brigade held the eastern sector of the Leopold Canal. Second Division was already in Antwerp, probing the German defences north of the Albert Canal. When ready, the division was to attack north to seal off, then take, South Beveland Peninsula while, simultaneously, 3rd Division cleared Breskens Pocket. Finally, after heavy bombing had breached Walcheren's dykes to flood the island and isolate its strong points, British Commandos were to assault Walcheren from the sea. Each of these complex operations was unique, and each is best described in turn: Breskens, Beveland, and Walcheren.

* * *

After reducing the compact fortresses on the Channel, 3rd Division moved to the Leopold Canal to conduct an entirely different type of siege. With their usual array of armour and special equipment like Crocodiles and AVREs unable to move in the sodden terrain, they had to rely even more than usual on infantrymen. General Spry devised a three-stage pincer attack. Immediately following a diversionary assault at the Isabella Polder on 5 October by the Algonquins, 7 Brigade would cross the Leopold Canal, open the Maldegem-Aardenburg road, and construct a bridge allowing vehicles into their bridgehead. Two days later, 9 Brigade would mount an amphibious assault across the Savojaard Plaat on the enclave's northern shore. In reserve, 8 Brigade was to exploit 7 Brigade's bridgehead on the Leopold and drive north and west towards Breskens and Knocke-Heyst.

Seven Brigade's crossing place was about nine kilometres east of Moerkerke, the site of the Algonquin's earlier ill-fated crossing, and about two east of the Maldegem road. Here, where the

---

[44] D Hist, German interrogation reports.

Neutralizing gun positions like this required modern siege techniques. (PA 167981)

Fortunately, their garrisons were not the finest. (PA 174410)

Lys and Leopold canals diverged, was a pocket of drier land and slightly more room to manoeuvre. The Regina Rifles on the left were to cross the 30-metre canal and swing left, or west, to secure the bridge site where the main road crossed over, while the Canadian Scottish on the right enlarged the bridgehead eastwards. In order to achieve surprise, the assault was to be silent — that is, without a preliminary bombardment — but the guns of both 3rd and 4th divisions as well as other field and medium regiments were to be available when their forward observers with infantry companies called for fire. One innovation was the positioning of 27 carrier-mounted Wasp flame-throwers to cover the initial assault, trials having found that

by inclining the carrier part-way up the slope of the bank its flame could be thrown not only against the opposite bank, but beyond it, where enemy slit trenches and dugouts might be expected to be sited.[45]

Each of the two assault companies in the leading battalions had eight canvas boats that soldiers of the North Shore Regiment carried to the canal. At 0530 the Wasps fired. The assault companies took the boats over the bank, launched them into the water, and paddled across. Both Scottish companies got over without serious difficulty, and engineers had a footbridge in place within the hour. The Reginas' left company — which was from the Royal Montreal Regiment, whose usual role was to protect First Canadian Army Headquarters — was badly hit. One platoon was almost wiped out on crossing; by noon, only 11 men were alive and unhurt, but they had held on. When the Reginas' other company was unable to launch, the reserve companies had to follow the RMR directly into the strongest point of the defences, deployed around the bridge site where the road crossed the canal. Opposing trenches were so close in the shallow bridgehead that artillery observers were unable to call in supporting fire.

Then began what was possibly the worst week of the war for these soldiers. The Winnipeg Rifles crossed over through the Scottish early next day, but

In places the bridgehead was little deeper than the Northern canal bank. Even protection was slight: slit trenches rapidly filled with water

and had to be dug out many times a day. Except in the bank they could only be a foot or so in depth. In consequence co-ordinated actions even on a platoon level were impossible. In front, the ground...was flooded.[46]

Not for three days were the battalions able to link up, and it was a week before sappers were able to bridge the Leopold, allowing the first tanks of the British Columbia Regiment to cross.

Although it would have been difficult to persuade the beleaguered soldiers in the bridgehead that opposition was slackening, 9 Brigade's operations on their flank had forced the Germans to disperse their resources. After leaving Cap Gris Nez on 3 October, the brigade had concentrated in the dock area north of Ghent to train for its amphibious assault across the Savojaards Plaat at the mouth of Braakman Inlet. There they met up with their helpful new transport — amphibious Buffaloes and Terrapins. The first was a large, tracked vehicle that moved comfortably both in water and on land while carrying a platoon of men, a jeep, a carrier, or a field gun. The wheeled Terrapin was smaller and less versatile but nonetheless useful. As they tried both vehicles out in the water, it was probably just as well that the soldiers did not fully realize the type of battle that awaited them. *"Had we been able to foresee the future,"* the Highland Light Infantry's Private Bradley recalled, *"we wouldn't have been very happy. That was probably the roughest deal we had throughout the whole war."*[47]

After only the briefest of familiarization training, platoons were to climb into their Buffaloes in the Ghent docks, swim the 35-kilometre Terneuzen Canal in darkness, and assault across the deep inlet against beaches east of the town of Hoofdplaat. The landing area had not been selected casually. In late September, a young Dutch resistance fighter, Pieter de Winde, had made a gutsy reconnaissance of the Breskens coast of the Scheldt on foot and bicycle, and noticed a gap in the German defences between Hoofdplaat and the western shore of Braakman Inlet. On the night of the 27th he set off in a

---

45 D Hist, unit reports.
46 D Hist, CMHQ Report 188.
47 D Hist, Bradley letters.

rubber dinghy to cross the Braakman and inform the Canadians. De Winde's boat sank and, in an extraordinary feat of courage and determination, he swam the rest of the way against tidal currents and gale-force winds to reach the Terneuzen shore, where he eventually found intelligence staffs to brief.[48]

Approaching the Braakman was not uneventful. The Buffaloes' loud airplane engines made sufficient noise while negotiating the canal in the night to cause anti-aircraft gunners in Flushing to open fire from across the Scheldt. Then damaged locks slowed them down and disabled several vehicles, causing Brigadier Rockingham to postpone the assault for a day. They waited apprehensively on the Scheldt, near the mouth of the canal, with vehicles and troops dispersed in farms, and happily avoided detection. Rockingham split his brigade into three groups. The first contained the North Novas and the Highland Light Infantry, along with Rockingham's tactical headquarters; the second was made up of the Stormont, Dundas and Glengarry Highlanders, mortars and machine guns of the Cameron Highlanders, and the main brigade headquarters; the last had medical and administrative units along with jeeps, carriers, and antitank guns. Each of the two leading flotillas was led over the eight-kilometre passage by a navigating motor launch, and artillery marked the beaches with night marker shells that had been flown in especially from Bayeux.

Estimated crossing time, under the guns of Flushing across the water, was a nail-biting hour and a half, but, extraordinarily, all worked as planned. Battalions found de Winde's gap, landed with little immediate opposition, and quickly consolidated a connected bridgehead 1500 metres deep. By then the Buffaloes were on their way back for the follow-up units, which were soon under way, screened by smoke laid down by generators in amphibious vehicles, storm boats, and smoke-floats. By noon, as the leading SDG companies were advancing on Hoofdplaat, one of their artillery observers could see Germans entrenched on the dyke that was to be their start line, and called for medium gunfire support. He later recounted:

After the fire lifted, the leading platoons opened fire, and the Wasps {flame-throwers} crept right in under the fire of the mediums. The stonk I called was slap bang dead on the target. After two squirts of the flame into the trees on the dyke, about a hundred Jerries came out of holes in the ground. The men were delighted. One sergeant was dancing around like a madman and promised me the best watch in the German army as a souvenir. I didn't get the watch until later...our advance continued and more prisoners poured in. Those mediums had terrified them as they had me too, for we were less than 200 yards away in a deep ditch. The fire became more intense as we neared Hoofdplaat, small arms and machine gun fire being augmented by 20mm. I thanked God for bringing smoke grenades.[49]

For one Dutch family sheltering in Hoofdplaat, it was a spine-tingling experience when the Canadians

succeed{ed} in reaching the harbour via the Scheldt embankment. There they {were} held up by two bunkers. I shall never forget the moment when the first Canadian entered the house. He looked around, saw we were civilians, calmly placed his rifle against the doorpost and started passing round cigarettes and chocolate.[50]

The German commander in Breskens, General Kurt Eberding, was taken completely by surprise by the landing on his flank, as he had been unaware of the Buffaloes and their amphibious capability. When Eberding sent his divisional reserves along with others from across the Scheldt to counter this threat, General Spry committed his own reserve, 8 Brigade, to exploit the opportunity that the surprise landing had given him. Instead of reinforcing 7 Brigade's bridgehead on the Leopold, as Spry had planned, he had it follow the 7th Reconnaissance Regiment across the Braakman and begin fighting its way south, dyke by dyke, towards Biervliet and Watervliet. Within a few days the entire brigade was in the eastern bridgehead and had taken over the left flank.

[48] Denis and Shelagh Whitaker, *Tug of War* (Toronto: Stoddart, 1984), 281-283.

[49] R.S. Spencer, *History of the Fifteenth Field Regiment* (Holland: The Regiment, 1945), 167.

[50] Personal, Pieter de Houck letters.

Fighting in the Scheldt was close and bitter, and with their backs to the sea German defenders took a deadly toll as the Canadians steadily squeezed them into a shrinking perimeter. With their own movements restricted to bare, open dykes, infantrymen were vulnerable to mortar and artillery fire, especially when the Germans fired their heavy anti-aircraft shells into trees, creating the effect of a deadly airburst; and when aircraft were grounded by bad weather anti-aircraft guns could concentrate on ground targets.

The first task was for 8 Brigade to link up with the Algonquins at the Isabella Polder and the Argylls at Watervliet. The Chaudières and the Queen's Own did so on the 15th, providing a land and road connection with the mainland that allowed not only supplies but artillery and heavy weapons into the area. Then the 7th Reconnaissance Regiment moved west to link up with the Leopold bridgehead, now occupied by a British brigade of 52nd Division, which had relieved 7 Brigade; 8 Brigade headed for Oostburg, in the centre of the pocket, alongside 9 Brigade, which made for Schoondijke and Breskens. As the noose tightened, artillery regiments sited south of the Leopold at right angles to the advance were able to surround the defenders with gunfire — with 13th Field Regiment firing from the rear, 14th Field from the flank, and 15th and 19th Field from the front.

> It subsequently turned out {that} this novel use of artillery proved particularly effective, because it caught the enemy from behind, thereby diminishing the protection of the dykes, and it was a very demoralizing factor to their defence.[51]

By the 19th, the Germans had been forced back to an inner line surrounding a shrunken island centred on Oostburg, which was also Eberding's headquarters. Fighting through these fortified towns was as difficult in its own way as moving along bare dyke roads. Here, Captain Martin saw

> blockhouses which the enemy had been at great pains to camouflage. Each concrete pillbox was fitted with a tile roof and its flat wall surfaces were painted so as to simulate civilian dwellings, with bricks, doors, windows and even lace curtains laboriously inscribed on them. One such disguised pillbox purported to be a public house and in its "window" appeared the legend "Cafe Groote Pint."

Typhoons and guns battered the town and, eventually, a Queen's Own platoon reached its entrance after fixing bayonets — swords, to riflemen — and charging. They and the Chaudières then cleared the streets of Germans.

Civilians trapped in the maelstrom could only wait it out. General Eberding later chided General Spry for causing unnecessary civilian casualties by bombarding towns like Oostburg. Spry responded that by choosing to fortify and fight in towns Eberding left him no choice but to fight for them; to protect the lives of his own men, he had to give them all the fire support he could. Civilians paid the price. One of them whose family was sheltering in Oostburg's ruins wrote:

> Now we are going through the worst night we have experienced. Continuously shells are exploding to the left and to the right of us, we pray that we may be spared. The ditch doesn't offer any cover of course....{We get away to a farm where} we can rest and have a meal now. We are in a shelter and a bit later we know that this farm is in the firing line. Machine gun firing and rifle firing. The bullets make a nasty noise when glancing off the wall. When it is quiet for a moment {someone shouts} "THEY ARE HERE !!!" At first it didn't get through to us. Then I storm outside and truly there is the first Canadian !! And although we have cursed them the last few days I want to throw my arms around him !! He told me that this region was a 2nd Normandy.[52]

Incredibly, some familiar echoes of normality survived in the midst of terror. The divisional Historical Officer was startled when he visited the North Novas as the battalion was fighting on the outskirts of Ijzendijke, a few kilometres north:

> The town crier of Ijzendijke made his appearance in the street, making his presence known by beating a brass gong. At the sound

---

51 W.W. Barrett, *The History of the 13th Canadian Field Regiment* (Holland: The Regiment, 1945), 83-85.

52 Personal, Pieter de Houck letters.

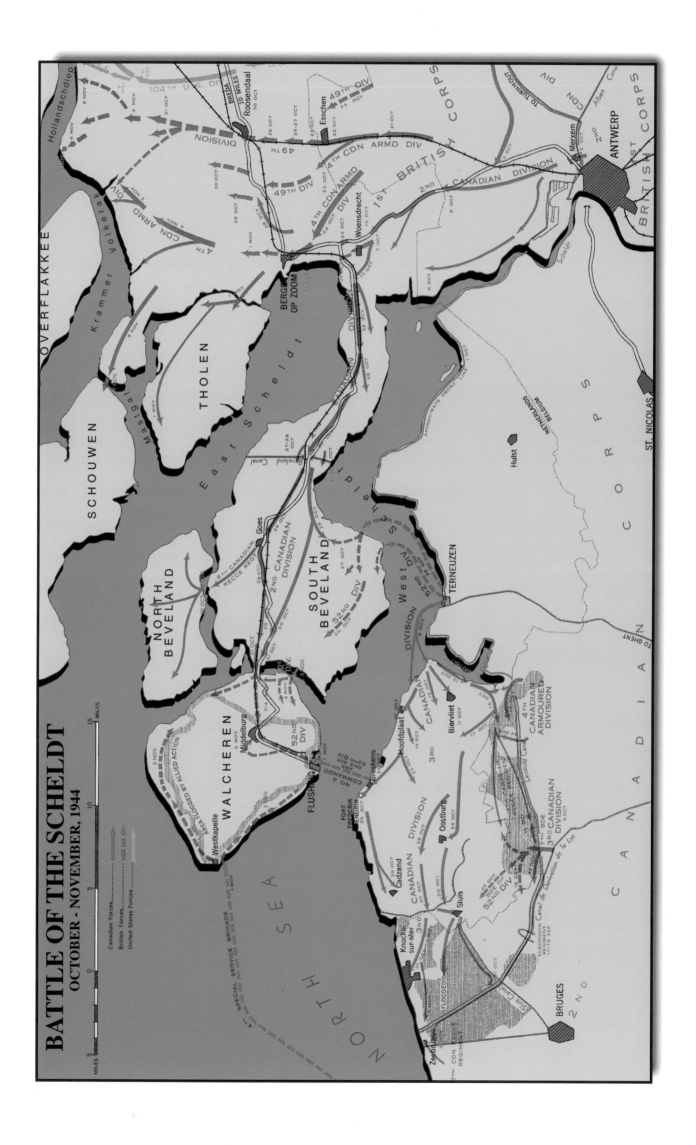

BATTLE OF THE SCHELDT
OCTOBER - NOVEMBER, 1944

the villagers looked from the doors and windows of their shattered houses and listened while he read some quite unintelligible announcement. This concluded he then stalked off to the next street to repeat the performance. Presumably in the course of the day he makes the rounds of the whole town.

A few days after Eberding was forced out of Oostburg, the SDG took Breskens, being shelled all the while by the guns at Flushing across the Scheldt. Seven Brigade passed through and secured the heavy Cadzand batteries a week later, while 8 Brigade took Sluis. Finally the North Novas moved into the suburbs of Knocke, where, at the golf course in Zet Houte, the leading company was met by a German major who said his commander wished to surrender. After Lieutenant Colonel Donald Forbes assured him that prisoners would be treated properly, the German took the company commander, Captain Winfield, to a large bunker where

a dozen colonels and majors sat around. They jumped to salute and offered Winfield a chair. A moment later he was led into a room where the major announced him and repeated the assurance Lieutenant Colonel Forbes had made. The General then indicated he wanted to surrender with all his staff and desired instructions. The staff, 100 in all, were marched off by Corporal Green and two men. General Eberding, commanding 64th Panzer Grenadier Division, walked out and was given a lift in a jeep by Lieutenant Veness who drove him down to Brigade Headquarters.[53]

* * *

While 3rd Division bled in the Breskens Pocket, 2nd Division fought its own war securing Beveland Peninsula. By mid-September units had moved into Antwerp — the 4th Field Regiment, for example, leaving Dunkirk shortly after midnight on the 16th, arriving in Antwerp late that day, and taking up gun positions pointing across the Albert Canal towards the northern suburb of Merxem. They stayed there for 17 days, supporting 4 Brigade during the bizarre days of the "streetcar war," when Germans north of the Albert Canal and Canadians south of it both commuted to battle

via Antwerp's functioning tram system. Although not safe by any means, the city had its pleasant moments:

Hotels and cabarets were doing a thriving business. Lights, music and pretty girls were everywhere, surrounded by all the evidence of good living. Battle stained, unshaven troops found themselves being served by waiters in tails.[54]

For those with different tastes, *"one could have afternoon tea in one of the most famous hotels in Europe among fashionably dressed people listening quietly to the hotel orchestra."*[55]

If September had its lighter moments, October was as bad a month for 2nd Division as it was for the 3rd in Breskens Pocket. The division's onerous task was to close the Beveland isthmus, then fight down the peninsula to Walcheren. Their immediate mission was to cut off German access to Beveland by capturing its base near the town of Woensdrecht. The plan called for 4 Brigade to cross the Albert Canal from its positions in Antwerp, secure the northern suburbs, and advance north, while 5 and 6 brigades formed a flanking pincer by crossing the Albert-Turnhout Canal further east, then swept in behind the enemy. On 2 October, while 6 Brigade moved out of its bridgehead, 4 Brigade attacked across the Albert Canal. As they reached Merxem, units were at first isolated, but they conveniently found a working civilian telephone line, which provided unorthodox but effective communications with the guns of 4th Field. During one particularly vicious counterattack, the Forward Observation Officer

shouted his fire orders from the top floor of the building; these were relayed from the ground floor over the public telephone to the artillery representative at battalion Headquarters in Antwerp, and thence to the guns.[56]

Once free of the built-up area, the brigade pressed north against withdrawing rearguards,

[53] Will Bird, *No Retreating Footsteps: The Story of the North Nova Scotia Highlanders* (Kentville, Nova Scotia: Kentville Publishing, n.d.), 221.

[54] D Hist, unit records.

[55] G.W.L. Nicholson, *Canada's Nursing Sisters* (Toronto: Samuel Stevens, Hakkert, 1975), 167.

[56] D Hist, Captain G.C. Blackburn, *The History of the 4th Field Regiment.*

who were being squeezed from the east by 6 Brigade's advance, and reached Ossendrecht, within a few kilometres of Woensdrecht, on the 6th.

Their rapid progress alarmed the Germans. General Von Zangen's task, besides delaying the opening of Antwerp's port as long as possible, was to hold the Antwerp-Tilburg-Hertogenbosch line south of the Maas, thus denying the Allies the secure river flank that would enable them to switch forces east towards the German border. The 2nd Division thrust threatened to split that line, and the Germans reacted strenuously by dispatching a strong battle group of paratroopers to stop the Canadians. For the next three weeks, until the Calgarys finally sealed the Beveland isthmus, 2nd Division bled in the sodden polders around Woensdrecht as one exhausted battalion after another tried to break through. The land they fought over had been reclaimed from the sea, much of it was flooded, and it was intersected at 800-metre intervals by four-metre-high dykes. All movement was under observation and direct fire from adjoining dykes and from the high ridge bordering Woensdrecht that controlled its approaches.

Once more, the terrain, and a general failure to appreciate German intentions and strength, produced over-optimistic intelligence reports and under-estimates of what was needed to clear them out. As it did elsewhere, close and personal fighting produced some unusual situations. On one occasion, while deploying their guns, 4th Field's batteries came under close small-arms fire. A patrol went out to find the Germans, but

by this time the gun position was under a hail of fire and all had been forced to take cover from this unseen enemy...the Troop Leader who, getting permission from R.H.Q. to fire over open sights at them, took charge of one of the guns. The sergeant of the gun laid the gun and fired it while the Troop Leader was on the trail directing the fire... After this affair was over and the guns were in position it seemed quite logical to learn that the most important of "D.F."{defensive fire} tasks, the "S.O.S." for the regiment, was directly behind them at 180 degrees to the bearing the guns were laid on.... The next morning the regiment fired many

targets and one minute would be firing directly to their front and the next minute would turn the gun directly behind them and blast away at Germans seen by a FOO somewhere in the bushland in that direction. Never was the truth that there is no "front line" in modern warfare so fully realized by the regiment.

The Woensdrecht stalemate was not broken until Montgomery, after a sulphurous exchange with General Eisenhower in October, finally gave Antwerp his highest priority. Instead of continuing to drain scarce resources east towards Arnhem, he redeployed them west to reinforce 2nd Division's struggle to open up Beveland. The 4th Armoured Division, operating under British command, was directed to secure the Canadian right flank and — along with 1st Polish, 49th British, and 104th American divisions — began a concerted drive towards Bergen op Zoom and Breda to drive the Germans north of the Maas.

With their right flank secure, 6 Brigade, supported by Fort Garry tanks, cleared the 22-kilometre stretch of the narrow peninsula as far as the canal that bisects it. In another four days of bitter slogging, 4 and 5 brigades reached the one-kilometre-long and 40-metre-wide causeway that carried a road, rail line, and bicycle path to Walcheren. A little more than halfway along, the Germans had cratered the route to form a ditch, which had filled with water, registered artillery and mortar targets, and sited tank and antitank guns to fire straight down the alley. The appalling tactical problem this presented was not helped by the continuing pressure placed on forward battalions to divert the Germans from the amphibious assault on Walcheren scheduled for 1 November. Not surprisingly, the Black Watch, which was first to make the attempt, was driven to ground at the near end, where they dug in. When the Calgarys tried to cross that night, 31 October, they found that the Germans had moved onto the causeway to avoid the heavy artillery barrage they knew would precede the next attack, and they were forced to ground as well. Next morning parts of two companies got to the far end before being driven back to the crater by a counterattack.

Late on 1 November the Maisonneuves were ordered to follow a barrage across the causeway before daylight next morning, with D Company leading. An hour or so after taking its objectives, the battalion was to be relieved by a British unit. In D Company, 16 and 17 platoons each had a dozen men and No 18 had 11; most were Canadian; a few were Belgian. Lieutenant Charles Forbes writes in his memoir it was raining and so cold his men had to work the bolts of their rifles continuously to keep them from freezing. His 16 Platoon's objective was the right-hand side of the dyke at the far end of the causeway, and Forbes moved towards the crater, telling his Bren gunners, the Arsenault brothers, to fire on anything that moved once they reached it. The 72 guns supporting the assault opened up on a 20-metre-wide target, making everything *"red with fire. The causeway looked like a steel beam being pushed into a hot furnace."*

> *The noise was deafening: My mouth open to mitigate the pain that the explosions caused in our ears, we approached the barrage. We slowed. The incredible was before us. We recognized steel helmets. They were ours. We saw coming out of the furnace, in front of me, soldiers running towards us, silhouetted against the curtain of fire and smoke. It was the Calgarys withdrawing. The barrage was falling on them. My head spun. Faithful to orders, the Arsenaults and others opened fire on them in enfilade. I could see them fall, cut down by their comrades. I stopped the machine guns and watched the Calgarys walk past, out of the barrage that was, in part, falling on their positions.... We came to the enormous crater where the Calgarys had taken position. And there I understood the terrible error. Obeying orders in full, my men had opened fire once past the crater. None of them knew that there were two.*

When Forbes and his few men struggled through the chest-deep water in the crater and out the far side, still with 500 metres to go, the Germans fired their own mortars, which bracketed them between two belts of fire: *"I have no words to describe this hell."* Extraordinarily, what remained of the company got to the far dyke, 16 Platoon on the left side of the road, 18 Platoon on the right. Forbes had five men left, and, with no comunications, they waited:

> *Time passed. Again, we lived in silence. Such silence that left room for imagination, anxiety, hope....*

> *Not a single cigarette, no matches. And hunger... bringing on stomach pains. We brought nothing to eat since we were expecting to be relieved at six.*

An hour later they ambushed a company of Germans trying to withdraw; after another four hours a tank approached along the dyke, but a Typhoon appeared and drove it away. Because the Germans now knew where they were, the men had to move out in the water; but the receding tide began to expose them. A messenger got through and told them to pull back.

> *My guys were gone. I threw myself to the top of the dyke to retrace our line of attack. Machine gun bursts kicked up the dirt around us. Carrière, one of my men, came out of nowhere and ran near me. He let out an expletive and showed me his hand, which had been shot right through. We ran and ran, to finally throw ourselves in the crater at the head of the roadway.*[57]

The Maisonneuves and 4 Brigade turned the battle over to a British brigade that had landed on the South Beveland shore, from Breskens. Having taken the peninsula against all odds,

> *a long line of weary, muddy infantrymen plodded slowly back down the road to meet the vehicles that would take them to the new area in Hofstade, a sleepy little Dutch village near Mechelen. The men were indescribably dirty. They were bearded, cold as it is only possible to be in Holland in November, and wet from living in water-filled holes in the ground for 24 hours of the day. Their eyes were red-rimmed from lack of sleep, and they were exhausted from their swift advance on foot under terrible conditions. Yet all ranks realized with a certain grim sense of satisfaction that a hard job had been well and truly done.*[58]

* * *

Walcheren remained. When the Canadians were first given the Antwerp problem in September, and assuming that it would take only a few days to clear Breskens and South

[57] Charlie Forbes, *Fantassin* (Sillery, Quebec: Septentrion, 1994), 175-184.

[58] D.J. Goodspeed, *Battle Royal: A History of the Royal Regiment of Canada, 1862-1962* (Toronto: The Regiment, 1962), 513.

Buffaloes were an invaluable addition to the armoured zoo, moving equally easily on land and water. (PA 191991)

A fought-over Dutch town, probably Oostburg, with a variety of transport including the ubiquitous Bren gun carrier. (PA 137194)

More carriers in a typically devastated landscape. (PA 131252)

Beveland, General Simonds had focused on the island. He persuasively argued that breaching the dykes with bombs would flood its interior and cut off supplies to the isolated German batteries and garrisons. Despite advice from senior engineers that bombing would not cut the high-earth dykes that rimmed the Walcheren saucer, and despite the reluctance of senior air force commanders to divert their heavy bombers from other targets, Simonds won his case. On 3 October, Bomber Command blew a 75-metre gap in the dyke near Westkapelle, and the following days made other breaches near Flushing and Veere. Simonds was less successful in obtaining bombers for continual raids on the 40 German batteries on Walcheren. Autumn weather limited flying, and these tactical operations ranked well below Bomber Command's priority strategic targets of German cities and industrial production facilities. In October, for example, Bomber Command flew 1106 sorties against factories and oil production targets, 10,930 against German cities, and just 1616 in support of ground operations. Moreover, heavy bombs were not the wonder weapons that their awesome destructive power made them seem, especially against guns emplaced in steel and concrete fortifications. Walcheren's 40 batteries would have required Bomber Command's undivided attention over several days to have any appreciative effect, and even then there was little assurance that it would be effective.

In the event, the limited bombing that was carried out was badly dispersed because of a failure of army staffs to establish firm targeting priorities, and most of the German guns were still firing on 1 November when No 4 Special Service Brigade sailed in landing craft for Westkapelle and No 4 Commando for Flushing. The previous afternoon, Simonds told his Historical Officer, he had received word that

> owing to the effects of bombing on civilian life and property at Le Havre, and the Prime Minister's desire to avoid a recurrence of such a situation... carpet bombing on Flushing would not be possible.

Boarding the frigate HMS *Kingsmill* in Ostend, Simonds told the amphibious force commander,

Captain W.F. Pugsley, that, in addition, restricted visibility made it *"uncertain until the last minute whether air support would be available for the assault on Westkapelle,"* and that he would have to decide himself, while at sea, whether to proceed or cancel.

The force sailed and, despite the lack of cover, its commander chose to go — directly into the fire of the powerful guns that neither bombing nor supporting naval fire had been able to suppress. Reckoning, correctly, that the German gunners would concentrate on the support vessels, rather than the landing craft, these small supporting ships let themselves hang as bait to allow the troop carriers to reach shore. It was an extraordinarily courageous and dedicated action. A third of the 27 supporting vessels were sunk, and another third damaged and disabled; 172 sailors were killed and another 125 wounded. The Commandos landed, however, and took their objectives quickly, with relatively light casualties.

Three days later minesweepers worked their way up the Scheldt to allow the first convoy of merchant ships to reach Antwerp on 28 November, almost three months after British troops had arrived in Antwerp. Leading the convoy was the Canadian-built merchant ship *Fort Cataraqui.*

* * *

Only those who experienced the Scheldt can truly know its reality, and the simple recital of chronology marking the progression of this or any other battle masks daily trials that words can barely and only inadequately describe. It takes a vivid imagination to share, however vicariously, conditions that the Queen's Own historian described.

> The fighting...was marked by the utter misery of the conditions and the great courage required to do the simplest things. Attacks had to go along dykes swept by enemy fire. To go through the polders meant wading, without possibility of concealment, in water that at times came up to the chest. Mortar fire, at which the Germans were masters, crashed into every rallying point. Spandaus sent their whining reverberations across the marshes. Our own artillery was deprived of

Antwerp's port facilities were indispensable... (PA 192023)

... and once the approaches were cleared, the ships were unloaded quickly, using all available technology. (PA 192024)

much of its effectiveness because of the great difficulty in reaching an enemy dug in on the reverse slope of a dyke... It was peculiarly a rifleman's fight in that there were no great decisive battles; just a steady, continuous struggle... Never forget the section — a corporal and five or six men. The sections fought the battle and without them, all the vast impedimenta in the rear would be useless. The perils were many; sloshing through the water, a rifleman might step on a mine; pushing aside the body of a dead enemy might explode a booby-trap; failure to search a captured dyke might result in a "silent" enemy firing from the rear. The section corporal must remember to fire at every innocent-looking haystack; and that a tug at an inviting piece of barbed wire would probably set off an automatic alarm. Yet soaking wet, ashen gray, inadequately reinforced, tired to the point of utter exhaustion, the men would push on. What provides the driving force?[59]

All units involved closely examined their Scheldt experiences for clues about that elusive driving force, among other things. Commanders were interested in tactics. After 3rd Division intelligence officers, assisted by Pieter de Winde, had interrogated General Eberding, the German commander of the Breskens Pocket, they took him to meet General Spry. The two commanders discussed their respective tactics. Eberding told Spry that 7 Brigade's initial crossing of the Leopold had *"forced him to commit the reserve battalions of his three infantry regiments,"* and when Spry's imaginative amphibious assault across the Braakman had outflanked his defences he had only ad hoc battle groups to send to that sector. Then, with his reserves committed on either flank, the centre of his position, facing 8 Brigade, was vulnerable. When Spry asked Eberding if he had intended holding Oostburg as a hinge on which to swing his defensive line until he reached the ring of concentric dykes around Cadzand and Zuidzand, the German *"replied that this was so, and he showed some amusement that {their} appreciations had coincided."* He also remarked that *"his men feared our flamethrowers more than any other weapons at our disposal,"* and

was generous in his remarks on the fighting ability of the Canadian soldiers. He said that they were very skilful and versatile in the use of ground, very brave and well provided with good junior leaders. He considered that the command, however, had been too timid in the choice of objectives, that it did not exploit success nor always penetrate deep enough to break up the defence.[60]

Commanders and staffs concluded that, although the nature of the ground had prevented them from deploying the usual array of supporting weapons, the operations demonstrated the fundamental worth of their basic infantry tactics. Because the only approaches were along dykes, operations had to be planned with limited objectives, one flooded polder at a time, and with vehicle movement of any kind so severely restricted the battle was left to small groups of infantrymen supported by their own mortars, artillery, and aircraft.

Both Germans and Canadians were agreed on the powerful effect of aircraft on the battlefield. Of the 27 days of operations, weather restricted flying to 17 days, during which No 84 Group flew 1733 sorties, medium and heavy bombers 508 more. Their missions were as follows: armed reconnaissance aircraft found targets; heavies bombed large gun positions; mediums took on enemy pivot positions like Breskens, Schoondijke, and Oostburg; rocket-firing Typhoons engaged headquarters, field guns, observation posts, and defensive positions; fighter-bombers gave close support; and fighter squadrons flew "Winkles," or area strafing, to disrupt communications. The busiest day was 13 October, when No 84 Group flew 502 sorties in support of troops from Dunkirk to South Beveland, more than half of them in support of 3rd Division. Of these, 150 were pre-planned sorties against casemates, heavy batteries, and selected concentrations of infantry. Another 134 were by four-aircraft stand-by, or cab rank, flights controlled by Forward Control Posts (FCP) against gun positions, strong points, houses, and dykes.

[59] W.T. Barnard, *The Queen's Own Rifles of Canada, 1860-1960* (Toronto: Ontario Publishing, 1960), 234-235.

[60] D Hist, Spry-Eberding correspondence.

Forward control procedures and communications between ground and air had much improved since Normandy, and on occasion response times were as short as 10-15 minutes, when aircraft were controlled from the ground by FCPs.[61] At times communications were more personal. A North Shore platoon commander told of an occasion when they themselves had just dodged fire from Spitfires supporting an adjoining unit:

> The enemy now started to mortar our position from the rear of an orchard 800 yards away and as luck would have it along came a flight of Typhoons from our own Tac Air who had been working with us for months. The flight leader came down to about twenty feet from ground level to see who we were. I stood up and used pantomime to tell him about the enemy mortars back of the orchard and he was a bright lad. Away he went to look at the place and went back and picked up his flight and the mess they made of Jerry's mortar position was beautiful to behold. Then the flight leader came back, waggled his wings and we cheered him on his way.

Another recalled an incident in that *"devil's dream of mud and dykes and rain"*:

> It was a mixed-up mess in every way and one day the Typhoons rocketed us by mistake and I had to grab a twelve-foot length of cellanese {sic} material which we used as air markers and run across an open field toward a wood which I knew held Jerries. But I had to go that way in order to attract the attention of the planes. As I neared the wood the Typhoons came in again and I had first-hand experience of a rocket bomb fairly near. There were seven German soldiers in the wood and I ignored them until I managed to signal the planes away. Then the Germans quickly surrendered, either grateful to me for saving them or awed by my new yellow weapon.[62]

The impact on individuals who endured these abominable conditions is as impossible to generalize as it is for one person to describe pain to another. As one young officer later wrote,

> No one has really been in the same places as anyone else; and I refuse to play the game of comparing experiences. The whole war seems to me a quite private experience.... Each man talks about a quite different war from mine, and ultimately everyone is separated from everyone by layers of privacy or egoism.[63]

Clashes could be very personal. One platoon commander was probing carefully along a dyke with his men spread out behind him.

> {I} went 50 yards and did not hear a sound or see a movement, then rounded a bend and came upon a dead German. This shook me a bit and I went around another bend and saw, 25 yards away, a young German crouched behind a dyke with a rifle across his knees. He was much more petrified than I but it seemed like ages before I could get my sten gun up and start shooting. The ground in front of him spurted jets of mud and he jumped up, threw his rifle and helmet away, and came running toward me with his hands up, shouting in German. There was no mistaking his intense desire to become a prisoner.

Soldiers always find their own ways to adapt to the most awful surroundings. A North Shore company commander visited his

> platoon positions and found everything in order. Then noticed two lads of No 10 Platoon lying almost on top of the dyke as if it were the firing point on a range. They had two pieces of brick between them and under the bricks were francs and guilders. So I stopped to see what was going on and found they were taking turns at firing. If a Jerry broke cover and one fellow fired and missed, he had to pay the other fellow. But if he made a hit the other lad paid him. I went back satisfied. With morale like that it would take a strong enemy to bother us.[64]

To stiffen their own soldiers' resolve, the Germans applied harsh discipline. One of Eberding's subordinates made clear that he would

> have the commander of a strongpoint shot summarily for cowardice in the presence of the enemy, if he is the first to retire without the order to do so, with the poor excuse that he wants to report the situation.[65]

[61] D Hist, AHQ Report 74.

[62] Will Bird, *North Shore (New Brunswick) Regiment* (Fredericton: Brunswick Press, 1963), 447ff.

[63] Donald Pearce, *Journal of a War* (Toronto: Macmillan, 1965), 179.

[64] Bird, *North Shore Regiment*, 449.

[65] Personal, Pieter de Houck letters.

In the circumstances it is little wonder that some Germans, as they were being pushed inexorably to the sea, became fatalistic about the outcome. One young conscript recorded the progression of his thoughts in a diary.

> *Wednesday 4 October. Am very ill. They left me in a foxhole some 100 metres from my room. I have a high temperature but I do not want to go to hospital, not for all the world. Now every man counts. That's why I, a conscript, shall join the battle again. Sunday 15 October. Little by little the struggle is drawing to an end. That's a good thing. For these people, Dutchmen and Germans together in a narrow space, go through inhuman experiences and the losses are severe. It would be a traitor's act to expose these people any longer to the force of arms. For us soldiers there will be only one solution: death or imprisonment. I had imagined the end of the war a bit differently but I must resign myself to the inevitable. The Canadians and the English are passing left and right. Only the paras seem to hold their ground...The artillery strikes home somewhere around here, the song of the front rings out on all sides.*[66]

There is some, albeit incomplete, evidence of ways in which the Scheldt operations tested the limits of human endurance, although we will never know the full toll. Physical casualties can be counted. By the end of October patients filled all 1200 beds in No 12 Canadian General Hospital (CGH), located in a former German facility in a suburb of Bruges. Both No 12 and No 16 CGH, sited at St. Omer during the Boulogne and Calais sieges, took in cases at a rate of 1000 each week; No 12's surgeons, assisted by a staff of Nursing Sisters, had completed 1860 operations. In 3rd Division alone, physical casualties numbered more than 2000, of whom 341 died, and another 400 were hospitalized as sick. The toll for 2nd Division was 2600, 465 of them deaths; almost 900 were hospitalized for sickness.[67]

Emotional costs are not so easily categorized. In 3rd Division, 421 battle exhaustion casualties reached medical treatment centres, in 2nd Division at least 200. Many more cases were handled within their units. None was typical, causes and reactions varying widely, but a Lake Superior officer described the situation:

> *Physical and mental fatigue, or battle exhaustion as we know it, has been without doubt a most important factor and a problem in this field unit. This was caused mostly by continued exposure to mortar, multi-mortar and artillery and SP fire. Also some men who had seen their buddies cut to pieces suffered a subsequent mental shock and had to be evacuated. After and during practically every action one or more men would have to be sent out for a rest or even evacuated in the more extreme cases. Usually we sent them back to the divisional administrative area for a week's rest.*[68]

At this stage of their combat experience, commanders and doctors alike had acknowledged two categories of battle exhaustion: soldiers new to battle who lost their self-control when introduced to the fear, noise, smells, and general chaos of battle; and experienced soldiers who burned out from over-exposure to cumulative stress. They also knew that at the core of battlefield effectiveness were those elusive but vital factors of morale and motivation. At this time, 3rd Division's field psychiatrist, Major Robert Gregory, became concerned about morale because now most of his patients were burnt-out cases. He reported that there

> *was one thing to note among all troops admitted for exhaustion — lack of morale or lack of volition to carry on. The foremost cause of this seemed to be futility. The men claimed there was nothing to which to look forward to — no rest, no leave, no enjoyment, no normal life and no escape. The only way one could get out of battle was death, wounds, self-inflicted wounds and going "nuts."*[69]

Moreover,

> *These are men who have been fighting for 4 or 5 months and had all it took to go through Caen, Falaise, etc. They have seen their units*

66 Personal, Pieter de Houck letters.

67 W.R. Feasby, *Official History of the Canadian Medical Services, 1939-1945*, Volume 1, *Organization and Campaigns* (Ottawa: Queen's Printer, 1956), 256-271.

68 NAC, RG 24, Vol 10, 480, "Battle Experience Questionnaire."

69 Terry Copp and Bill McAndrew, *Battle Exhaustion: Soldiers and Psychiatrists in the Canadian Army, 1939-1945* (Montreal: McGill-Queen's University Press, 1990), 143-144.

Operation Relax, as 3rd Division arrives in Ghent... (PA 192033)

... and the soldiers meet their hosts. (PA 192034)

decimated. Finally they broke down, often after an experience which was not new to them, e.g., loss of a friend or a tank destroyed. In attempting to determine why they broke when they did, I have asked many questions and think the answer is as follows: For months they have had only the type of sleep one gets when eternally on guard. The gradually settling in winter weather without a roof over one's head plays a part; more important is the inability for the subject to see anything except misery and danger in the future; a future which he tells himself must terminate eventually but looks like forever to him at this stage. Most important of all, I think, he has had a feeling, ridiculous as it may be, that he will never actually die, he now begins to feel he is a marked man, that there is a bullet with his name on it.

One intractable difficulty was distinguishing between medical and disciplinary cases. Invariably, the further back from the front the more inclined observers were to classify anyone who displayed untoward behaviour as a malingerer or a coward. Front-line soldiers were more tolerant, realizing that each of them had his own breaking point. One psychiatrist described the futility of simplifying complex behavioural explanations:

The attitudes of the RMO's are of two types. (A) A few RMO's believe that the contagion of exhaustion is heightened by allowing any considerable number of men to be evacuated. These officers make evacuation very difficult and exert pressure on combatant officers to keep the man who is merely "jittery" in the line. The result is that the evacuations for exhaustion are relatively few but there is a possibility that the efficiency of the unit may suffer to some extent. One RMO stated that he was blamed for the large number of AWL's in his unit as the combatant officers felt that these men would normally have been evacuated for exhaustion earlier. (B) The majority of RMO's, yielding perhaps to pressure from fellow officers, feel that the contagion is greater if such men are kept in the line where they demoralize their comrades, and consequently evacuate most cases as they arise.

Other behavioural complexities intervened to affect combat effectiveness. In a questionnaire that many wounded officers completed while recuperating in England, one officer explained how contagion and demoralization could affect morale and battlefield performance.

This is a subject upon which I hold very strong views. Men can be physically and mentally tired yet maintain high morale. But if one man cracks his fear is contagious. One man can ruin the morale of a whole company. On several occasions men were sent to the MO for "nervous exhaustion." They were worthless in an infantry battalion because of their nervous condition. Yet in a few days they would be returned to the battalion. The very next attack, or as soon as we came under heavy fire, these men would crack again. On one occasion, the battalion plan called for the four rifle companies to push deep into a wood held by the enemy, then attack a strong enemy position from the rear. We were to move all night, attack at dawn. When I returned from the battalion "O" Group at 2300 hours, I found men crying, others vomiting. All felt dejected. All this was caused by two men, both of whom had been sent out before but had been returned. Those two men had to be left behind. Had the men in the company not been very tired, the rantings of two men would not have had much effect on them. Even so, had those two nervous wrecks not been returned to us as reinforcements the morale of the company would never have been affected.[70]

Field psychiatrists, as well as other medical officers, were placed in an unenviable position, having responsibilities not only to their patients but also to the army as an institution. One of their most important functions was to conserve manpower. Receiving a soldier with shattered nerves, the psychiatrist had to restore him quickly and send him back to the combat situation that had made him a patient in the first place. Return rates varied with circumstance and, despite Major Gregory's advice, most were returned to combat after a short rest. We do not know how effective these men were, or their eventual fate, during the war or after. The most useful, as well as humane, alternative was to send burnt-out cases to Special Employment Companies where they worked in field hospitals, loaded ammunition, and performed many other non-combat chores.

---

70 "Battle Experience Questionnaire."

56

What kept soldiers going under these abominable conditions? It certainly was not simply the earning of their dollar-a-day. Psychiatrists concluded that there was no unique personality that ensured endurance, or otherwise.

In some, it is a case of my father went through it OK, so I guess I can. In others it seems to be a question of I couldn't let the boys down. Others seem to have a sort of intense sense of responsibility which makes it quite impossible for them to give up and accept illness or at least disability.[71]

For most, it seems, motivation came from unique combinations of concern for comrades, selflessness, fear of showing fear, and sheer cussedness in not letting the other bastards prevail. Infantrymen put it simply:

These were your brothers; you could not let them down.... With nothing to look forward to but pain, deprivation and death, life becomes so intense and so utterly stripped of pretense, cant and falseness, that we were all bound as brothers in the real sense of that word.[72]

These ordinary Canadians, who were called upon to do extraordinary things as a matter of course, took great and deserved pride in what they had achieved. They likely shared the sentiments of Private Bradley, who wrote to his mother, *"When the enemy gets into strong positions, the war becomes very brutal. The guy that has the best technology and the best infantry is the guy that's going to win those battles."* Bradley was convinced that he was in the best platoon, in the best company, in the best battalion.

Even Jerry will admit we're pretty hot stuff. Our Brigade, which is all Highland outfits, has been going since D-Day, has never given up an inch of ground to Jerry in all his counter attacks of which we've had plenty. We took out Caen, were the spearhead in the breakthrough south of Caen, took out Boulogne, Cap Gris Nez, and Calais, landed in the Scheldt and fought through to take out Knocke-sur-Mer....[73]

Considering the terrain and that the German garrison was three times larger than originally estimated, it is little wonder that the Canadians battled for 27 days rather than the three to four that staff officers initially thought would be required to conduct their methodical, grinding advance. Third Division's staff calculated that, of the 137 days of campaigning since D-Day, infantry battalions had been active in combat between 104 and 108. At last, both 2nd and 3rd divisions got a week's rest, the former around Antwerp and Brussels, the latter at Ghent. Captain Martin explained that Operation Relax

was conceived some time ago when it was considered that the fighting efficiency of 3rd Canadian Infantry Division was being impaired by continuous fighting and that it needed a genuine rest in comfortable surroundings.

Consequently, when the burgomaster of Ghent graciously offered to billet all 15,000 or so men of the division in private homes as guests, they gratefully accepted.

Many were understandably apprehensive about turning 15,000 soldiers, just released from a month of bitter misery and death, loose in a large city. Martin, for one,

hoped that {Ghent's} citizens do not have cause to regret their generosity, for the Canadian soldier on leave from the fighting front is not noted for his gentility.... It remained now only to demonstrate the truth of the thesis that soldiers fresh from the line could be safely introduced into a more genteel milieu.

He need not have worried. As they arrived from the front, the soldiers were given billeting cards with addresses, met their hosts, and dispersed to homes all over the city. Martin continued in his war diary:

The entry of the first troops (7 Brigade) was not unlike a triumphal procession: an endless line of vehicles of every sort rumbled through the streets, which were crowded with cheering civilians. As events proved, neither military nor civil powers had cause to doubt that it could be done, and it was even considered that an important precedent had been established. Discipline, certainly, was not that of the parade square, but this had never been the intention, and serious breaches were so few as to be negligible. The cheerfulness of the Canadians

---

71 Copp and McAndrew, *Battle Exhaustion*, 149-161.

72 Shaun Brown, "The Loyal Edmonton Regiment," MA thesis, Wilfrid Laurier University, 171.

73 D Hist, Bradley letters.

57

delighted the civilians and their behaviour generally was much admired. One point of etiquette, which might not occur to North Americans, was remarked on: the Canadian private soldiers knew how to use a knife and fork.

Lieutenant Donald Pearce of the North Novas, who was among the happy visitors, also was relieved to see that *"the troops have responded by acting for a change like gentlemen, as if they had somehow caught the character of the city."* That character, Pearce thought, was defined by Ghent's *"fine views, quiet buildings, all silver-grey...as if everything in it had arisen at one time, and that a long time ago...{with} tremendous dignity and peace."* Besides their wonderful city, it may have been Ghent's citizens who captured the hearts of the soldiers. They had plastered the windows of shops with signs reading: *"Soldiers of the Allied Nations — thank you for the quick liberation of our dearest Belgium."*[74]

---

[74] Pearce, *Journal of a War,* 81-82.

(PA 190972)

CHAPTER III

WINTER

The weather having turned cold some days ago has now frozen ground solid and ditches are fit for skating — and hundreds of Dutch people out on them. They seem to love skating and not a sign of a hockey stick anywhere. Their skates are long thin metal blades with a curl up at front end and all set in a piece of wood with straps to put on ordinary shoes. And the children carry them on a string around their necks all the time, ie, going to and from school. Our soldiers have started skating too and it is becoming common to see them arm in arm with a Dutch girl on their way to the ice. Must have developed a common language.[75]

While the Canadians were enjoying a Belgian respite from their ordeal in the Scheldt, General Simonds personally briefed groups of officers in Ghent and Malines on the course of the campaign. He told them that the key to future operations was whether the Germans decided to fight on the near side of the Rhine to keep Allied guns out of range of their cities, or retire beyond the river in order to use it as a barrier. Simonds thought the

former more likely and was so confident that it would spell the end of the war before New Year's that he placed bets on it. In the event, despite holding on to the Rhine's west bank, the Germans fought on for another five months.

First Canadian Army's winter role differed from its previous ones. In early November, units relieved British and American troops deployed along the Maas and Waal rivers where they remained in defensive static lines until their next major operation in the Rhineland in the early spring of 1945. Having returned to First Army after recovering from his illness, General Crerar assumed responsibility for a 300-kilometre front extending from Dunkirk to Nijmegen. He deployed I British Corps, including 1st Polish and 4th Canadian Armoured divisions, in the west, and II Canadian Corps, with the 2nd and 3rd Canadian and the 3rd and 49th British divisions, around Nijmegen. Several command changes accompanied the switch in roles. General Simonds returned to II Corps; General Foulkes

---

[75] D Hist, Brigadier N.E. Rodger diary.

59

left 2nd Division to take command of I Canadian Corps in Italy, and was replaced by Major General A.B. Matthews. Major General H.W. Foster also went to Italy to command 1st Canadian Infantry Division, and its commander, Major General C. Vokes, took over 4th Armoured.

With the Germans also on the defensive in these months, relatively few units were in direct contact with the enemy at any one time. Comparative quiet allowed divisions to rotate brigades, and brigades battalions, between the front line and rest areas, while reconnaissance regiments filled gaps along deserted stretches. Static lines produced fewer casualties, and the operational pause came at an opportune time, because the four to five months of active operations since Normandy had cost the Canadians dearly. By late fall, the toll of killed and wounded, which had stripped infantry battalions of most of their originals, was staggering. In the Scheldt operations alone, there were more than 6000 casualties, between 75 and 80 per cent of them infantrymen, a rate of loss comparable to the worst battles of the First World War. Although replacements arrived, there were never enough of them, and sustaining the combat effectiveness of battalions became perhaps the most intractable problem commanders at all levels had to face.

Heavy losses gave rise to Canada's "manpower crisis," or more properly its "trained infantryman crisis." When Canada went to war in 1939 it had been impossible to foresee accurately the eventual scope and shape of the country's military commitments, or predict that within a few years more than one million men and women of a population of scarcely 12 million would be in uniform. National commitments to the war effort accumulated piecemeal without an effective allocation of personnel resources among the services. Competition was not eased when, to preserve a semblance of national unity, two armies were formed — a volunteer force to fight anywhere, and a conscript one to serve in Canada only. Warping allocations further, planners assumed that the war would be a mechanized one and gave priority to finding tradesmen to man specialized units, leaving the remainder to the infantry. Finally, wastage rates, the cold

calculations of expected casualties on which planners based their recruiting and training requirements, had been determined according to British experience in North Africa; these figures seriously under-estimated actual infantry losses in the riflemen's war that characterized fighting in Italy and northwest Europe.

Reinforcement problems had first surfaced in Italy in December 1943 when 1st Canadian Infantry Division lost 4000 men to the enemy or to sickness, and even with replacements the division was left more than 1000 men short, most of these from rifle platoons. It must be kept in mind that the fighting point of an infantry division is not large: perhaps 3000 riflemen of the division's full establishment of 18,000, and, while men were available, few of them were trained to fill the right holes. By the summer of 1944, with Canadians taking heavy casualties in both Italy and Normandy, infantry shortages became acute. Unable to send trained infantrymen from the Canadian conscript army overseas, personnel administrators canvassed static units for drivers, storemen, mechanics, and anti-aircraft gunners, as well as former infantrymen who had been employed in administrative jobs. They were to be given a crash course in infantry survival and sent to battalions in the front line. There were, however, too few of them, and complaints that those who did arrive were inadequately trained grew in volume, as the Minister of Defence, Colonel J.L. Ralston, learned when he visited Italy and Belgium in the fall of 1944. Ralston ordered the complaints investigated and eventually left the government when he advocated sending overseas conscripts then serving in Canada.

It is difficult to evaluate the validity of the complaints about inadequately trained reinforcements. When on Ralston's instructions investigators examined the training records of replacements, they concluded that most of them met acceptable standards. The investigators argued that fighting commanders would never be satisfied no matter how good the replacements were. This reliance on paper records ran strangely counter to innumerable anecdotal reports of men arriving in units inadequately prepared for combat. For example, during the Scheldt fighting, the Black Watch diarist reported that

Locating mines was a routine if nerve-wracking job for sappers... (PA 116748)

... but prodding to expose and then disarm them was worse. (PA 191995)

almost half of 379 men in its rifle companies had at most a month's infantry training, and that

the previous training of a man listed as for instance one month on paper, probably represents considerably less time actual training. This assumption is borne out by the fact that very few men arrive with knowledge of the Piat {infantry antitank weapon} or elementary section and platoon tactics. Some reinforcements have never fired the bren {gun} or handled grenades.

Leaving aside academic debate about how many anecdotes are needed to complete a theory, the length of time spent on training was not necessarily a valid indication of the quality and effectiveness of that training. One example will illustrate how a soldier could slip through the system. A private, on arriving in England, failed basic tests on the Bren light machine gun, the Thompson sub-machine gun, grenades, and the PIAT. One of his instructors interviewed him to determine why he had not learned such elementary skills, and the soldier's story was a long one. Having enlisted in Toronto on 7 March 1944, he proceeded to Brantford, Ontario, for eight weeks' basic training, which he completed on 26 May. The young soldier

stated that in that time of eight weeks he was exempt trg {training} for four weeks on light duty and was excused all but two route marches,

which, nonetheless, did not prevent him from proceeding to the Advanced Training Centre at Camp Borden for a week, where he was again put on light duty. Posted to a training centre in Calgary for two months, he was excused for three weeks due to a gas-stove explosion. By his own account he received little weapons instruction, nor did he ever throw a hand grenade. He fired one smoke bomb and two high-explosive bombs from a two-inch mortar, but failed to achieve the necessary standard on both rifle and Bren gun. Having completed, at least on paper, his Advanced Infantry Training on 5 August, supposedly in accordance with the standard syllabus, the recruit then went on two weeks' leave before sailing overseas on 1 September. In his three weeks at Number 2 Canadian Infantry Reinforcement Unit he was employed as a hut orderly, and though he fired the rifle and the

Bren he threw no grenades and received no training on the two-inch mortar; he saw the Thompson sub-machine gun and the PIAT for the first time, firing three dummy bombs from the latter. In all, in Canada and England, the soldier seems to have acquired 12 weeks' training at most. The officer who interviewed him noted:

It is realized that this may be an exceptional case but it is such cases that tend to pull down the general efficiency of a draft.[76]

Many of the engineers, gunners, and other tradesmen who had been remustered as riflemen were potentially first-rate infantry soldiers. Lieutenant Colonel V. Stott of the South Saskatchewan Regiment reported that he had

interviewed several of these men and by talking to them and sizing them up {had} made the following observations: (a) Gen standard of physique and type of man is good. (b) Above average in intelligence.

The problem was that reinforcement and training depots had not taken advantage of their potential to instruct the recruits properly. Their one-month training syllabus had included nine days of leave, and only three hours indoctrination on each of the PIAT, the Sten machine pistol, the Bren, the rifle, and grenades, allowing trainees only enough time to throw three grenades, fire two live antitank bombs, two magazines of ammunition on the Sten, and 70 rounds through the Bren. There was no organized range practice, no time spent in field craft, no instruction on fire orders or target recognition, very little indoctrination on the German army, and only two route marches. Stott concluded:

The above gives some indication of why these men do not come to a fd {field} unit equipped for infantrymen the way they should be, and it is very important to an inf{antry} bn {battalion} that regardless of what type of rfts {reinforcements} are received, these rfts must know something about inf. In many cases they arrive at the fd unit one day and are up fighting in the front line the next day. In my opinion it takes more than a month to attain for

76 Besides that contained in unit war diaries, the above and following information concerning reinforcements is in the NAC, RG24, volumes 9777, 9897, 9900.

other arms something of an inf perspective, and if only 1 month is to be allotted the trg of these men, that month should contain 31 full days of trg....

Every effort is being made to train these men when they arrive at the unit, but in the majority of cases this is impossible owing to the fact that these men are needed as rfts for the front line and cannot be trained back at B Ech {echelon}. It is being done whenever possible.

When men like this reached a front-line battalion much depended upon the condition of the unit when he arrived. If his platoon was not in action, and a soldier had a chance to meet his new mates and non-commissioned officers, they could at least partially prepare him for the combat that was fashioned to kill or maim him. If he went straight into battle on arrival, a soldier's chances of surviving were drastically reduced. As well, shortages drove down morale by putting additional burdens on fewer and fewer men. One infantry officer described it well:

Men worry about the arrival of reinforcements. They don't mind being understrength so long as they know reinforcements will definitely arrive in the near future. But they never knew when they would come. The strength of a section would often be reduced so that you did not have enough riflemen to put in an attack.... Lack of reinforcements was a constant topic with the men. They felt the risk of becoming a casualty was greater, because the strength of a platoon was less. Definitely, lack of reinforcements lowered morale.

The result was a vicious circle, producing more casualties and lowering a unit's ability to fight. French-speaking battalions were especially vulnerable. On 1 September Le Régiment de Maisonneuve was short 276 riflemen, Les Fusiliers Mont-Royal 333. An officer in the former described their problems in a questionnaire:

Fatigue was a serious problem with our unit due to the lack of rest. We had numerous cases of first class soldiers going AWL for a few days. The reason given by them on their return was that the only way they could get any rest was by going AWL. It was more or less impossible for the unit to send any LOB {left out of battle} personnel to the rear as for a long

time rifle companies were fighting with an average of 40 other ranks. Where we did begin to receive reinforcements they were so poorly trained that some could not even strip a bren gun. Others had never fired a two-inch mortar or PIAT. Some had absolutely no infantry training of any kind.[77]

The Army acknowledged a serious fault line in the reinforcement system and took steps to improve it. But finding suitable instructors was difficult, for many of those best qualified to teach were also those most needed in their battalions at the front. Nevertheless, Major General J.H. Roberts, who had commanded 2nd Division during the Dieppe raid and was now responsible for reinforcement units in Britain, requested five battalion commanders, two of them French-speaking, and 25 officers capable of commanding companies, 10 of them French-speaking, to help prepare new soldiers for battle. Roberts also requested 200 battle-wise NCOs, all to be detached for three months and subject to recall if it became operationally necessary. In early January 18 officers and 196 NCOs went to Britain to take up training duties, with more to follow in subsequent weeks.

Divisions in the field also did what they could to ensure that replacements underwent realistic training in battalion rear echelons, to fire weapons, throw grenades, practise battalion battle procedures, and learn the basics of combat discipline before they went into action. It is well that there was time during the inactive winter months to replenish, and at least one battalion commander was grateful for the long interval between costly operations:

It took me all winter to get my battalion into adequate shape to break out on the Rhine. If we had really got involved in another long-drawn-out, head-knocking operation again, we'd have been in big trouble.[78]

* * *

The pause in ground operations did not apply to those Canadians involved in the continuing air

77 "Battle Experience Questionnaire."
78 D. and S. Whitaker, *Tug of War* (Toronto: Stoddart, 1984), 217.

war, and for Royal Canadian Air Force squadrons it was business as usual. Air power had grown geometrically in importance in the course of the war, and Canadians flew in all the varied missions of the Second Tactical Air Force, which supported 21st Army Group. Second TAF was composed of 2 Group (medium bombers), 85 Group (night fighters), 83 Group (fighters in support of Second British Army), and 84 Group (fighters in support of First Canadian Army).

Interdicting German supply lines — bombing bridges and strafing railways and vehicle convoys to disrupt the enemy's communications — was the principal task of the RCAF pilots concentrated in 83 Group, who represented about a quarter of those flying Second TAF's fighters and fighter-bombers, and who accounted for more than half of the rail cuts and a third of the locomotives.[79] Providing close support for the army was the other main task, and the day-fighters had followed close behind the ground advance to keep their short-range aircraft within striking distance of the front.

By this time, long-range American fighters had broken the back of the German fighter forces, so these posed less of a threat to pilots than other hazards. With so much of their bombing and strafing conducted at extremely low altitudes, anti-aircraft fire — or flak — was the main danger they faced, and, with the front now static, the Germans had time to deploy anti-aircraft batteries in greater numbers. Second TAF noted in late November that the Germans were concentrating on protecting vulnerable points with anti-aircraft guns, and that the increasing intensity of flak suggested that they were moving *up batteries from deeper in the Reich, to make a 20-mile protective belt between the Rhine and the Ruhr rivers.*

The pilots' other main hindrance was bad autumn weather. Low cloud, rain, or snow so often masked ground targets that squadrons had to bomb blind. With newly developed techniques, Ground Control Interception radar (GCI) could track a dozen Spitfires, eight Typhoons, or six medium bombers, and the GCI controller could guide pilots close to a target, keeping the planes above 3000 metres, beyond the range of light anti-aircraft fire. Operational

researchers later reported that this technique was as effective as visual bombing methods.

After dark, 409 and 410 (Night-fighter) squadrons, flying all-purpose twin-engined Mosquitoes, provided cover to front-line troops, since what was left of the German air force preferred to attack after dark. Night-flying operations, relying on mottled green electronic displays and the unemotional voice of a ground controller, may not have seemed as dramatic as free-wheeling aerial combats. Each time they went up, however, night-fighter crews had a better statistical chance of shooting down an enemy aircraft than pilots in the Spitfire squadrons — needing just 34 sorties for each victory compared to the day-fighters' 119. Over the course of the campaign, the two Canadian squadrons serving in Second TAF claimed a total of 53 enemy aircraft destroyed, while their own casualties amounted to 21 aircrew — with more than half the latter dying in flying accidents.

* * *

While the army's small fighting point marked time during the winter pause, behind them was a vast organization that included large numbers of administrators, logisticians, doctors and nurses, truck drivers, laundry technicians, and a host of others whose day-to-day work went on as usual. Among them were engineers responsible for keeping open the roads and bridges the army and air force needed to keep troops supplied with the food, ammunition, and other material resources they would require when the tempo of the campaign picked up. The engineers' huge establishment permeated all levels of First Canadian Army. Answering directly to Army Headquarters were three works battalions, two tunnelling companies, two road-construction companies, various mechanical, equipment, park, and workshop companies, and four field companies. Each corps and division headquarters had direct authority over three field companies and a park company, for a total of more than 6000 sappers.

In the winter of 1944-45, their top priority was constructing and maintaining roads,

[79] Air force records cited here and below are in D Hist.

Sappers also had to maintain all types of roads, and adapted 19th-century techniques when necessary. (PA 140645)

a continuing task whose lack of glamour was matched only by its dire necessity, and whose scale of operations matched that of most provincial works departments. Already over-taxed by the large numbers of heavy vehicles using them, the roads failed under bad weather much more rapidly than usual. Road crews had to deal with three causes of collapse: softening of the material below the pavement or surface, road sides (verges) failed into ditches when vehicles ran too close to the edge, and delay in repairing potholes. Proper care and maintenance was mandatory, the 2nd Canadian Road Construction Company cautioned its sappers, because

> There are many verges now which would not have collapsed or even needed extra metal IF THE DRAINAGE HAD BEEN ATTENDED TO in the first instance. The solution {was to} IMMEDIATELY inaugurate works to drain water off the surface of the roadway and its verges, as well as a two-foot margin of safety to either side. Only with CEASELESS attention to DRAINAGE

could roads be kept open indefinitely.[80]

Field engineers, whose usual jobs were to lay or breach minefields, build bridges, demolish pillboxes, and the like, also focused their efforts on maintaining roads. The 11th Field Company reported that during November *"hundreds of tons of rubble have been hauled from Nijmegen"* to resurface routes. Though one war diary referred to the winter period sarcastically as *"some rest,"* at least sappers were able to obtain help from civilian labourers, even if only after *"continued pressure by the Burgomaster."* There were 15 field companies or squadrons in the theatre, and since it was not unusual for an entire unit to be working on one stretch of road, the scope of the task is obvious. Strict priorities had to be established so that the most important lines of communication could be kept open. As 7th Field Company reported in December, one route *"has had a pretty bad goinover {sic} in the last few days,"* making it necessary to *"descend on it like a bunch of bees or it will disappear completely."*

Roads were put to good use, trucks continually making round trips between front-line supply dumps and depots in Antwerp, the Channel ports, and all the way back to

Normandy. Convoys had to negotiate all manner of obstacles, natural and bureaucratic. The adventures of one 18-vehicle detachment can serve as an example. The convoy left its camp in Holland on 8 December and arrived in Bayeux two days later. The operators of No 14 Army Ordnance Depot (AOD), however, where drivers and their helpers were to pick up stores, had not been warned of their arrival. After waiting about for several hours the men went to Carpiquet Airfield where they stayed overnight in their vehicles. The AOD finally located their cargoes and they spent the next two days loading and sorting out paperwork before the vehicles started for home on the 12th. Refused accommodation at Rouen, the convoy made its way to Poix for the night, and the drivers returned to their platoon lines on 14 December, after a six-day, 1200-kilometre journey. Fortunately their collective sense of humour was still intact:

> The journies {sic} in the area of No 14 AOD and its several sub parks to pick up the required stores was a nightmare of thin soupy mud, and treacherous pot-holes, the worst stretches of road ever seen outside a northern Canadian muskeg. Within an hour of our arrival vehicles and men were plastered from head to foot with mud, illiciting {sic} comments from some of the less hardy members of the expedition, as to where abouts of issues of hip waders for the use of, and small row boats. Two days spent in the dump and vehicles and men assumed a brownish hue, covered with a coating of ruddy mud.

Their impression of their fellow logisticians, though, was less than flattering:

> The organization of the AOD appears to the layman as being so vast and cumbersome, as to be almost unwieldy, it requiring much sweat and hard words to get the necessary papers through.

Soldiers quickly adapt to circumstances, whether cushy or miserable, and units rotating through defensive positions made them as habitable as they could. Gunners in 4th Field, for example, despite *"cold, wet and foggy"* weather, lived in dugouts near their guns and made themselves

---

80 Unless otherwise noted, this and the following material is from unit war diaries in the RG24 Series at the NAC.

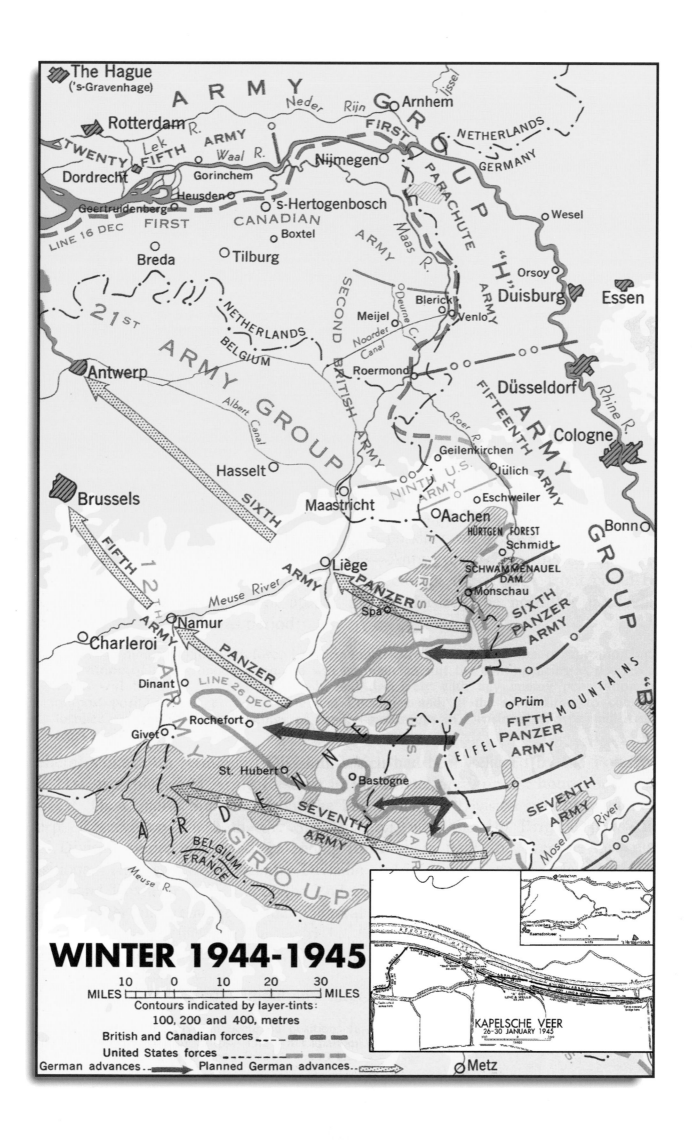

WINTER 1944-1945

10   0   10   20   30

MILES ⊢┼┼┼┼┼──┼──────┼──────┼ MILES

Contours indicated by layer-tints:
100, 200 and 400, metres

British and Canadian forces   — — —

United States forces   — — —

German advances   ──→   Planned German advances ◁═══▷

KAPELSCHE VEER
26-30 JANUARY 1945

quite comfortable, having underground stoves, beds, easy chairs, rugs, etc., from the smashed houses in the area. Everyone slept underground except R.H.Q. {regimental headquarters} personnel who had the only building in the district, a large modern one looking like a summer hotel perched on a hill overlooking the gun positions. Work never ended on the dugouts and by the time the regiment finally did leave there were many who were sorry to leave them behind. Most of these underground habitations were shacks built in a hole and covered with earth. The 14th Battery built an Officers' Mess in this manner which was more comfortable than many battery messes in England, and one major built a complete log cabin underground. All dugouts had batteries and electric bulbs, and the 2nd Battery had proper electric lights, the power being brought in off a nearby line.[81]

Airmen also improvised imaginatively to improve their lot. At Eindhoven, home of RCAF Typhoons, the electricians of No 143 Wing used a German stock of underground transmission cable and overhead transmission wire to string more than 15 kilometres of wiring for permanent lighting in quarters and working buildings. Other tradesmen rigged up oil-drip stoves from German furnace boilers, not unlike those fashioned in many prairie homes years before. An aircraft drop tank made a hot-water tank that, with some rubber tubing and a stirrup pump, fed an adequate shower. Bits of wood and pipe, a piece of steel runway matting, and strips of inner tubes made a bed. According to an RCAF Historical Officer, Flying Officer Carl Reinke,

The erks showed amazing ingenuity in what they were able to assemble from the parts of abandoned and partially destroyed German equipment. They made everything run that had ever been intended to run, including tractors, diesel locomotives which they found on small-gauge station rail lines, road rollers. They built individual power units out of parts of German aircraft generators, motorcycles, and so on. They set up telephone communications between individual tents, using equipment from Gerry dugouts. From old automobile engines, water-bowser frames and Gerry pumps they built pumps to move oil from drums (in which it arrived) to bowsers, putting it through a pressure filter en route, substituting the whole for the small capacity pumps issued with the bowsers. They built their own trailers by attaching wheels from a German vehicle to one of the German cupboards which were to be found everywhere.[82]

There was time during the winter for rest and recuperation leaves that gave soldiers an opportunity to see something of Europe beyond their slit trenches and shelled-out buildings. A lucky few, who had volunteered for service in the early days of the war, returned to Canada for a time, but these were a mere handful. Generally, day-trips or breaks of up to a week allowed officers and men to make their way to Paris, Brussels, and other cities. Leave centres were set up in several locations to accommodate men at affordable prices, and they could either eat free at army-run restaurants or pay going prices at civilian ones. The air force even operated a ski resort in the Alps. Reinke found that

in Paris, by general consensus — including American opinion — the leave arrangements for Canadians {were} tops in quality...{the troops} revelled in the ultimate luxury of the Palais d'Orsay, bordering on the south bank of the Seine. All was gilt and maroon velours and satins and crystal chandeliers there.

David Marshall agreed:

Our room was the biggest hotel room I had ever seen. It was luxurious. Two big beds, a bathroom with a bath tub with hot and cold water, and a funny bathroom fixture that shot water straight up.

Brussels was closer, and the Auxiliary Services — operated by the Salvation Army, Canadian Legion, YMCA, and Knights of Columbus — ran several hotels and canteens, while Education Officers arranged tours of Brussels. For one city excursion, a staff member would meet a small group of soldiers, give them a city guide, and take them to the "Blue Pool" for a swim: "towel, soap and swimming suit {were} free, {while} valet service and seamstress {were} available, also Cdn cigarettes and chocolate bars at the canteen." Reinke elaborated:

The Blue Pool was a unique part of the leave arrangement for Canadians. It was basically

---

81 D Hist, "History of 4th Field Regiment."

82 D Hist, "Fighter Wings on the Continent."

Parcels from home were always welcome, but especially at Christmas... (PA 192026)

... when soldiers shared them with Dutch and Belgian children. (PA 184087)

a beautifully large swimming pool with a snack bar attached, where the elusive "cokes" could usually be obtained, just like home. But in addition, an army or air force lad just in from the front line or camp, dirty and unkempt, could get himself completely renovated there, with little effort on his part. On entering the place, he would go through a line like a clothing parade at an equipment depot. He would turn in his dirty, wrinkled uniform to be sponged and pressed while he was in swimming. He would turn in his dirty shirt, socks and underwear and be issued with other, clean clothing from the large stock always on hand. There were also two barbers in the place. So, altogether, he might arrive looking like a tramp and leave looking fit for any parade.

After leaving the pool, soldiers went to City Hall Square for a tour of the old Lower Town, followed by lunch at the Maple Leaf Club (at 20 to 25 francs, the equivalent of a dollar), and, finally, a two-hour tram ride around the city. There were innumerable pubs and varied nightlife. Another possibility was a trip to nearby Waterloo, and during the last two weeks of November many also saw an exhibition arranged by Canadian War Artists at the Palais des Beaux Arts, featuring works by Orville Fisher, George Pepper, and Will Ogilvie.

* * *

Life for units in the line was generally dull and routine. Both sides regularly shelled one another, and line-crossers moved back and forth across the Maas and Waal rivers. Some were agents infiltrating opposing defences, and others were helping paratroopers who had evaded capture at Arnhem get away to safety. In one extended section of the front, Manitoba Dragoon armoured cars covered a division's normal frontage. Arriving in the Roosendaal area on 7 November, the regiment settled into a system of patrolling that continued for several months. It was for the most part a cold, boring, and uneventful time, as recorded in a typical war diary report:

There was very little activity along the complete front today and a patrol from "C" Sqn {squadron} took a small boat into the R Maas and sailed about the river, but did not cross to the other side. The patrol saw nothing of interest on the other side, nor did they draw any fire. Contact was established by telephone with resistance movement on the Island of Schouwen ... and some interesting infm {information} believed to be quite reliable was reported through "B" Sqn. Some gun posns {positions} were given and also the time and routes of small enemy naval convoys were reported. We have an air support LO {Liaison Officer}, Lt R Berry, attached to us, but the dull weather has grounded aircraft, and this area now has a low priority, it will be difficult to direct air support on enemy on Schouwen.

For the first few weeks, patrols replaced one another with unrelieved dullness, the only excitement being the desertion of 15 German soldiers — Armenians captured on the eastern front, who had volunteered for duty rather than starve in prison camps. As the weather grew colder, opposition warmed up, with shelling and mortaring continuing intermittently for weeks but inflicting few casualties.

The most vital sector of the lengthy Canadian front was that around Nijmegen, bordering Germany and connected by the large bridge over the Waal with the island leading to the Rhine at Arnhem. Over the weeks the enemy tried several times to demolish the vital bridge — for example, by using the river current to float mines, against which it was difficult to devise countermeasures. Sappers strung booms across the river, but floating debris tended to accumulate against them until they broke from the strain. On 15 November, the Germans did manage to damage the bridge when a mine with 150 kilograms of explosives detonated on contact.

For infantry units in the line, the winter fighting came to assume the flavour of the trench lines of the First World War. Particularly reminiscent was the perceived need to dominate no man's land. While a soldier in his slit trench overlooking the sodden Dutch countryside around Nijmegen saw the area immediately around him as the most crucial piece of ground on the front, commanders necessarily had wider perspectives. They continually monitored enemy activities to determine whether the Germans

Training for Kapelsche Veer. (PA 131782)

were moving troops in or out of the sector, and the quality of those troops, in order to evaluate their strength and capabilities as well as to deduce their intentions. For example, movements of tanks or parachute units into a particular area might well signal a pending attack that required countermeasures. Accordingly, in December General Crerar instructed:

It is becoming increasingly important that Cdn Army patrols dominate No Man's Land and water and that the enemy be prevented from obtaining information as to our dispositions and intentions by action {of} his own patrols or by infiltration of agents.

Patrolling took several forms. Small standing patrols of a few men deployed in front of trench lines with a field telephone or radio gave warning of enemy forays; larger ones ambushed them. Reconnaissance patrols moved into enemy territory to gain what information they could about defensive positions, troop movements, and routines.

Larger fighting patrols used reconnaissance information to attack German outposts and take prisoners who could provide valuable data about unit identifications. Intelligence staffs could assess enemy morale by questioning prisoners and deserters, such as one 18-year-old named Edgar Knuf. His interrogator reported that Knuf had been conscripted into the SS on 15 June 1944 and had served in a variety of training and holding units before ending up in the 1st Battalion of the 22nd SS Panzer Grenadier Regiment of the 10th SS Division. Now in the line against the Canadians, Knuf's morale declined as living conditions deteriorated over the winter and he saw his company lose 20 men in a month to mortar fire and sickness.

Hot rations came up at 1800 hrs each day {but}... they were always cold and greasy by the time they got up to the fwd {forward} lines. They were supposed to get 6 cigarettes per day but got tobacco without papers instead. PW {Knuf} said tobacco was dried grass. Nothing was done to improve drinking water or to control its use. PW believed this was the reason for about 50% of his unit suffering from Diarrhoea. PW has had the illness for 4 weeks and was in a sorry condition. {One night} Knuf was on outpost duty and when he returned to his
position he found his trench full of water and his bread, chocolate {the first he had seen in months}, tobacco and everything ruined. That was too much for him and he deserted.

In the course of the winter, both sides increased the tempo of patrolling, which included large-scale raids that were also reminiscent of the trench warfare of the First World War. Perhaps the most spectacular of these was Operation Mickey Finn, 2nd Division's most ambitious assault of the winter. The raid was prepared and executed by D Company of the Black Watch, heavily supported by an artillery battery of the 5th Field Regiment, two platoons of 4.2-inch mortars, a company of medium machineguns of the Toronto Scottish, and three-inch mortars from both the Calgary Highlanders and the Black Watch itself. They planned in minute detail, according to their diarist.

During the day Maj E.W. Hudson had found a piece of ground, near his Company area, resembling very closely that upon which the men would be fighting and had had the advance to the assault rehearsed a few times "dry." Times and distances were closely checked and the whole planned with the most minute detail. Trenches were constructed on the practice ground according to the dimensions shown in the Div{isional} Int{elligence} Sum{mary} as being the type used by the enemy in front of the Reichswald.

H-Hour was set for 2000 on 7 December, the company deploying with No 16 Platoon on the right, No 18 on the left, and No 17 in the centre, with support weapons positioned on the flanks and artillery on call. Before the assault began, mortars dropped smoke to mask houses on the left of what was to become a small battlefield, while machine guns covered the right; infantry slowly made their way to within 50 metres of the enemy, who was being shelled. Artillery lifted from the objective and began pounding a small ridge further back, which might harbour German positions, and a known gun emplacement off to the right. Support weapons continued to fire at the houses on the left and the woods to the right, the whole serving to isolate the small German garrison. Platoons *"went in with everything going and while it lasted, action was fast and furious."* Only a severe wound or the capture of a prisoner made it

Behind the front, military policemen kept traffic moving in all conditions. (PA 192021)

permissible for anyone to withdraw before the scheduled time of 2015. Getting out proved more difficult than moving in, the enemy's mortars having registered the area through which the Canadians had to withdraw and the company *"sustained several casualties in the initial stages of the mortaring and Lieut T.W. MacKenzie was one who could not be evacuated and must be listed as missing."* They took one prisoner and killed or wounded possibly 50 Germans in the night's grim work, while losing nine of their own men.

At this time the Germans introduced a different category of indiscriminate slaughter when Hitler ordered that V2s be targeted exclusively against London and Antwerp. These rockets were the second of Hitler's weapons of revenge, the earlier V1 having consisted of a flying one-ton bomb propelled by a pulse-jet engine. Its successor, a crude ballistic missile, was able to rise to the statosphere, then plunge to earth without giving any warning. The first V2 exploded in Antwerp on 16 October and the first V1 on 16 December, and they continued to fall until March 1945. In all, almost 6000 missiles hit the Antwerp region, causing more than 11,000 civilian and military casualties. One of the worst single incidents was a V2 attack that demolished the Rex cinema on the Keyserlei, killing 567, of whom 296 were Allied soldiers. A Canadian doctor, Major J.B. Hillsman, wrote that the attacks made Antwerp

> *a very unpleasant location at this time.... These flying bombs were not very dangerous from a percentage viewpoint but all mathematics were thoroughly driven out of your mind by their terrific blasts. All the windows of the Hospital had been blown out and the bombs were falling irregularly every ten or fifteen minutes. You just sat back and waited for them and never relaxed. It soon began to get on our nerves and the Hospital was moved to St Michelle, Holland.*[83]

Canadian Nursing Sisters serving in army hospitals in Antwerp, Ghent, and other targeted areas also closely observed the random destruction of these diabolical weapons.

> Their eleven weeks' stay in Antwerp had been an eventful experience for the nursing sisters of the two hospitals.... [They] learned to keep doors and windows open, because of the blast.

Ceilings were coming down; but by taking cover in slit-trenches dug in a small adjoining park, all escaped injury. There would be sombre memories of a horribly full morgue and wards crowded with badly-injured civilian patients, all victims of a hit by a V-bomb on a packed Antwerp theatre.... It was the misfortune of No 20 Canadian General Hospital to reach Antwerp about the time that the rocket attacks on that city were nearing their peak. "Fifteen minutes after our arrival," recorded the unit diary on December 18, 1944, "a V-2 greeted us — giving some of the boys a bit of a scare."[84]

Rockets were just a part of the German attempt to reverse allied gains of the previous months. Their most important operation was the December offensive that drove a large wedge into American forces in the Battle of the Bulge. As early as September, Hitler had ordered his commanders to form an armoured reserve able to stage a decisive counter-offensive when they judged the Allied Armies to be unbalanced. Their intention was to punch an armoured fist through the widely spread First Army, split the Allied front before ground and air forces could react, and drive the 150-200 kilometres to Antwerp. Attaining almost complete tactical surprise, Field Marshal Von Rundstedt's Army Group B began the offensive in the middle of December, with 6th Panzer Army directed on Antwerp and 5th Panzer Army to its left on Brussels. Their leading units achieved sufficient immediate tactical success to alarm Allied commanders, but the attack lost its momentum and strong counterattacks on both flanks of the enemy salient finished it.

Few Canadians were directly caught up in the German offensive. Several Forestry companies were evacuated from the Ardennes where they had been cutting timber. The 1st Canadian Parachute Battalion was sent to the area as part of 6th British Parachute Division, where it patrolled actively for several weeks. The possibility of a serious enemy breakthrough, or

---

83 J.B. Hillsman, *Eleven Men and a Scalpel* (Winnipeg: Columbia Press, 1948), 114ff.

84 G.W.L. Nicholson, *Canada's Nursing Sisters* (Toronto: Samuel Stevens, Hakkert, 1975), 166-167.

paratroop landings, did sound an alert, however, especially in normally safe but vulnerable rear areas. At No 10 Canadian General Hospital, German prisoners became excited at such prospects. Their enthusiasm alarmed "some of the [nursing] sisters who... anxiously walked the corridors all night, unable to put from their minds the fear of being taken prisoner."[85] Major J.E.G. Labrosse, a Canadian Civil Affairs Officer, was one of those responsible for rear-area security:

> *When the Allied High Command realized the situation, after a few days orders were given that all Civil Affairs Detachments stationed in France should be sent forward to the Ardennes Sector to patrol roads, control traffic, arrest and question suspects.... All units stationed in the town {Enghien} were assigned a sector in the District to patrol from darkness until dawn. Two officers and men were detailed every night for duty being relieved every two hours. Guards were doubled up around every military vital point especially the Pol {petrol, oil, and lubricants} dump near the town, in case Parachutists were dropped. Anybody met on the road after darkness was obliged to identify himself quickly; otherwise he would be taken into custody for questioning. After curfew hours anyone found on the streets or highway was arrested at once and taken to Military Police Headquarters in the town. A daily troop train due about 2300 hrs at the station of a small town situated near Enghien had been machine-gunned for five consecutive nights by a German lone wolf. The British AA Battery located in Enghien had tried every night to get him and their perseverance was rewarded, on the fifth night they shot him down.*[86]

The Canadians most directly involved in stopping the German attack were the air and ground crew of RCAF fighter squadrons. On 17 December, Second Tactical Air Force came in to support Ninth US Air Force, leaving only a few units to cover the northern front. Pilots flew their patrols largely behind German lines opposite First US Army, serving as an advance protective screen against Luftwaffe fighters and fighter-bombers, while also reporting and interdicting movement on the ground. When the skies finally cleared on 23 December, five days of intense aerial

activity followed, and on Christmas Eve, as airfields instructed their personnel to carry weapons, the tactical air forces launched so many sorties that air traffic controllers were almost overwhelmed. Ground and air defences stopped German tanks and infantry, but German aircraft were more active than they had been in months, and on Christmas Day No 83 Group fighters sighted no fewer than 31 Me 262 jets. A few weeks earlier one of these new aircraft had killed several men of the Stormont, Dundas and Glengarry Highlanders as they were forming up in a Dutch town for a church parade. Squadron Leader J.E. Collier, commanding No 403 (RCAF) Squadron, was able to claim one of the German jets when he came upon an enemy pilot whose concentration was focused on ground targets. Collier got to within 50 metres — whites-of-the-eyes range — before opening fire. The jet then opened throttle, increasing its range until Collier ran out of ammunition. Some rounds struck home, however: with white smoke trailing from his port engine the German pilot baled out. An hour or so later a long queue of airmen waiting for Christmas dinner on B88, at Heesch, in Holland, took cover when Flight Lieutenant Jack Boyle of No 411 (RCAF) Squadron shot down another Me 262 *"right over base."* In his case, Boyle was just pulling out of a steep dive, in which he had built up *"excessive speed,"* allowing him to keep up with the marauding Me 262 long enough to shoot it down. The jet crashed about five miles from the strip.

Piston-engined aircraft were also in evidence and, in all, RCAF fighter pilots claimed 18 destroyed that Christmas weekend, while losing 11 of their own. No 439 Squadron, whose ground attack duties had limited its aerial victories to a single enemy aircraft, shot down two more on 29 December. For 126 (RCAF) Wing, the 29th proved *"a day of many highlights,"* with 11 enemy shot down, five of them credited to a single pilot, Flight Lieutenant Richard Audet, the only member of Second TAF to accomplish such an extraordinary feat. His combat report deserves to be quoted in full.

> *I was leading Yellow section of 411 Squadron in the Rheine/Osnabruck area when Control*

85 Nicholson, *Canada's Nursing Sisters*, 167-168.
86 D Hist, AHQ Report 12.

reported Huns at Rheine and the Squadron turned in that direction. An Me 262 was sighted and just at that time I spotted 12 e/a {enemy aircraft} on our starboard side at 2 o'clock. These turned out to be mixture of approximately 4 Me 109s and 8 FW 190s.

1st Combat

I attacked an Me 109 which was the last a/c {aircraft} in the formation of about 12 all flying line astern. At approximately 200 yards and 30° to starboard at 10,000 feet I opened fire and saw strikes all over the fuselage and wing roots. The 109 burst into flames on the starboard side of the fuselage only, and trailed intense black smoke.

I then broke off my attack....

2nd Combat

After the first attack I went around in a defensive circle at about 8400 feet until I spotted an FW 190 which I immediately attacked from 250 yards down to 100 yards and from 30° to line astern I saw strikes over cockpit and to the rear of the fuselage, it burst into flames from the engine back and as I passed very close over top of it I saw the pilot slumped over in his cockpit, which was also in flames....

3rd Combat

My third attack followed immediately on the 2nd.

I followed what I believe was an Me 109 in a slight dive. He then climbed sharply and his coupe top flew off about 3 to 4,000 feet. I then gave a very short burst from about 300 yards and line astern and his aircraft whipped downwards in a dive. The pilot attempted {to} or did bale out. I saw a black object on the edge of the cockpit but his chute ripped to shreds. I then took cine shots of his a/c going to the ground and the bits of parachute floating around. I saw this aircraft hit and smash into many flaming pieces on the ground. I do not remember any strikes on this aircraft.

The Browning {machinegun} button only may have been pressed.

4th Combat

I spotted an FW 190 being pursued at about 5,000 by a Spitfire which was in turn pursued by an FW 190. I called this yellow section pilot to break, and attacked the 190 up his rear. The fight went downward in a steep dive. When I was about 250 yards and line astern of this 190 I opened fire, there were many strikes on the length of the fuselage and it immediately burst into flames. I saw this FW 190 go straight into the ground and burn.

5th Combat

Several minutes later while attempting to form my section up again I spotted an FW 190 from 4,000 feet, he was at about 2,000 feet. I dived down on him and attempted a head-on attack. I slowed down to wait for the 190 to fly in range. At about 200 yards and 20° I gave a very short burst, but couldn't see any strikes. This a/c flicked violently, and continued to do so until he crashed into the ground.

Audet's attack lasted just 10 minutes. He continued flying until 3 March, when he was killed by flak while attacking a railway siding.

Not directly affected by the Ardennes battle, First Canadian Army's main concern was to counter any potential move that Germans facing them might mount in support of the main offensive. Parachute landings seemed possible and II Canadian Corps divided its area into seven zones, with a brigade or division in each responsible for clearing out any airborne troops that might drop in. Intelligence staffs concentrating intently on German activities across the Maas depended on a number of sources. By identifying the parent units of prisoners, analysts could plot their movements from one sector to another. Wireless interceptions located enemy headquarters, and Dutch underground sources provided information about defences and troop movements. When weather permitted flying, tactical aerial reconnaissance and air photographs were invaluable. At this time, First Army intelligence had identified the 6th Parachute Division and 711th, 712th, and 346th Infantry divisions opposite them. In the following days their sources identified troop movements and

Ground crews beating the weather to keep their aircraft maintained... (PL 41727)

... so that pilots could get airborne. (PL 41857)

four more parachute divisions, as well as activity on airfields from which an attack might be launched. By the 21st, the regular Intelligence Summary, INTSUM, concluded:

The evidence is reasonably conclusive that the enemy is preparing a large paratroop landing to take place very shortly to disrupt the communications of the Armies dependent on Antwerp and Brussels.

Over the next few days, prisoners, air reconnaissance, aerial photographs, and captured enemy agents provided other suggestive if not entirely conclusive evidence of a pending operation.

On Christmas Eve, Brigadier N.E. Rodger, II Corps Chief of Staff, recorded in his diary that the senior staff amused themselves by composing limericks capturing the essence of a Corps order that would adequately counter any threatened paratroop landings. The winner,

*2 Canadian Corps though festive, will
Hold tight as hell from Elst to Mill.
While pushing piles and grouping guns,
Will hold the line against the Huns.*

naturally prompted other would-be poets to respond, the best coming from the commander of 49th British Division. He was upset because, on asking the 7th Canadian Reconnaissance Regiment, which was patrolling in his sector, what they intended to do about a German patrol that was prowling around their area, they had replied, "*Nothing.*" The British divisional commander signalled to II Corps:

*We acknowledge your message with
hundreds of thanks.
We don't quite approve of your holiday
pranks.
We think it far better
To send out a letter
Instructing your Recce to look after our
flanks.*

More seriously, the accumulation of incomplete evidence could not be ignored, but when, at 1800 on Boxing Day, the senior Intelligence Officer, Lieutenant Colonel Peter Wright, briefed the Army Commander, General Crerar replied, "*I've just been talking to Monty and he doesn't think there's anything in it.*" Wright then telephoned his concerns to his counterpart at 21st Army Group Headquarters,

Brigadier E.T. Williams, who agreed and said he would speak with Montgomery. At 2000 Crerar called Wright to tell him, "*I've just been talking to Monty. He thinks there might be something to this threat across the Maas,*" and said he was ordering troop movements to prepare for the worst eventuality.[87] The possibility of a subsidiary enemy attack against the Canadians depended on the success of the main offensive, and by early January, with the Germans clearly stalled in the Ardennes, Wright's intelligence team detected signs that the threat had receded and the alert was downgraded.

The possibility that the Germans might suddenly appear in their midst, however, was enough to disrupt most unit plans for Christmas. The 4th Field historian recalled the days before the normally festive season.

Certain memories of the period leading to Christmas stand out; the seductive voice of "Mary of Arnhem" and her radio program of sentimental American dance records trying to entice the Canadians to desert...the road building program and the mud...the vapour trails in the sky left by V-2's...the snow that came and went...the officers playing field hockey and being beaten by the Nijmegen girls' team...the allotment of coal, two pounds per man per day, and the smoking stoves...the reaction to news that U.K. leaves were to start for all with six months' active service...and the beginning of the rumours of the Ardennes salient.

Rumours, and the increased alert that followed, meant that for these gunners "Christmas was spoiled to a great extent for the regiment by a German airborne landing scare," as they and others manned their guns. In the mess of John Morgan Gray's counter-intelligence unit, *the menu {for}*

Christmas dinner in an old monastery had a picture of Santa Claus in a German helmet swinging down in a parachute and carrying a German Schmeisser sub-machine gun under his arm. As a caption we borrowed a brave sentiment from Henry V: "And gentlemen in England now abed shall think themselves accursed they were not here."[88]

The scare also ruined Christmas preparations in David Marshall's troop. The South Albertas

[87] S.R. Elliot, *Scarlet and Green* (Toronto: CISA, 1981), 291.
[88] J.M. Gray, *Fun Tomorrow* (Toronto: Macmillan, 1978), 299.

Flying Officer Dick Audet "shooting a line"... (PMR 98252)

... but the Germans struck back with a vengeance on New Year's Day. (PMR7 4318)

and the rest of 4th Division had spent the winter watching the Maas, squadrons rotating in and out of the line, six days in and three out, and had planned to celebrate the occasion with

> *tables set in a large room with festive bunting and decorations. Each soldier was to get a pint of beer, canned turkey, mashed potatoes, creamed carrots, peas and peaches and a mince tart for dessert. There were also cigarettes, cigars and an orange, a small parcel from the Women's Auxiliary and a diary from the Sally Ann.*

While anticipating the occasion on Christmas morning, they were instead ordered to man their tanks and move.

Most units, like the Sherbrooke Fusiliers, observed the custom of having the officers serve dinner to their men, but not without interruptions. One company of the North Shore Regiment came out of the line for Christmas dinner *"with all the trimmings and it was really a treat,"* the company commander told their unit historian, until it was spoiled by a German patrol. Bernard McElwaine, a subaltern in the same battalion, described his Christmas in his journal.

> *Dec. 24. Clear cold night. Patrol goes out with blacked faces and all. In front, in a wood, is a Jerry outpost. We hear horses at midnight each night bringing in supplies. Mickey throws over three-inch mortars. The horse bolts and the Germans swear.... Christmas morning. Breakfast tinned bacon, compo tea, porridge, bread and margarine. Mud is frozen and sun shining. Little tree decorated with tin foil. Platoon comedian appeared in tux and top hat taken from wreckage... Dinner was roast meat, tinned carrots and peas, compo tea, tinned plums, bread and margarine.... Jan. 4. Had our Christmas dinner on the 30th. Real turkey, plum pudding, oranges, candy and beer. An old German headquarters behind the lines was scrubbed clean, wired for light and decorated. Tables came from old shutters, sides of a house and old boxes. Decorations from the woods. Jerry rendered some music on a bugle. Our 25-pounders threw over a few gifts.*[89]

Many units captured the spirit of the season by adopting local children for the day, providing them with a feast and entertainment. One city official expressed his gratitude for the gesture in a letter to a nearby engineering unit.

> *It is my privilege as burgomaster of the town of Mol to express my thanks for the Christmas party you are giving these poor children, whose fathers, as you know, will not be able to be near their dear ones this Christmas-tide, owing to the misfortunes of war.*
>
> *Your kind action touches us all the more deeply when we take account of the fact that your men have made it possible by saving their own personal rations.*
>
> *We know too that this Christmas-tide spent between our children, will carry your thoughts across the Ocean to the ones so dear to you that you have left behind to fight for the freedom of our little peace-loving nation.*
>
> *But one day when the world is again at peace and you will once more be able to spend Chrismas in your homes, surrounded by your families, we would like you to think of these poor little children who will be telling their parents of the nice party you prepared for them at Christmas-tide 1944.*

It was a bittersweet time for soldiers, some of whom were spending their fifth or sixth Christmas away from home. Private Bradley, who usually didn't tell his mother about the hard times, possibly spoke for many others when he wrote:

> *Well, here it is, Christmas over and done with and I'm none the worse for it. I can't complain about the setup we had for Christmas day even though we were in the lines. But it's not the same when you're away from home: that was the third one, and I hope to hell there's not a fourth one. We have been very lucky to find ourselves in good positions. I find it hard to believe, myself, after some of the mud holes we have been in, in this part of Holland. The place we're in now could be classed as a mansion, and the lights, the gas, and the furnace which heats the whole house just right is perfect. On Christmas we used up our army rum we had been saving for said occasion: boy, is that ever powerful stuff. Well, on the 25th we had a show and after that we had the turkey, you'd like it very much. All in all it was a pretty good do, except for a few cases of home sickness including yours truly,*

---

[89] Will Bird, *North Shore (New Brunswick) Regiment* (Fredericton: Brunswick Press, 1963), 492-494.

Alex Colville, 1920-
Infantry near Nijmegen, Holland, 1946
Oil on canvas

Canadian War Museum (12172)

Campbell Tinning, 1910-
Dutch Resistance Headquarters, 1945
Watercolour

Canadian War Museum (13877)

William Ogilvie, 1901-1989
Troop Officer Receiving Information, n.d.
Watercolour

Canadian War Museum (13631)

Alex Colville, 1920-
Cutting Firewood near Nijmegen, n.d.
Watercolour

Canadian War Museum (82457)

Alex Colville, 1920-
Anti Aircraft Gun near Nijmegen Bridge, 1944
Watercolour

Canadian War Museum (12113)

Bruno Jacob Bobak, 1923-
Liberation of Almelo, 1945
Watercolour

Canadian War Museum (11942)

Alex Colville, 1920-
Flak Over Nijmegen Bridge, 1944
Watercolour

Canadian War Museum (12158)

Molly Lamb Bobak, 1922-
Canteen, Nijmegen, n.d.
Oil on canvas

Canadian War Museum (12017)

Molly Lamb Bobak, 1922-
CWAC on Leave in Amsterdam, 1945
Oil on canvas

Canadian War Museum (12037)

Campbell Tinning, 1910-
Spring in Arnhem, 1945
Mixed Media

Canadian War Museum (14002)

Campbell Tinning, 1910-
Young Dutchman after the War, 1945
Watercolour

Canadian War Museum (14035)

Campbell Tinning, 1910-
The End of it All, 1945
Watercolour

Canadian War Museum (13879)

and the rum did not help any. I hope you had a good time; I guess the house was packed with the folks. I hope you all got my cards in time. I sent them as soon as I got them, and I'm not sure whether they got there in time or not.

Operationally, New Year's proved far busier than Christmas. In one last, desperate gamble, the German air force, having succeeded in accumulating a fighter force of some thousand aircraft, most flown by novice pilots from training schools, set out at first light on 1 January 1945 to attack 11 major Allied airfields. These were excellent targets. Atrocious weather and transportation difficulties had forced British, Canadian, and American airmen to concentrate their resources on bases with permanent runways, which the Germans had used themselves. Three of them — Eindhoven, Heesch, and Evere — were homes to RCAF wings.

Two of the latter, Nos 39 and 143, were based at Eindhoven, where Canadian Spitfire and Typhoon pilots found themselves the objects of massed and determined strafing attacks for the first — and last — time in the war. They were taken by surprise, with eight Typhoons from each of Nos 438 and 440 squadrons lined up for take-off. The two that did get into the air were shot down by swarming German fighters; another 14 were shot to pieces on the ground. Having destroyed all the aircraft on the runway, the attackers circled and strafed Eindhoven for more than 20 minutes, their main opposition coming from three squadrons of RAF Regiment anti-aircraft gunners.

Others fought back as well. One of them was Sergeant W.L. Large, of 438 Squadron:

{I} was down the road from dispersal waiting to see the Sqn take off when I saw a number of e/a making an attack on the airfield. I first thought this was a hit and run raid, but after the second and third wave had passed over and I saw e/a circle the field and continue their attacks from out of the sun, I figured they were playing for keeps and therefore hurried back to dispersal where our Bren guns were kept. There I saw F/Sgt McGee and we decided to take a whack at anything flying over the dispersal. We each took a Bren gun and two boxes of clips and stood outside the dispersal door and waited for

any Jerry who came within range .... One aircraft coming from the south turned off the runway and made a steep climbing turn about 120 yards away from us at a height of not more than forty feet. We both fired, each emptying a full magazine at him. We saw strikes down the engine cowling in the direction of the cockpit and saw small pieces fall off.

Three days after the attack a burnt-out FW 190 was discovered near the airfield — sufficient evidence to give Large and McGee credit for one enemy aircraft destroyed. The attackers lost 10 pilots killed or missing and six captured, but left Eindhoven a shambles; 13 were dead and dozens wounded, 31 aircraft were left burning or shot up, and many buildings were damaged, while several bomb and petrol dumps added flames and explosions to the general confusion.

At Heesch and Evere the Canadians got off more lightly, but losses were nonetheless serious. In all, Second TAF lost 127 aircraft destroyed and 133 damaged, while US forces lost another 36. It was not, however, the decisive blow the Germans desperately needed, and their own losses of 300 aircraft with 214 pilots, a third of them to their own anti-aircraft fire, was catastrophic. After two disastrous months in which almost 800 pilots had been killed or fallen into Allied hands, the operation was a defeat from which they never recovered.

* * *

In the aftermath of the German offensive, with its accompanying threat of spoiling attacks in its own sector, First Canadian Army became concerned about a German salient on the Canadian side of the Maas near Kapelsche Veer, in 1st Polish Armoured Division's sector. In effect, the German position formed a bridgehead on the south bank, from which elements of 6th Parachute Division could launch a disruptive attack. On the night of 30 December the Polish tried but failed to eliminate the salient, and a second attempt on 7 January could do no better. On the 13th and 14th, a British Commando unit tried once more but was also unsuccessful.

Military operations can easily develop a momentum of their own and, presenting a challenge as well as a threat, the Kapelsche Veer salient had to go. Fourth Canadian Armoured Division's 10th Infantry Brigade was told to do it, and it detailed two battalions, the Lincoln and Welland Regiment and the Argyll and Sutherland Highlanders, for the task.

The outline plan for the assault noted that about two companies of enemy troops were dug in on the Canadian side of the river and, at first look, the German position seemed precarious. With the river to the north, the paratroopers faced Canadians to east, south, and west. Bisecting the salient, forming a ridge of high ground from east to west, was a dyke. Against the salient would be sent two companies of the Lincoln and Welland Regiment attacking from the east, another from the west, and a special party in boats to try to land from the north. Training and reconnaissance began on 17 January, the same day that Typhoons and Spitfires attacked the enemy's positions, with RAF officers on hand to observe results. Wasp flame-throwers arrived on the 21st, and officers of the Toronto Scottish (Machine Gun) Regiment came the next day, *"amidst a thick veil of secrecy."* Later the boat crews were timed over a two-kilometre stretch of water to determine how long it would take them to reach the objective.

The attack went in on the 26th, but problems arose immediately; the boat party was unable to get into the water at the correct time due to ice, and as it paddled its way close to shore towards German positions it came under fire and had to take cover on land. By 0830 both A Company, advancing from the east, and B Company, coming in from the west, reported they were breaking into the salient, but subsequent counterattacks forced A Company to withdraw. By 1000 both companies had lost all their officers and B was completely cut off by *"what battle-experienced veterans described as 'the heaviest mortar barrage ever'."*

Both sides tried to reinforce — but here the Canadians had the advantage, as the enemy had to move its troops across the river by boat, in the face of Canadian mortar and small-arms fire. The Lincoln and Wellands were joined by A Company of the Argyll and Sutherland Highlanders, reinforcing the eastern attack, and

the general plan was now to work up gradually from both East and West and literally dig out

all the enemy that were firmed up on the bridgehead.... The general atmosphere, cold, windy, muddy and exposed to the elements as well as to enemy fire, was as unpleasant as possible. Rations and rum were taken up to the forward troops under cover of darkness.

The battle continued for five long days, the Canadians taking enemy-held ground a metre at a time and then digging in to prepare for the next assault, with tanks literally blasting small pockets of German paratroopers out of their positions. By the time it ended on the morning of the 31st, with the Canadians in control of the area, the Lincoln and Wellands had lost 300 men. The salient was, however, eliminated.

General Simonds lost his bet on the timing of the end of the war. While American and British counterattacks soon restored the December front, the Ardennes offensive had demonstrated that the Germans were going to fight to the last regardless of the ultimate consequences to their people. With the Red Army closing from the east and Canadian, British, and American armies preparing to cross the Rhine into Germany, the end was clearly at hand. But another costly spring campaign, and more appalling losses for all concerned, was unavoidable, as the Germans, defiantly or resignedly, fought on. What sustained them — to inflict and take countless more casualties in a hopeless cause? One of their officers later told his interrogators,

The greatest phenomenon of Nationalism was its ability to convert the German pessimism of the last war into the illusionism of this one. Men between thirty and forty years of age, who had seen the world, nevertheless believed all of Goebbels' propaganda with a naivety and faith difficult to understand....This universal faith in a miracle that would be wrought by Adolf Hitler, was something...impossible to comprehend. It was the style to be cheerful and hopeful, whereas in the last war it was the thing to be gloomy and disillusioned. This strange reaction existed even though men knew they had not been told the dark truth about Russia, and that the over-all picture was extremely dark.[90]

---

90 D Hist, German interrogation reports.

CHAPTER IV

SEAWARD

*The sunwashed yellow and white houses fronting the esplanade were in plain sight as HMCS **Haida** eased her way some three miles offshore, HMS **Kelvin** screening her to seaward. Through the binoculars observers could see the upperworks of several sunken ships. People could be seen moving around and gathering in clusters to look seaward.*

There was drama in this moment. For the ships it was one of the objectives of the long years of fighting, the reward for the ceaseless patrols off the land when they could venture within sight of the coast only at night. This was another D-Day and it was all their own.

Tense and expectant, they studied the town across the sunlit waters. If the Germans were here they could expect gunfire at any moment. Faintly to their listening ears came the rattle of small arms fire, a machine gun, but nothing stirred the water in their vicinity. The shooting seemed to be along the beach, among the entanglement of wire and wooden crosspieces erected on the sands as a defence against invasion.

Something was happening on top of a square stone tower overlooking the harbour. A flag was breaking out. Slowly it shook loose in the faint breeze and its colours were read eagerly. It was the red, white and blue of the tricolour of France.[91]

Canadian sailors did not liberate many towns; that was left to the Army. What they did share with soldiers in the European theatre over the last months of the war was a bitter struggle against an enemy who refused to quit.

Although the Royal Canadian Navy's main effort during this time continued to be trade defence in the North Atlantic, approximately 75 of its vessels served in European waters. These warships contributed to almost every aspect of the maritime war by escorting convoys, attacking enemy merchant vessels and warships, hunting U-boats, and sweeping mines. Like sailors from other navies, Canadians found that, even with victory a certainty, the face of battle retained its grim character; during this final period of the war the RCN lost seven vessels and the lives of

---

91 W. Sclater, *Haida* (Toronto: Paperjacks, 1980), 263-264.

87 sailors. Also unchanging was the ceaseless struggle of sailors against the sea, which on certain terrible occasions seemed to conspire with the enemy. Times like this reveal much about the character of the Canadian sailor and his ships. The ships, of course, are "people" too. Their personalities played a full part in the intense, close, unique dynamics of each crew. Navies, no less than other armed services, are more than complex machines and huge organizations; they are people.

* * *

As First Canadian Army liberated the Channel ports in September and October, Allied coastal forces worked seaward, defending Allied convoy routes from hit-and-run raids by enemy motor torpedo boats (E-boats) and harassing German coastal shipping attempting to flee or supply the beleaguered ports. The 29th and 65th RCN MTB flotillas — each equipped with eight small, fast boats packed with an armament of six-pounder and 20mm automatic cannons, machine guns, and torpedoes — were only peripherally involved in these operations as both were moving to bases away from the action.

Initially, the 29th flotilla was relieved with the move to quieter waters. From June through the beginning of August it had carried out a gruelling schedule of operations in the Baie de la Seine off the Normandy beachhead that had taken a severe toll on men and equipment. Finally, they transferred to Ramsgate, a quiet fishing hamlet 30 kilometres up the coast from Dover. In his memoirs, the flotilla's leader, Lieutenant Commander Tony Law RCNVR, recalled idyllic days at the new base:

> Life was pleasant at Ramsgate and the weather was glorious. In the mornings the Flotilla worked hard cleaning their ships, and in the afternoons they would have "make and mends." Officers and crews alike took advantage of the sandy beach beneath the white cliffs, and after the weary, dreary days of Normandy, it was marvellous to relax and soak in the sunshine until we were tanned to a lovely copper colour. Interspersed with bouts of sunbathing and refreshing dips in the cold, salty sea, the 29th often played great games of baseball or American football in the hot sands. Then, around seven or eight o'clock, a unit of boats would proceed to sea on the nightly patrol, while those who were not on duty would hire the old taxi and drive over to M. Lucy's in Margate for a super meal with a bottle of good white wine as the finishing touch.[92]

The only drawbacks to Ramsgate were that some crews had to sleep in their cramped MTBs, and the port was occasionally targeted by those same long-range German batteries across the Channel that Canadian troops were overrunning.

Throughout the autumn, the 29th was occupied mainly on anti-E-boat operations known as "Z" patrols. In these, two or three MTBs lay stopped in fixed "Z" positions 12-15 kilometres seaward of Allied convoy routes along the British east coast. Interceptions were rare because E-boats could outrun Allied MTBs, but the Germans took advantage of an intelligence coup as well. In September 1942 they had recovered a chart from a burned-out British MTB showing the various "Z" positions, and, because they remained unaltered throughout the war, E-boats could attack convoys and escape by avoiding the defensive positions. Allied naval commanders attributed the enemy's success to effective use of radar; ironically this same rationale was often used by German naval officers to explain Allied successes that actually resulted from Ultra intelligence. The upshot for Canadian MTB sailors was that "Z" patrols were largely uneventful, to the point that some referred to them as "Zizz" patrols on account of their sleepy nature.[93]

A high point for the two Canadian MTB flotillas came at the beginning of November, with Operation Infatuate, the assault on Walcheren. The 65th flotilla had a static role, providing flank protection against E-boat attack that, in their sector at least, never materialized. The 29th had a more active role, patrolling near

---

[92] C.A. Law, *White Plumes Astern* (Halifax: Nimbus, 1989), 115.

[93] F.H. Hinsley et al., *British Intelligence in the Second World War*, III, pt 2 (London: HMSO, 1988), 454. H. Frank, "E-Boats in Action off the Coast of England," *Marine-Rundschau* (July-August 1987), 8. Law, *White Plumes Astern*, 136.

Lieutenant Commander J.R.H. Kirkpatrick RCNVR. Known as "Kirk" or "The Brain," the commander of 65th MTB Flotilla was recognized throughout coastal forces as an outstanding leader. (PMR 94300)

German bases in northern Holland in order to cut the Germans off at their source. Soon after Law reached his patrol position off the Hook of Holland, he sighted enemy ships forming up outside of the harbour. Splitting his force, his and another boat distracted the escorts while the two other MTBs attacked a merchant ship with torpedoes, one of which hit home. Over the next three hours, the enemy escort frustrated further attacks by the Canadians before the Germans withdrew into harbour.

The night was not over. Returning to their patrol position the MTBs encountered the "Four Horsemen of the Apocalypse" — a standing patrol of four heavily armed flak trawlers that, as Law's account shows, were firmly established in Coastal Force lore:

> *I knew that these bullies were far from gentle and that no matter what was done they would always gain the upper hand, especially on a moonlit night.*
>
> *We spent the night playing a game with one another which mainly consisted of hitting shells back and forth. No one was getting hurt but we were having the life scared out of us. As soon as we manoeuvred into a nice torpedo position and were ready to pull the lever, what would happen? The Four Horsemen would alter course towards us, and just to keep the game lively they would slam out a few more 88mm's.*

After three hours of this *"game,"* Law came to the startling realization that *"both teams...had been assigned to the same patrol position."* The match ended when Law detected what he thought were two E-boats heading south towards Walcheren; he engaged, but the quarry — actually two British MTBs — escaped under cover of smoke. Law's boats made their way back to port but all had been damaged in the actions with German forces, and one sailor had been killed.

Activity for the two Canadian flotillas ebbed after the Walcheren operation. Again they found themselves involved mainly in routine anti-E-boat patrols interspersed with an occasional offensive sweep. These operations were not helped by the rough winter seas, which were difficult for the small, fragile MTBs to manage. Another problem — made worse by the weather

— was the difficulty of navigating along a stretch of coast infamous for its dangerous shoals and ever-shifting sandbanks. Although all boats shared the same challenges, some were better able to withstand them.

The most capable boat in the 65th was *MTB-748,* commanded by the flotilla leader, Lieutenant Commander J.R. Kirkpatrick RCNVR. As lead boat, *748* had the best trained sailors in the flotilla but it also had the benefit of Kirkpatrick's outstanding leadership. A pre-war graduate of the Royal Military College, Kirkpatrick had fought in Coastal Forces since early in the war and had earned a reputation for bravery and audacity. A master of tactics — his officers dubbed him "The Brain" — and a thorough professional, especially when it came to maintaining his boat, Kirkpatrick set high standards to which his crew readily responded. Of course, sailors being renowned for their individuality, there were exceptions: *MTB-748* had the most accurate gunner in the flotilla but this sailor was unhappy in MTBs and wanted to transfer back to escort duty on the North Atlantic. When this request was denied, he forced his own release by staging a one-man mutiny — Kirkpatrick had no choice but to send him to cells.

Despite the fact that their gunnery deteriorated with the departure of the recalcitrant gunner, *MTB-748* continued to excel. On the night of 15/16 November, for example, the boat was one of two assigned to an anti-E-boat patrol off the Scheldt estuary. Ordered to intercept a distant contact, the two MTBs were forced to run at full speed for some 20 minutes, putting great strain on their Packard engines. One MTB was forced to drop out; *748* could keep up the torrid pace because her engines were, in the words of her navigating officer, *"so well kept, so well maintained."* Arriving at the interception point alone, Kirkpatrick did not hesitate to attack six E-boats that he found stopped, laying mines in the Scheldt. *MTB-748* made two high-speed passes down the enemy line, engaging each boat in turn. Although ordered to withdraw so that a more powerful frigate could engage, Kirkpatrick made a final firing run before breaking off.[94]

---

94 D Hist, D.B. Wilson memoir.

*The crew of Kirkpatrick's **MTB-748** at Ostend during the winter of 1944-45. Their good spirits can be at least partly explained by the fact that the operation scheduled for that night had just been cancelled. (PMR9 4325)*

On another occasion Kirkpatrick took advantage of the skill of his navigator to demonstrate to his British counterparts that Canadians were as good as, if not better than, the Royal Navy. A thick fog had suddenly descended over the approaches to the MTB base at Ostend, Belgium, shutting down the port for three days. Numerous vessels were stranded at sea, including an MTB with several high-ranking officers onboard. According to *MTB-748's* navigator, Lieutenant David Bryce Wilson RCNVR, nobody else wanted to do it, but Kirkpatrick

> *volunteered the services of the 748 to go out and bring in this boat-load of admirals and anybody else that we could find out there. So I was asked, would I volunteer for this? And I thought "Well, this is one of those political situations, Kirk had practically committed us, and the prestige of Canadians; I don't really have a choice."*

Kirkpatrick and Wilson went back to *748* and eased carefully through the narrow, fog-shrouded entrance to the harbour *"on our errand of mercy"*:

> *Well, we were going out into the fog slowly and were using our loud-hailer to search for our target (and to avoid collisions). We kept encountering anchored boats all over the place, and to each one we'd give a course and speed and distance; we'd tell them exactly where they were; exactly what course they should steer to clear the breakwaters and go on in. We must have rescued about a dozen or so boats before we found the one that had all the high ranking people on it; and having found them our job was done. We didn't have to go and look for any more boats so we just told them to follow us and we led them back in. And this apparently was well received; Kirk's stocks went up at the Coastal Forces Mobile Base.*

As the two RCN MTB flotillas settled into a largely uneventful winter, other Canadians involved in the war at sea had the opportunity to take the fight to the enemy. One area where the Allies had consistently tried to apply pressure was the Norwegian coast; throughout the war Germany had run convoys through Norwegian waters to supply its northern bases and bring valuable iron ore back to its factories. Quite apart from the importance of stopping this shipping,

the Allies knew from signals intelligence that Hitler was especially concerned about possible Allied landings in Norway; thus naval operations in the area fuelled these anxieties and tied down large numbers of German troops.

Achieving these aims was no easy task. Urgent demands elsewhere throughout the war made it difficult to cobble together enough forces for a sustained offensive. Geography was another problem. Norway was a considerable distance from British bases — 500 kilometres at the nearest point — and its sinuous, craggy coast provided formidable natural defences to the German ships as they scuttled from port to port. Deep fjords cut into coastal mountain ranges made perfect hiding places, and a long series of rocky islands known as the Inner Leads that ran just off the coast sheltered the inshore channels.

After the Normandy invasion the Allies increased their efforts to interdict this shipping. In August, neutral Sweden stopped insuring any ships carrying trade to Germany and in the next month closed her harbours to German vessels altogether. Finland also stopped trading. These diplomatic measures forced the Germans to increase their shipping through Norwegian waters, and the Allies responded with a campaign that included anti-shipping strikes and mine-laying by aircraft, MTBs, and submarines. Their success was such that in October the Germans restricted convoys to night-time passage through the most vulnerable area, a stretch of coast in southwest Norway between Aalesund and Lindesnes. In response, British naval commanders decided to ignore the danger posed by minefields and shore batteries and, for the first time in four years, mount anti-shipping sweeps with cruisers and destroyers.[95]

Force 2, the cruisers HMS *Kent* and *Bellona* and four destroyers, including HMCS *Algonquin,* conducted the first sweep, dubbed Operation Counterblast. The force commander, Rear Admiral Roderick McGrigor RN, selected an area south of Stavanger as his target because there were no fjords and the high cliffs along the coast would allow his ships to manoeuvre close

---

[95] S.W. Roskill, *The War at Sea*, III, pt 2 (London: HMSO, 1961), 163-165. F.H. Hinsley et al., *British Intelligence in the Second World War*, 493-494.

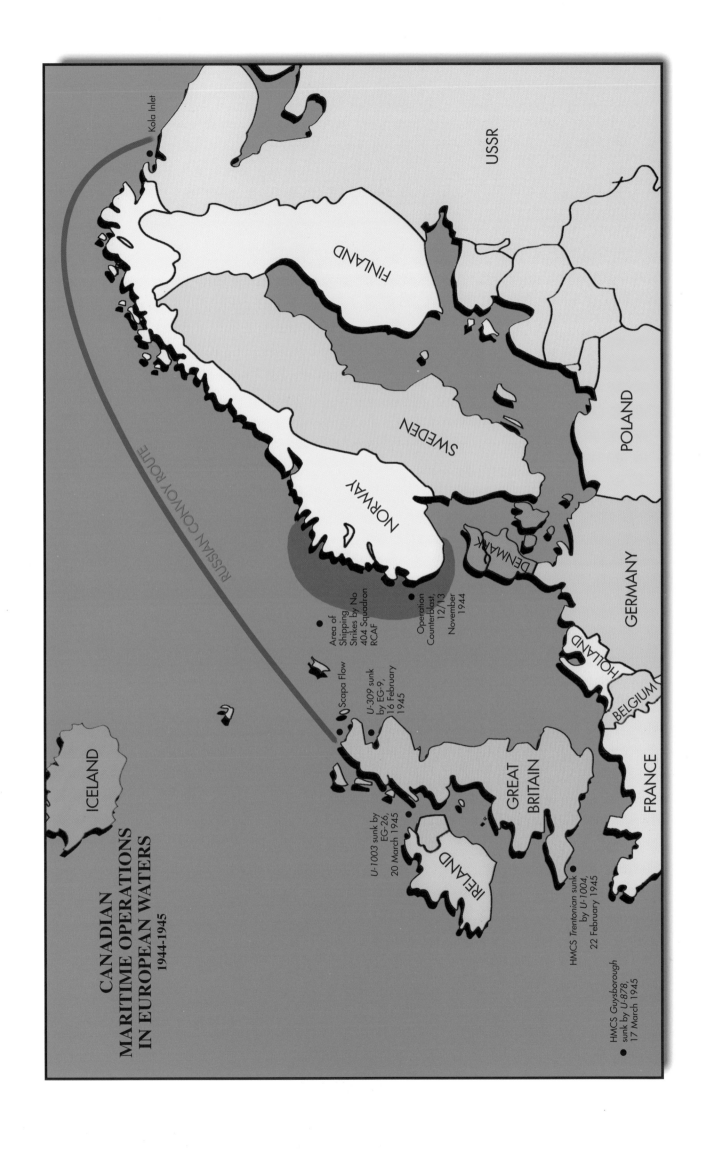

CANADIAN
MARITIME OPERATIONS
IN EUROPEAN WATERS
1944-1945

Kola Inlet

USSR

FINLAND

SWEDEN

NORWAY

RUSSIAN CONVOY ROUTE

ICELAND

Area of
Shipping
Strikes by No
404 Squadron
RCAF

Operation
Counterblast,
12/13
November
1944

DENMARK

POLAND

GERMANY

HOLLAND

BELGIUM

Scapa Flow

U-309 sunk
by EG-9,
16 February
1945

U-1003 sunk by
EG-26,
20 March 1945

GREAT
BRITAIN

FRANCE

IRELAND

HMCS Trentonian sunk
by U-1004,
22 February 1945

HMCS Guysborough
sunk by U-878,
17 March 1945

inshore. He planned to attack in line-ahead with the cruisers leading the destroyers; *Algonquin* was the fourth ship. McGrigor instructed his captains that *"the objective must at first be to cripple as many ships as possible so as to prevent them escaping, finishing them off at a later stage."*

Force 2 reached its destination at approximately 2000 on 12 November. After manoeuvring to avoid contacts off Stavanger, the warships proceeded southeast about 16 kilometres from the coast. Navigation was straightforward; not only did radar give accurate fixes but lighthouses *"were burning for short periods in what appeared regular intervals with maximum brilliancy."* Three small radar contacts were passed by because McGrigor, tipped off by Ultra, was after bigger game. Finally, at 2150, his patience was rewarded when *Kent* obtained

> *a number of radar contacts indicating a northward bound convoy. There appeared to be three or four lines of ships, the furthest and largest group being some 5 miles on the quarter of the nearest line and only about 2 miles off-shore.*

Proceeding across the path of the convoy — in effect achieving the treasured naval objective of capping its "T" — at 2314 McGrigor gave the order to open fire. With the initial range just 4600 metres — virtually point-blank in this type of warfare — and the escort comprising only two minesweepers and four small submarine chasers, the result was akin to slaughter. According to *Algonquin's* captain, Lieutenant Commander D.W. Piers,

> *Many targets were plainly visible and quickly engaged.* **ALGONQUIN** *opened fire on an escort vessel at an initial range of 5400 {4937 metres} at 2314 and obtained a hit with the first salvo. This target was also being engaged by other ships ahead: it burst into flames within a minute. Fire was shifted at 2317 to a merchant ship at an initial range of 8000 yards {7315 metres}. Using No. 2 gun (B) gun for starshell illumination and the remainder of the main armament firing S.A.P., this second target was also reduced to flames by the first few salvoes.*[96]

As the Allied warships poured shells into them, those merchant ships that could headed for the coast to gain protection from shore batteries.

Meanwhile, *"in the face of hopeless odds,"* three courageous escorts attacked the destroyers at the rear of the line. After avoiding several near misses, *Algonquin* joined other ships in engaging an escort just 2700 metres on the starboard beam; it was quickly a mass of flames.

By this time, *Kent*, the lead ship, had run past the convoy and was only three kilometres from shore. McGrigor therefore led around to port *"in order to re-engage the rear ships of the convoy and at the same time to avoid masking the fire of our own ships astern."* In *Algonquin*, Piers noted that as the line turned it came under accurate fire from 105mm shore batteries; *"most of our ships were near-missed and straddled on several occasions, but no hits were obtained."* Now heading south, *Algonquin* joined the other ships in firing upon a merchant ship, which blew up, and then engaged an escort, which burst into flames. McGrigor ordered the destroyers to make one final pass and, despite more near misses from shore batteries, they set ablaze the three ships still visible.

Counterblast was unquestionably an outstanding success. In all, two of four merchant ships and five of six escorts were sunk. The local German naval commander noted that the addition of major warships to operations against the iron-ore convoys made the situation *"extremely critical."* Not surprisingly, Allied naval commanders praised the action. Among the captains of the warships involved, a common sentiment was the pleasure of being in offensive action after being on the defensive for so long.

One amusing note followed Counterblast that, like Lieutenant Commander Kirkpatrick's bragging about his navigator, sheds some light on the sometimes tenuous relationship between British and Canadian naval personnel. *"Two days after we were in Scapa Flow,"* Lieutenant Commander Piers recalled,

> *the Admiral aboard the cruiser* **Kent** *gave a little party at night, a dinner for the officers involved in this action, and it was a very pleasant affair. The Admiral was able to stand up and say what a fine lot we were and we were very pleased of course with our modest success. Following dinner, we had the usual*

---

96 NAC, HMCS *Algonquin, Report of Proceedings.*

wardroom shenanigans. The young officers vying with each other with various forms of games and sports, and swinging from the chandeliers, or deckhead I should say. Jumping and leaping and having a good time all around, and this went on for awhile. I, as captain, had stayed rather aloof from the gymnastics that were going on although I enjoyed something like that. After this had been going for about half an hour, it seemed that the senior officers were getting rather bored with it all and one of ship's officers in the **Kent,** *who was a Commander by rank, looked at me and by this time we did not have our Canada badges on and had not yet been introduced, and I presume since I was standing aloof from all this, and dressed rather formally for an evening dinner and standing close to the Admiral, he came up and murmured over my shoulder, "I say, old boy, how are we going to get rid of these bloody Canadians?" Whereupon I looked at him and said, "I don't think we'll have any trouble sir, I'll just get my officers and we'll be off." It was one of those lovely moments when you can say almost anything you like, and our friend of course was duly embarrassed, and apologized.[97]*

There were no more parties — *"lovely moments"* and all — celebrating cruiser-destroyer sweeps off the Norwegian coast, because there were no other successful operations of that type. At the end of December, a force including the destroyer HMCS *Sioux* twice made unsuccessful sweeps; the first was frustrated by poor weather, the second was detected by radar allowing the Germans to clear all shipping from the area. Then, in April 1945, the destroyer HMCS *Iroquois* participated in a sweep that intercepted shipping, but the attack was so poorly led that it inflicted only minimal casualties. These failures, however, did little harm to the overall objective because other anti-shipping forces were getting the job done. Coastal Command strike squadrons, including No 404 RCAF, were particularly successful.

Although No 404 became one of the most effective maritime strike squadrons in Coastal Command, its story is not well known. Formed in April 1941, it spent its first two years flying reconnaissance missions or escorting

anti-submarine patrol aircraft over the Bay of Biscay. In April 1943, now flying Bristol Beaufighters, No 404 joined one of the first maritime strike wings and for the remainder of the war helped refine anti-shipping operations to a devastating art. One of the keys to the success of this campaign was 404's pioneering use of rocket projectiles, or RPs. Experience soon taught that this was a formidable weapon — especially the armour-piercing variety — against thin-skinned merchant ships. "Dry" hits that exploded against a ship's superstructure could cause some damage and suppress flak, but "wet" hits, when RPs entered the sea short of the target and exploded beneath the waterline, were more destructive, punching holes in the hull or damaging vital machinery.

In September 1944, after achieving great success in the Normandy campaign, No 404, with three RAF squadrons (one Beaufighter and two Mosquito) collectively known as the Banff Wing, renewed the offensive in Norwegian waters. Just flying the operations in this sector was a challenge: they entailed long, low-level flights over the North Sea from Scotland to Norway — two places not known for their fair climates — and flak over convoys was usually intense. The wing overcame these obstacles and sank a number of vessels, but enemy attempts to confound the strike wing made targets increasingly scarce. Convoys sailed at night and at first light would seek shelter in fjords — it was too hazardous to enter the narrow inlets during darkness — where fighter-bombers could not reach them without prohibitive losses. In response, the wing began using the "Drem" system. Flying across the North Sea at night in loose formation to avoid collisions, they would circle off the Norwegian coast at a pre-arranged location marked by flares, then attack convoys at sunrise before they entered the fjords. The wing first tried "Drem" on 9 October 1944, sinking two ships and damaging another.

Poor weather hampered the Banff Wing's operations throughout the winter of 1944/1945 but it still took a steady toll of shipping, forcing the Luftwaffe to increase its fighter strength in Norway. On 9 February, the combination of

---

[97] D Hist, D.W. Piers biographical file.

Germans, geography, and a difficult target led to 404's worst day of the war. Attacking a destroyer, two minesweepers, two flak ships, and a smaller escort located up a narrow fjord, 32 Beaufighters, including 11 from No 404, met a hail of intense flak from the warships and positions on the surrounding hills. To make matters worse, they were bounced by FW-190 fighters who eluded their Mustang escort. Although they helped put the large destroyer *Z-33* out of the war, 404's losses were staggering; six of 11 aircraft were shot down, and of the 12 missing air crew only one survived to become a prisoner of war.

Replacing their losses, No 404 continued flying strikes, sinking two merchantmen on a particularly successful mission on 24 February. Following that the squadron began attacking lighthouses in an effort to disrupt navigation on the treacherous coast during darkness; by the end of March they had extinguished 15. In May, after converting to longer-ranged Mosquitoes, the squadron flew two missions deep into the Skagerrak, its RPs helping to destroy a U-boat, a minesweeper, and a merchant ship.

Since they had been formed in the spring of 1943, Coastal Command strike wings accounted for almost 300,000 tons of shipping in northern waters. Along with mine-laying by the Fleet Air Arm, Bomber Command, and submarines, and direct attacks by warships and naval aircraft, they almost completely decimated the German merchant marine and brought the transport of vital war materiel to a virtual standstill.

The Germans failed to achieve the same result against the Allies' main shipping commitment in northern waters, the famous Russian convoys. From the time of the Soviet Union's entry into the war in 1941, the Allies had convoyed valuable lend-lease supplies of aircraft, vehicles, munitions, and other war materiel from the United Kingdom to ports in North Russia, most to Murmansk. As a symbol of Allied solidarity, and American and British support for Stalin, the Murmansk convoys took on a political aspect that grew to equal, if not exceed, the logistical benefits. The Germans fought hard to stop them. Although the British planned and executed the convoys, there were nonetheless Canadian ships on three quarters of those run from October 1943 until the end of the war.

Much has been written about the Russian convoys, primarily from a British perspective, and part of their attraction lies in the sheer challenge that they posed. The Royal Navy's Home Fleet, which was responsible for running the convoys,

had to provide for safety on passage to and from a destination some 2000 miles [3200 kilometres] distant. The route was open to U-boat passage throughout its entire length, was limited to the westward and northward by ice and to the eastward and southward by an enemy-held coast, well provided with anchorages whence surface forces could operate at will, and airfields from which aircraft could dominate 1400 [2250 kilometres] of its furthest east, and therefore most vulnerable waters. The whole route, moreover, including the terminal ports at each end, lay within the range of enemy air reconnaissance, for which he was not lacking in resources, and at two points was crossed by routine German meteorological flights. British shore based air support [including RCAF squadrons] was confined to what could be given from Iceland and Sullom Voe [in the Shetland Islands].

Quite apart from enemy interference were the great navigational difficulties in these Arctic waters — strong and uncertain currents; frequent gales, which would disperse the convoys and drive the ships many miles from their routes; no sun sights or W/T beacons to enable them to check their positions. And ice, in one form or another, was an ever present danger.[98]

In geographic terms more familiar to Canadians, the task facing the Home Fleet was akin to running convoys between Bahamas and St. John's, Newfoundland, with the eastern seaboard of the United States and Canada in enemy hands. The entire route would lie within easy range of enemy aircraft; submarines and surface ships could sortie from well-defended ports like Norfolk, New York, Boston, Halifax, and Sydney; and the convoys would have to

98 Admiralty, *Arctic Convoys, 1941-1945* (London: HMSO, 1954).

*HMCS **Algonquin**, the Canadian participant in Operation Counterblast, in the Shetland Islands. These isolated islands often served as a refuelling site for destroyers operating in northern European waters. (PA 157804)*

With an armament of eight armour-piercing rocket projectiles, four 20mm cannon, and six .303 machine guns, No 404 Squadron's Bristol Beaufighters were formidable strike aircraft. They sunk both merchant ships in this attack. (R E3711)

withstand an extreme arctic climate with some of the worst weather conditions that could be encountered at sea, including ice packs that restricted freedom of manoeuvre. It was an imposing challenge.

Canadian sailors, who were used to the travails of the northwest Atlantic, did not find conditions on the Murmansk run as rigorous as did their British counterparts. The cold and the seas were about as bad, but the average Russian convoy took only six to eight days to reach its destination, as opposed to the 10 to 15 it took to escort a slow convoy across the North Atlantic. Still, as Lieutenant Pat Budge, executive officer of the destroyer HMCS *Huron* and by reputation one of the toughest sailors ever to wear an RCN uniform, later recalled, the Murmansk run could be a trial for even the most hard-bitten Canadian:

Usually, in looking back at our seatime, we sailors only remember the good times. The Russian run was an exception. It was winter, and it seemed that gales were forever sweeping over the dark, clouded sea. The dim red ball of the sun barely reaching the horizon as the ship pitched and tossed, the musty smell of damp clothes in which we lived, the bitter cold, the long frequent watches that seemed to last forever. This on a diet of stale bread, powdered eggs and red lead {stewed tomatoes} and bacon. The relief to get below for some sleep into that blessed haven — the comforting embrace of a well slung hammock. There was no respite on watch for gun, torpedo or depth charge crews as every fifteen minutes would come the cry "For exercise all guns train and elevate through the full limits" — this to keep them free of ice. This was another problem, as the watch below would be called on deck to clear the ship of ice — the only time the engine room staff were envied. Each trip out and back seemed to last an eternity with nothing to look forward to at either end except that perhaps mail would be waiting for us at Scapa Flow.[99]

Most of what has been written about the Russian convoys concentrates on the period 1941 to 1943 when powerful German warships such as the battleship *Tirpitz* and the battle-cruiser *Scharnhorst* threatened the route. By the final year of the war, however, this menace had been largely eradicated. *Scharnhorst* was sunk on

Boxing Day 1943 — three Canadian destroyers were escorting the convoy that the battle-cruiser was attempting to attack when it was caught and destroyed by British forces in the Battle of North Cape. *Tirpitz* had twice been temporarily put out of action by midget submarines and naval aircraft but it was not until 12 November 1944 that Lancasters from Bomber Command capsized the battleship. Some German surface forces, mainly destroyers and older cruisers, still posed a slight threat to the Murmansk run but the main danger came from U-boats and Luftwaffe torpedo bombers based in northern Norway. Although each convoy was unique, the outbound *JW-64* and homeward-bound *RA-64* of February 1945 can serve as an example. This choice also highlights HMCS *Sioux,* a capable ship that has never received the attention it deserves.

Commissioned in February 1944, *Sioux* had spent a busy year escorting two Russian convoys, screening Home Fleet operations against Norway, and participating in the Normandy invasion. During this demanding time, the 220 officers and sailors who formed the destroyer's crew, many of whom had never been to sea before, meshed into an efficient working unit. *Sioux* was not a flashy ship and this was largely due to the calm personalities of the captain, Lieutenant Commander Eric Boak RCN, and his executive officer, Lieutenant Doug Bruce RCNVR. Both had been in the navy since before the war — Bruce as a reservist during pre-war summers — and many months of hard service on the North Atlantic had instilled a quiet confidence that mixed well with the youthful exuberance of the ship's company. According to Petty Officer George Vander Hagen, another wise veteran,

*We had a good lot in **Sioux**. That was the finest ship I ever served in and one of the most efficient I've been in. Doug Bruce was an excellent First Lieutenant, Boak was a good Captain, and I had Stubbs and Haddon and Pullen to judge him by. We had a bunch of characters. The cook wasn't a cook but he was full of fun. Dave Rollins was the mess-deck moaner. Every ship had one and we had Rollins. If you said good morning he'd prove it*

99 D Hist, address by Rear Admiral P.D. Budge, 19 September 1981.

wasn't. And our forger — one day the Gunner's Mate was in a fury because the flotilla Captain Gunnery Officer was coming and the Captain was ashore and had not signed the gunnery log, the magazine logs and all the rest. We had this kid in the gunner's party, he said, "What's the problem?" Then he signed the Captain's name just as nice as you please. You couldn't tell the difference...He had it exact. The Gunner's Mate said, "What did you used to do?" and the kid said, "I was a forger." We had a real cross section of humanity in that ship.[100]

In *JW-64* and the returning *RA-64* the escorts and merchantmen were faced with all the elements that gave Russian convoys their notoriety. Twenty-seven transports carrying lend-lease material to the Soviets sailed from the Clyde on 3 February and met their through escort northeast of the Faeroe Islands three days later. Because of the potential opposition, the Russian convoys were in essence fleet operations with an escort far more powerful than that which accompanied North Atlantic convoys; in this case two escort carriers, a light cruiser, nine Fleet destroyers, 10 smaller escorts, and two support groups of eight frigates. The operation was commanded by Rear Admiral Roderick McGrigor, of Counterblast fame.

As the escort joined, *Sioux* taking position in the outer screen, the convoy was sighted by a Luftwaffe meteorological flight. From then on, patrol aircraft shadowed *JW-64* intermittently to its destination. Grumman Wildcat fighters from the escort carriers drove off the shadowers during the short Arctic days but only one obsolete Fairey Fulmar night-fighter was available for interceptions after dark, and it crashed upon landing after its first flight. But even with the benefit of shadowing reports, the Germans had trouble finding the convoy. On 7 February, 48 JU-188 torpedo bombers took off to attack but they failed to locate the main body, even though some were engaged by escorts in the outer screen. Seven of the bombers did not make it home.

When they detected a convoy in time, Group North, the German naval command in the Arctic, usually deployed a U-boat patrol line at the entrance to the Barents Sea between Bear Island and North Cape. This gap was just under 480 kilometres across and U-boats should have been able to locate convoys with certainty. Their commanders, however, were not bold in the face of the strong convoy escorts, and the British commanders, with the additional advantage of Ultra intelligence about the enemy's intentions, usually managed to skirt the submarine patrol lines. *JW-64* was no different. The eight U-boats of Group Rasmus were waiting in the gap, but McGrigor guided the convoy around the northern end of the patrol line unharmed.

On the morning of 10 February, poor communications caused *JW-64* to be taken by surprise. Radar detected an aircraft approaching from the south, but, on the basis of an incomplete signal received from British naval staff in Murmansk, it was thought to be a Soviet patrol plane. Shortly afterwards, *Sioux* was positioned in its night cruising station on the starboard wing of the convoy when

a JU 188 appeared from a bearing of Green 90 (240° true), about 50 feet off the water and 3000 yards {2743 metres} away, flying directly towards the ship. At about 1500 yards {1371 metres} the plane dropped a torpedo and banked away to starboard, flying-up between HMCS Sioux and HMS Lark, who was about 3500 yards {3200 metres} away. Ship went "Full ahead together, hard-a-port," and steadied up on a course 060°, Starboard Oerlikons opened up on the plane just before the torpedo was dropped and followed him out of range, also one round from "B" gun was fired at him but was short. Enemy's port engine was seen to be smoking heavily before he disappeared into a snow flurry.[101]

Boak immediately reported the encounter to McGrigor, who later reported that

this was the only warning received of the torpedo attack which was on its way. It was fortunate for us as it gave the screens time to start moving

---

[100] Quoted in H.E. Lawrence, *Tales of the North Atlantic* (Toronto: McClelland and Stewart, 1985), 213.

[101] NAC, HMCS *Sioux*, "Narrative of Air Attack on Convoy JW-64, 10th February 1945."

into their anti-aircraft positions and brought everybody to the alert.[102]

Fifteen minutes later, 30 JU-188s attacked the convoy through snow flurries and low cloud. *Sioux* sighted

> *a group of about 12 to 15 aircraft...bearing 130° steering about 350° about 50 feet off the water and at 5000 yards {4572 metres} range. Opened fire with main armament, which in conjunction with **Lark's** and **Whitehall's** fire turned them away. One plane which was closer than the others, due to his turn towards, appeared to be continually hit by the Bofors {40mm} gun and when last seen was about 100 feet off the sea diving towards it. A snow flurry unfortunately obscured any definite result.*

While the starboard wing broke up this attack, Wildcats and anti-aircraft fire from escorts prevented other torpedo bombers from getting through to the merchant ships. The defences broke up a second assault 40 minutes later. McGrigor claimed seven JU-188s destroyed, four probables, and eight damaged — *Sioux* modestly claimed one probable, one damaged — against the loss of one Wildcat. In spite of the sweeping claims of Lord Haw-Haw, the German radio propagandist to whom sailors listened with glee, no ships were damaged.

Apart from occasional aircraft that shadowed from a distance, the Germans left *JW-64* alone for the next two days. On the afternoon of 12 February the Russian local escort met it off the entrance of Kola Inlet, and when darkness came the merchant ships filed through the entrance, heading for Murmansk, some 40 kilometres away. Just after the last transport entered, the corvette HMS *Denbigh Castle* was torpedoed by a U-boat. It was towed to shelter but it proved to be past the point of repair and was abandoned.

As if the rigours of escorting the Russian convoys were not enough, Home Fleet destroyers also had the misfortune to operate from two of the most unaccommodating ports anywhere. Their home base at Scapa Flow in the barren, desolate Orkney Islands north of Scotland was just an anchorage with little else to offer. There were few facilities ashore and destroyers spent most of their time moored at isolated buoys. The only place they went alongside was the destroyer tender HMS *Tyne* when they required minor repairs, but this was an unpopular berth as the British admiral who used *Tyne* as a flagship was renowned for his irascibility. The weather at Scapa was consistently dreadful, and all sailors could do with their time off was watch movies, visit other ships, or, on rare occasions, go ashore to play sports or to drink a beer in the canteen.

But Scapa was paradise compared to Kola Inlet. Layovers there usually lasted two or three days, and on the few occasions when sailors went ashore Soviet authorities restricted their movements and the members of the local population were aloof and inhospitable. Occasionally, events such as one hockey game in which *Algonquin* defeated a Soviet squad 3-2 in a forerunner of the hockey summits of recent times bridged the gulf between the Commonwealth sailors and their Russian hosts, but usually, as at Scapa, ships or flotillas organized their own activities, or the crews simply slept.

The crew of *Sioux* was therefore likely not too disappointed when after the passage of *JW-64* they did not have their usual layover in Kola Inlet, but were instead dispatched on a mission of mercy. Allied intelligence had learned that the Germans had cut off supplies to the Norwegian inhabitants of Suröy Island, just west of North Cape. Their position was becoming desperate and the Norwegian government-in-exile asked that they be evacuated. Accordingly, three British destroyers from *JW-64* took the civilians off under the cover of darkness, with *Sioux* keeping guard in case the enemy intervened. They rescued 499 Norwegians, mostly women and children, without incident. Upon return to Kola Inlet the evacuees took passage aboard merchant ships returning to the British Isles with convoy *RA-64*.

Against previous returning convoys, the Germans had deployed U-boats off the entrance of Kola Inlet to attack before the merchant ships formed up with the escort screen. Admiral McGrigor attempted to frustrate them by sweeping the area with a support group the

[102] D Hist, Rear Admiral R.R. McGrigor, "Operation Hotbed — The Passage of JW-64 and RA-64."

*Destroyers of 26th Flotilla, including **Algonquin** and **Sioux**, file slowly out of foreboding Scapa Flow for a Russian convoy. After being commissioned in February 1944, the two Fleet "V"-class destroyers were among the busiest ships in the RCN, escorting Russian convoys, participating in the Normandy invasion, screening fleet operations, and conducting anti-shipping sweeps. (PMR 92553)*

night before *RA-64* sailed and then flooding the area with patrol aircraft the next morning. Results were mixed. In exchange for one U-boat destroyed, the Allies lost a merchant ship and a corvette; the U-boats also damaged a frigate that had to be left behind. The enemy submarines, however, did not succeed in holding contact with *RA-64*.

After two uneventful days, weather and Germans intervened. First a gale of 110-kilometre-per-hour winds and a heavy swell hit *RA-64*. The convoy scattered badly and escorts had to spend most of 18 and 19 February rounding up stragglers. This took on some urgency, for a Luftwaffe reconnaissance aircraft found the convoy on the morning of the 19th, and Ultra revealed that torpedo bombers could be expected the next day.

Once again, *Sioux*, by chance at the point of attack, was instrumental in breaking up the raid despite sea conditions that made accurate gunnery difficult. "*At 1004 the first aircraft,*" according to Boak's report, "*was sighted passing down the starboard side*":

Fire was opened with all armament and planes were driven off. At 1009 numerous planes were sighted in front of snow squalls, off the port bow about 6000 yards {5486 metres} away. One of the planes closed to torpedo {merchant ship} number 103. Fire was opened and aircraft released torpedo which eventually exploded at end of run between 9th and 10th columns. The plane went down the port side being heavily engaged with close range weapons. At the same time a plane coming in from the starboard quarter was also engaged and driven away.

The former plane was reported by Bofors and After supply crews to explode and crash astern starboard wing column.

At 1012 all guns fired simultaneously at about 4 visible targets, the main armament having a good run at an aircraft on the starboard beam about 6000 yards away. Due to excessive rolling and pitching this plane was not hit although driven away when it closed to about 4000 yards when the Bofors tackled it.[103]

Boak calculated that *Sioux's* guns forced nine JU-188s to break away before they could reach

an effective attack position. The bombers torpedoed no ships and six failed to return.

The final obstacle that confronted *RA-64* was a hurricane that hit on 22 February. Winds of 130-150 kilometres per hour and 15-metre waves battered the convoy. "*It is difficult to describe wind and sea of this primeval force,*" recalled Lieutenant Hal Lawrence, an officer aboard the Canadian destroyer.

That afternoon Sioux rolled to fifty-six degrees {over 45° is considered hazardous}. Marc had a good grip on the compass stand but the rest of us on the bridge ended up in an untidy heap on the port side. With massive seas looming over our head, Sioux picked herself up, hesitated, dipped slightly again, lolled for a full six seconds — a very long six seconds — and righted herself. She was a good girl, Sioux.

In the convoy, abused engines broke down, cargoes shifted, decks split, steering gear went wonky, ice-chipped propellers thrashed. Merchant ships dropped astern and sometimes stopped. There was little we could do to help. The seas continued at awful heights, spindrift streaming from boiling crests. Sioux shuddered as wave after endless wave pounded her thin sides.[104]

Over the next four days the convoy struggled towards home in the face of high winds and mountainous seas. Many of the destroyers ran low of fuel and most were detached to the Faeroes. *Sioux,* one of only three to complete the entire voyage without refuelling, finally left the convoy on the evening of 26 February, shepherding the escort carriers back to the barren yet welcome shelter of Scapa Flow.

Sioux played a key role in the successful passages of *JW/RA-64*. Despite what can only be described as atrocious weather conditions — several destroyers had to put into dry-dock to repair weather damage — the ship had performed magnificently. Deployed on the convoy's most threatened quarter, *Sioux* had reported enemy activity promptly and the

---

[103] D Hist, HMCS *Sioux*, "Report of Air Attack on Convoy JW-64 [sic], 20th February 1945."

[109] H.E. Lawrence, *A Bloody War* (Toronto: Macmillan, 1979), 168-169.

tenacity of her anti-aircraft barrage had helped prevent torpedo bombers from penetrating to the merchant ships. In recognition of what was undoubtedly his ship's finest moment, and symbolic of the performance of other Canadian ships on the Murmansk run, Lieutenant Commander Boak was awarded a Distinguished Service Cross by the RCN and the Knight of the Order of St. Olaf by the Norwegians.

* * *

Canadian warships, like those of other navies, acquired unique personalities. Even two vessels of the same type, involved in the same operations from the same base, could have completely different styles. HMCS *Algonquin* and HMCS *Sioux,* sister ships in the same flotilla at Scapa Flow, are good examples. *Algonquin* was a "pusser" ship, naval parlance meaning that things are done by the book. For example, Lieutenant Commander Piers, the commanding officer, insisted that his sailors always wear regulation dress. In *Sioux,* by contrast, Lieutenant Commander Boak set a more informal tone. Sailors dressed in a variety of gear — hockey sweaters, usually the Maple Leafs, being the most popular.[105] Despite such differences, and there were others, the destroyers were equally competent and each fulfilled its duties with skill and professionalism.

Both *Algonquin* and *Sioux* were "happy" ships, another specific naval term that describes a warship whose crew members cooperate smoothly and efficiently in all their diverse functions no matter what the circumstances. This requires leadership and firm discipline at all levels, something that is difficult to attain in war when so many inexperienced officers and ratings go to sea. In a happy ship, ordinary sailors receive effective guidance and training from the senior ratings and petty officers who played perhaps the most critical role in the ship, acting as linchpins between the lower deck and the wardroom. They, in turn, have a good working relationship with officers, especially the First Lieutenant, or executive officer, who is responsible for the ship's routine and is, according to one officer, *"the focal point for all requests, complaints, demands,*

threats, pleas, from above and below."[106] Finally, at the top of the ladder, the captain, whose responsibility is absolute, is respected by the lower deck and the wardroom for both his disciplinary style and his professional ability. In happy ships, which are also the most effective ships, trust and respect flow both ways. The importance of these subtle, complex dynamics is best shown by the rare occasions when the system breaks down. There were only a handful of such incidents in the RCN during the war.

One of these breakdowns occurred onboard the corvette HMCS *Rivière-du-Loup* in January 1945. Although the captain was popular with the crew, the First Lieutenant was not. The lower deck thought his discipline too severe — a common complaint among sailors — but, more importantly, they had no respect for his professional ability. Twice they thought the First Lieutenant had put their lives in jeopardy: once when he allowed the ship to lag five kilometres behind a convoy when its correct station was at the front of the formation, and another time when he stopped the ship to exercise launching Carley floats even though U-boats were thought to be in the vicinity. Ab Saunders, a young Able Seaman on board the corvette, said, *"We didn't trust him."*[107]

On 10 January 1945 matters came to a head. The previous night *Rivière-du-Loup* was alongside in Belfast when word spread that the captain was going into hospital. Thinking that the First Lieutenant would take the ship to sea — in fact, a temporary commanding officer had been assigned — 47 sailors, after discussing the situation through the night, locked themselves in the forward mess when they were called to duty the next morning. Although this is commonly termed mutiny, the sailors had committed a traditional, centuries-old act of protest against an unpopular officer. In accordance with this practice, they waited in their mess until a senior officer came on board and listened to their grievances. Afterwards, they

---

[105] D Hist, interview with L.B. Jenson. Jenson was *Algonquin's* executive officer, while the interviewer, Hal Lawrence, was an officer in *Sioux.*

[106] Lawrence, *A Bloody War,* 189.

[107] Author's interview with A. Saunders.

were led to a bus through armed guards and taken to a British escort carrier berthed nearby. There they were given coffee and sandwiches, and told of the legal ramifications of what they had done.

The flag officer in command at Belfast took the sensible view *"that this indiscipline had been a foolish escapade on the part of young ratings rather than insubordination of a serious nature."* A board of inquiry (which included a Canadian officer), perhaps wanting to send a stronger message, thought differently. Although it was admitted that the sailors *"did not fully realize the seriousness of their crime,"* they had nonetheless committed *"an act of mutiny."* But the board of inquiry also made clear

> *that the main cause of this refusal of duty was general lack of discipline on board over a long period...caused by injudicious and tactless handling of the ratings.*

Blame was assigned to the First Lieutenant, to petty officers and senior ratings who had given him little assistance, and to the captain for allowing the situation to get out of hand. All of these men were drafted to other ships. They were the lucky ones: 44 of the 47 ratings who had refused duty were sentenced to Belfast Gaol for 42, 60, or 90 days, the heaviest terms being given to those who had served longest in the navy.[108]

The remainder of Ab Saunders' war shows that the mutineers were at least given a second chance. He recalls that they were well treated by the guards at Belfast Gaol. Placed two to a cell and allowed to pick their own cellmates, they received square meals, two exercise periods a day, and much-coveted cigarettes. Like the others, Saunders was released early and was sent to the RCN manning depot HMCS *Niobe*. He was eventually drafted to the frigate HMCS *Matane*, where he was assigned duty as the petty officers' messman *"so they could keep an eye on me."* Staying with the ship until it went around to British Columbia after the end of the war in Europe, Saunders volunteered for duty in the Pacific but was demobilized when the atomic bombs ended the war with Japan. To this day he has no regrets about his stance in *Rivière-du-Loup.*

* * *

Since HX-1, the first eastbound trans-Atlantic convoy, had left Halifax on 16 September 1939,

the primary role of the RCN had been to help ensure the safe and timely arrival of the merchant ships that sustained Britain. The long, bitter campaign to win the war against the U-boats had been fought mainly on the North Atlantic, but this changed with the invasion of Normandy. The Germans responded to the landings by concentrating their submarines in the waters around the British Isles, initiating a coastal-waters campaign that continued to the end of the war. Canadian escorts played a prominent part in this grim but little-known struggle, as they had in the ocean campaign.

The success of the U-boats in shallow inshore waters surprised the Germans as much as it did the Allies. The U-boats had been fitted with schnorkel breathing tubes that allowed them to recharge their battery-driven underwater propulsion system while running submerged. This had been a desperate measure to try to save the submarines from Allied radar-equipped aircraft that had become expert at pouncing upon surfaced U-boats. During the Normandy operations the submarines found that they could not only survive, but also maintain attacking positions close to Allied ports — something they had dared not try since the first months of the war. The reason was that sonar in warships, the only reliable equipment for finding submerged submarines, proved to be of limited effectiveness in coastal waters. Recalled one veteran U-boat hunter,

> *In shallow water a U-boat, finding herself in danger of being chased, can look at the chart and go to ground among a lot of boulders or in a valley in the sea bed, leaving us the task of combing the bottom and deciding which of the knobs are boulders or old wrecks and which may conceivably be the enemy. Add the complication of manoeuvring to get over the top of, or even to remain in contact with, a small bump on the bottom, while the tidal stream relentlessly sweeps the ship away, and it can be appreciated that this sort of search calls for the exercise of much faith and patience.[109]*

[108] NAC, "Board of Inquiry, Refusal of Duty — HMCS *Rivière-du-Loup."*

[109] D.E.G. Wemyss, *Walker's Hunting Groups in the Western Approaches* (Liverpool: Liverpool Daily Post and Echo, 1948), 139.

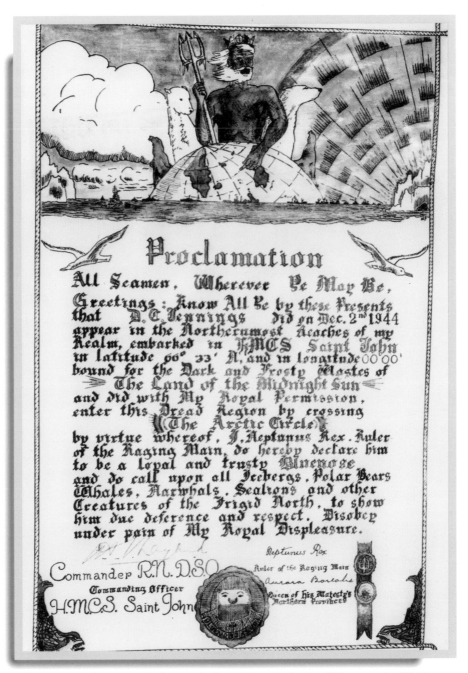

*Sailors crossing the Arctic Circle were inducted into the Order of Bluenoses by "Neptunus Rex" and "Queen Aurora Borealis." The crews of at least 15 Canadian warships joined this exclusive club during the Second World War; in this case the new Bluenoser was Lieutenant D.C. Jennings of the frigate HMCS **Saint John.** (PMR 924307)*

Moreover, because the geography of coastal waters forced shipping to follow fixed, well known routes, instead of actively searching for targets as they had to on the open ocean, U-boats could lay on the bottom and wait for targets to come to them. Allied navies eventually evolved countermeasures to cope with these new challenges, but it took time.

A post-war Royal Navy staff study divided the coastal-waters campaign into three distinct stages. In the first, from the invasion in June to the abandonment of U-boat bases on the Bay of Biscay in August 1944, U-boats achieved limited success but took heavy losses. In the second stage, lasting from September through November 1944, U-boats were redeployed to Norwegian bases and activity sunk to "a very low ebb." In December, the third and most intense phase began, and remained the major commitment of the U-boat fleet until their surrender in May 1945.

The shipping that the Germans strove to sink was vital to the advance of Allied armies across northwest Europe. Naval officers responsible for routing convoys had to balance two concerns: getting the materiel to its destination quickly; and ensuring that it arrived at all, by selecting the safest route (which was also usually the longest and slowest). During the second phase of the coastal-waters offensive, British authorities shifted the North Atlantic convoy lanes south from their usual approach to the British Isles north of Ireland to a route through the southwestern approaches into either St. George's Channel or the English Channel. This forced U-boats to make a longer passage from Norway, thus decreasing their time on station and increasing opportunities to intercept them. As the fall came to a close, many merchant ships continued to unload in Britain but an increasing number headed directly to liberated ports such as Cherbourg or Le Havre. In December, when the Scheldt was finally cleared of Germans and mines, much of the shipping proceeded directly across the North Sea to unload their cargoes at Antwerp, close to the allied armies that required them.

The valuable transports received protection from three sources. Maritime patrol aircraft — Liberators, Sunderlands, and Wellingtons — flew over the convoys themselves and patrolled focal areas such as the entrances to the English and St. George's channels. Close escorts consisting of corvettes, minesweepers, or trawlers accompanied convoys throughout their passage. Anti-submarine support groups, normally comprising four or five destroyers, frigates, or sloops, patrolled independently where U-boats were suspected or where geography forced shipping to follow fixed routes. When a convoy was known to be in danger, or had been attacked, the support group in the area would reinforce the close escort.

The unsung members of this triumvirate were the close escorts, of which 19 were RCN corvettes that had been on this tedious but necessary duty since May 1944. Coastal convoys normally consisted of about 10 merchant ships, usually coasters, LSTs, or larger transports, that proceeded in one or two long columns. These formations were slow — the rate of advance was about seven knots — unwieldy, and notoriously undisciplined. Their escorts (there was often just one) had to shepherd them constantly, leading them through narrow, mineswept channels, coaxing or bullying reluctant — or just plain ornery — skippers back into station. If a convoy was attacked, the close escort was usually under orders not to counterattack but to lead its charges out of danger, leaving the hunt to support groups. This tactic made good sense — close escorts lacked the modern equipment and training required to kill U-boats in shallow waters — but it added to the thanklessness of the task. The RCN corvettes escorted hundreds of coastal convoys in the last year of the war, and although the work was valuable it was exceedingly unpopular.

Apart from occasional runs ashore by thirsty sailors, the dreariness of this duty was interrupted only by poor weather or the sudden appearance of the enemy. HMCS *Moose Jaw's* report for October 1944 provides examples of the problems caused by autumn gales and high seas. On 11 October, while secured alongside HMCS *Louisbourg* at a buoy in Milford Haven, *Moose Jaw* sustained damage to its hull from the pounding of its sister ship. The corvette escorted three convoys that month. One was forced to seek shelter. On another convoy the skipper of the ship carrying the Commodore decided on his own authority to put into a bay to ride out a storm. The Commodore was unable to transfer to another ship or appoint a deputy and, according to the captain of *Moose Jaw*, "*the convoy became confused and badly scattered.*" The corvette was left to pull the formation back together. Other corvettes struggled with difficult situations that month: HMCS *Trentonian* had to corral a tow that broke lose in the middle of a convoy, and *Mayflower's* captain thought conditions so unpleasant that he "*found that the decision whether or not to plow ahead in bad weather and risk damaging one's Ship is every bit as hard to make in the {English} Channel as in the North Atlantic.*"

The beginning of the most intense phase of the U-boats' inshore offensive in December reduced weather to secondary concern. That month four U-boats entered the Channel, and two of them were successful. *U-486* struck first on the 18th, attacking a convoy off Falmouth and sinking one merchantman. HMCS *Algoma* was part of the escort but was unable to detect the assailant. The submarine then proceeded to cause havoc over the next 10 days, sinking two transports, a frigate, and a landing craft, and damaging another escort, before escaping to Norway.

U-772 arrived on the heels of *U-486*. On 23 December it claimed a merchant ship far up the Channel off the Isle of Wight, and then lay low. Six days later, HMCS *Calgary* was escorting a convoy westward off Portland Bill when a large explosion erupted against the port side of the second-last ship in the port column. *Calgary,* the lone escort, immediately began a search for the attacking submarine — *U-772* — but three minutes later a second explosion staggered another transport. *Calgary* dropped a number of depth charges on doubtful echoes but the submarine escaped. Fortunately, both its victims made port, but *U-772* was not so lucky. The next night a Wellington patrol aircraft from No 407 Squadron RCAF flown by Squadron Leader Cameron Taylor detected the submarine's schnorkel with its radar and destroyed *U-772* in a skilful, low-level attack.

The December losses in the English Channel, and others in the Irish Sea during January,

prompted naval leaders to take stronger defensive measures, including an expanded deep-water mining campaign and intensified warship and aircraft patrols. These measures, which continued until the end of the war, helped, but the U-boats continued to take a toll, including, in February, a Canadian corvette.

On the afternoon of 22 February, conditions were almost perfect as HMCS *Trentonian* escorted the convoy BTC-76 — 14 ships in two columns — eastward through Falmouth Bay. The wind was light, the sea calm, and visibility 16 kilometres. The corvette, the lone escort, was zigzagging in front of the convoy when, at 1320, an explosion shook the coaster *Alexander Kennedy,* the second ship in the starboard column. On *Trentonian's* bridge, the officer of the watch immediately rang the action bells and ordered the helmsman to alter to port towards the convoy. As the escort turned, the sonar operator detected a contact in the path of the convoy. By this time the commanding officer, Lieutenant C.S. Glassco RCNVR, had arrived on the bridge and, considering that the "*bearing and distance from the torpedoed ship placed the echo in a highly improbable position for it to be a submarine,*" steadied on a southwest course on the assumption that the U-boat, following a favourite tactic, had attacked from a position inshore of the convoy.

As *Trentonian* approached the convoy at 14 knots, Glassco ordered its anti-acoustic gear streamed and asked the Commodore on which side the *Alexander Kennedy* had been torpedoed. Upon learning it was the starboard side, and not the port as he had suspected, Glassco immediately headed for the seaward side of the formation, passing under the lead ship's stern. At 1330, just as *Trentonian* cleared the starboard column of the convoy, "*a heavy explosion was felt on the starboard side aft and the ship slewed to starboard.*" A torpedo, obviously intended for another ship, hit in the shaft tunnel and split the engine-room bulkhead. The engine-room flooded immediately and the corvette settled slowly by the stern. After receiving damage reports, Glassco concluded *Trentonian* could not be saved and at 1334 ordered abandon ship. All but six sailors were rescued.

The U-boat had picked its attack area well, for the large force of escorts that searched for it until the next morning was unsuccessful. The report of the leader of the support group that led the hunt describes the frustrations of shallow-water searches:

It appeared that everything possible which could have been done to provide against the U-boat's escape was done on this occasion and an armada of small ships was quickly mobilized to guard the avenues of escape. Some loopholes, however, always arise and no scheme is entirely watertight when 50 percent of the vessels engaged are distracted by "non-sub" contacts. Falmouth Bay is notorious for its "non-subs" which flourish as daisies on a summer golf course and, ever since the summer campaign, this area has proved the despair of hunting groups.

Like a very wet gopher on the same golf course, *U-1004* burrowed its way out of Falmouth Bay despite being heavily depth charged.

It is doubtful that any of the Canadian corvettes engaged in close escort in British waters ever attacked an actual U-boat, but RCN support groups were in a much better position to hit back. Not only had they received more intensive training but they had more modern equipment, including the latest models of sonar, radio navigation gear to provide exact positioning, and echo sounders to help differentiate bottomed U-boats from wrecks. Most support groups had this equipment — and the fire power to match — but only some had the intangible savvy or wiliness needed to locate and kill submarines in inshore waters.

One of these was the RCN's Escort Group (EG) 9. With a strength of four to six River-class frigates (depending on refit schedules), EG 9 had been involved in the inshore campaign from the beginning. The group was not only experienced, but successful, having killed two U-boats in British waters since August 1944 to go with two previously destroyed on the North Atlantic. Much of the success derived from the group's leaders. Its senior officer, Commander A.F.C. Layard RN, had led anti-submarine groups since the dark days of the Battle of the Atlantic. Although Layard's personal diary indicates that the long hours he had spent at sea throughout the war were taxing his nerves, he was well supported by the individual captains in the group. Officers

such as Lieutenant Commanders Clarence King RCNR and William Stacey RCNR were among the best naval reservists in the RCN and, like Layard, they had spent the war fighting U-boats. Similarly, the frigates' sonar crews had had a wealth of experience.

The skill of EG 9 was demonstrated by its efficient dispatch of *U-309* on 16 February 1945. Providing support for a small convoy off northeast Scotland, the frigate HMCS *Saint John* detected a bottomed contact as it led the way across Moray Firth. A model shallow-water kill ensued. *Saint John,* with Layard acting as its captain as well as group SO, first made a slow pass using its echo sounder to trace an outline of the contact, to help classify it and see if it was indeed lying on the seabed. At the same time it used the radio navigation aid GEE to fix the exact position of the contact, to see if there was a known wreck there. Because *"there was no plotted wreck in the vicinity,"* Layard later reported, *contact was attacked with 5-charge pattern. This first attack brought oil to the surface which increased when attacked again by H{edge}/H{og}. A Third attack with 5 D{epth}/C{harge}'s dropped in line by Echo Sounder produced more oil and a certain amount of debris — mostly splintered wood but which included pages from a German Signal Log, a tube of boracic acid marked in German "Medical Stores Kiel" and a small aluminum flask. Several more attacks were carried out before dark but more oil, which was classified diesel oil, and more wood were all brought up.*

Further depth charges brought up more debris over the next two days but *U-309* was probably destroyed in the first attacks.[110]

Another kill the next month by EG-26 demonstrates that good fortune can sometimes be as important as skill. Just before midnight on 20 March, while on passage to a training session off Lough Foyle in Northern Ireland, a lookout in HMCS *New Glasgow* exclaimed *"low flying aircraft approaching!"* In fact he had been deceived by the loud whooshing noise made by a schnorkel and quickly changed his report to *"object in the*

[110] D Hist, naval records, Senior Officer, 9th Escort Group, ROP, 3 March 1945.

(PA 180509)

The elements of a ship's company; if trust and respect flowed freely among them the result was usually a "happy" ship. At top, ratings in their cramped, stuffy mess deck, where they ate, slept, and enjoyed what little free time they had. In middle, some of **Algonquin's** officers, perhaps fresh from a bout of wardroom gymnastics in the flagship, relax in their wardroom. At bottom, chiefs and petty officers, the glue that held it all together, in this case from **Algonquin.**

(PMR 92462)

(PMR 92524)

water very close!" Both reports got the immediate attention of the captain and officer of the watch, who sighted a schnorkel just 45-90 metres ahead. Seconds later, *New Glasgow* smashed into the contact, the frigate lifting up with the impact, but despite the efforts of EG-26 and two other RCN escort groups no further sign was found of what had obviously been a submarine.[111]

New Glasgow had literally run down *U-1003*. Reports from prisoners of war confirm that the U-boat had been schnorkeling when it was suddenly staggered by a violent impact from astern. Although the sailor on the radar warning set had monitored signals close by, he had failed to warn his captain. The collision caused the submarine to list 30 degrees and plunge violently downward 60 metres to bottom. The "circular saws" of EG-26's anti-acoustic torpedo gear could plainly be heard above, and several depth charges shook the boat, but after an hour or two *U-1003* was able to creep away. It was only when the U-boat surfaced 24 hours later that the extent of its damage became apparent. The schnorkel and periscope were wrecked, a 20mm gun and antenna ripped away, and the conning tower buckled. An approaching contact forced *U-1003* to dive, but the main hatch could not be sealed tightly and the conning tower flooded. After another 20 hours the U-boat surfaced, hoping to make repairs or beach on the nearby Irish coast, but, after another contact approached, its captain decided to scuttle his boat. Four hours later, the frigate HMCS *Thetford Mines,* on passage to Londonderry for repairs, came upon 31 survivors in the water and *New Glasgow* was credited with the kill.[112]

Despite the increasing effectiveness of Allied anti-submarine forces against schnorkel-equipped U-boats, the German submarines claimed victims right up to the end of the war. Among them was the minesweeper HMCS *Guysborough,* in March 1945. A ship with an excellent record and a veteran of the sweeping operations off Normandy, *Guysborough* was returning to European waters after a refit in Canada. On 17 March, sailing independently, the Bangor-class minesweeper was on the final leg of its journey approximately 400 kilometres north of Cape Finisterre. *Guysborough* was maintaining a sonar watch and towing CAT gear (an anti-acoustic torpedo noisemaker), but was not zigzagging because the daily U-boat report radioed by shore authorities did not indicate that any submarines were in the vicinity and the captain wanted to conserve fuel.

In the early evening an acoustic torpedo from *U-878* exploded against *Guysborough's* stern. The CAT gear should have attracted the torpedo away from the ship's propeller noise, but in accordance with standard procedure it was streamed at 228 metres, apparently too close to confuse the torpedo — a regulation that was changed when *Guysborough's* fate became known. Immediately after the explosion the ship settled by the stern and took a slight list to port but, despite the fact that part of the stern had been blown off, the ship appeared to be in no danger of sinking. Damage-control parties plugged leaks and shored up the after bulkhead while the rest of the crew mustered on the upper deck and all boats and floats were lowered.

Approximately 90 minutes later, a second torpedo hit amidships on the starboard side. The vessel now began to settle rapidly and the captain, Lieutenant B.T.R. Russell RCNR, gave the order to abandon ship. Russell made a final quick search of the upper deck before jumping himself. According to later accounts, all but two of the sailors aboard were seen in the water. *Guysborough's* motor cutter was holed too badly to be of use, and the whaler had overturned, but five Carley floats had been cut away. Four were lashed together by one group of 48 sailors but the other 42 survivors crowded around the remaining float, which drifted away from the others.

The ship had sent a distress signal after the first torpedo hit, and the C-in-C Western Approaches immediately dispatched vessels to the scene, but *Guysborough's* sailors were in the frigid 8°C sea for 19 long hours before the first arrived. Forty-nine men died in the meantime, including 36 of the 42 on the single Carley float. One who survived, Chief Petty Officer Maurice Benoît, left a poignant account of the time on the overcrowded raft.

[111] D Hist, HMCS *New Glasgow,* Report of Proceedings.
[112] D Hist, Admiralty, "Report on the Interrogation of Survivors of U-1003."

*The doomed minesweeper HMCS **Guysborough**.
(PA 133877)*

*Although this photograph is of survivors from another sinking, it illustrates the small size
of a Carley float, one of which 42 **Guysborough** sailors clung to when their ship went
down. Also, these sailors are wearing the RCN life-jacket, which was responsible for saving
many lives but which was costly in **Guysborough**'s case. (PMR 94306)*

I was just coming from the chartroom to the bridge when the torpedo struck, and was thrown about 40 feet away from the ship by the force of the explosion. At that time I think I was alone in the water, and I swam for about half an hour before I came to the Carley Float, which was already supporting 40 men. I increased the number to 41. A little later we heard someone calling for help and Joseph Norvel Gouthro and I swam out and brought in one of the officers, who was pretty badly wounded. It was a sad disappointment to us both when he died a few minutes later.

Recognizing that *"things did not look very good,"* the survivors organized themselves. Married men with children were placed next to the float *"where they would have the best chance of survival."*

We did pretty well, considering the circumstances, until the evening. When it got dark it became a whole lot colder than it had been and it had not been exactly warm at any time. But with the darkness a cold wind came up, and that was what got a number of the boys who had been holding on with all their strength and will until then. It was not long before quite a few started to complain about the cold and to say that they didn't think they could hold on much longer. There was nothing that anybody could do about it, you just had to hang on.

The RCN had designed a new life-jacket during the war that was popular with sailors and was credited with saving many lives. Unhappily, on this night an overlooked flaw killed some men.

The wind was very strong as well as cold, and the sea was quite rough. I am afraid that that fact accounted for the loss of quite a few men. If we had better luck with the weather there would have been more survivors.

Twice the Carley Float turned over, and this was one of the worse things that happened in the whole business. Some of the fellows had tied themselves on to the float and when it turned over they couldn't get loose, but were held underneath it and drowned. 8 of them died the first time this happened and 5 more died the second time.

Some sailors had secured themselves to the float by a snap hook on the life-jacket but their fingers were too numb to release it when the float flipped over. Because of this tragedy, a three-metre line was later attached to the snap hook, and this enabled trapped sailors to float free.

By 0100 there were only 20 sailors left. Because they could not all get near the float they fastened themselves to those who could.

Right at the beginning our morale had been very good. We did a lot of singing to pass the time, and to keep ourselves as cheerful as possible in the circumstances. Every now and then the singing would stop and someone would start a prayer, and very soon the rest of us would join in. Coder {John Charles} Gleason was the only one who had a watch that was still working, and every now and then he would sing out the time to the rest of us. That was the only way we could feel really that time was passing. The whole experience seemed to be as if there were no such thing as time, as if it would just go on forever, and as if you might slip from life in{to} death without time having anything to do with it.

We were beginning to feel that way in the early hours of the morning. You couldn't say that the morale was going. Nobody was afraid. Time didn't matter any more. In fact after a while we told Gleason not to let us know what the time was. It just made it seem as if it was going on longer.

The last time he gave us the hour which was around three o'clock in the morning there were only 11 of us left. Another went sometime between then and dawn.

We didn't really expect to be picked up at all. Daylight is always supposed to make you feel better, but the coming of dawn didn't seem to make any difference. The sea was there still, and the sky, and I guess the wind was still just as cold only we couldn't feel very much by that time. By noon there were just the six of us left. The fellows died without complaints. They just seemed to go to sleep from the cold. One minute they would be talking to you and the next they wouldn't be there any more. It made you realize what a very thin line there is sometimes between life and death.

The crique inside Ostend harbour after the accident that decimated the 29th MTB Flotilla on 14 February 1945. (PA 180511)

It was 1400 on 18 March when the frigate HMS *Inglis* found the two groups of survivors. Too weak and numb to pull themselves up the scramble nets, the sailors, including Gouthro and Gleason, had to be hoisted aboard. Benoît recalls,

It was certainly a wonderful feeling to realize that after all we had been through we were saved and alive, and with friends. I think maybe the best thing of all was when we met over 30 {other} survivors of the **Guysborough**.[113]

The *Guysborough* disaster came on the heels of another tragedy that decimated one of the RCN's two MTB flotillas. Both Canadian units had passed a largely uneventful winter. The 65th divided its time between Ostend and Great Yarmouth and carried out defensive patrols along the Thames-Antwerp convoy route and one offensive sweep, but encountered no German forces. The 29th moved to Ostend in mid-January and met the enemy only once in 13 operations.

During this time Lieutenant Commander Kirkpatrick attempted to unite the two Canadian flotillas at one base. After the fall of Walcheren, Coastal Forces planners considered opening a new base at Veere on the eastern shore of the island so that they could extend operations further up the coast, allowing them to clamp a more effective blockade on E-boat bases and improve their chances of intercepting German coastal convoys. When he learned of this plan, Kirkpatrick suggested that Veere be used as a Canadian MTB base. Apart from obvious national reasons, the two flotillas would complement each other operationally and could share spare personnel, something they could not do with the RN flotillas with which they normally served. Ultimately, the plan to establish a base at Veere fell through, and Kirkpatrick's plan to unite the two Canadian flotillas working side by side faded away.[114]

This was unfortunate, for on 14 February the 29th flotilla was virtually destroyed by a tragic accident that took place within the safe confines of Ostend harbour. On the afternoon of 14 February, four of the 29th's MTBs were preparing for that night's operations. MTB-464 was carrying out its armament check at sea when one of its engines cut out because of water in the

fuel system. This had become an all too common problem, apparently because fuel pumped ashore from a tanker was contaminated with water. Base maintenance staff claimed it was too busy to handle the problem and instructed motor mechanics to pump the water out of their fuel tanks into buckets and then throw the contents over the side.

When *MTB-464's* chief motor mechanic discovered a recurrence of the problem on 14 February, he sought assistance from the base staff. Finding no one, he began to fix the defect himself and, rejecting the slower bucket method, used the bilge pump to force water directly into the harbour. He instructed a stoker to watch over the side to inform him when the water was drained and gas began to flow into the harbour. *MTB-464's* First Lieutenant came by while the pumping was underway and, when told what was going on, *"made no comment other than 'O.K.'."* Over a 20-minute period, they pumped approximately 190 litres of fluid over the side. The motor mechanic later told a board of inquiry *"that he took these steps as he considered it his duty to make the boat operational in time to go to sea at 1730 that day."*[115]

Subsequent investigations concluded that *464's* fuel was likely discoloured by sludge, making it difficult to discern it from the water being pumped out of the tank. Certainly, the smell of high-octane fuel pervaded the harbour area. Testimony revealed that several officers and ratings, including the captains of four MTBs, *"all noticed the smell of petrol yet none gave any warning."* At approximately 1600, somebody spotted flames between two MTBs tied together in a "trot" just downwind from *464;* minutes later powerful explosions shook Ostend harbour.

The inner basin was packed with coastal craft. Sixteen MTBs were berthed in a small "crique" or basin off the main harbour that was approximately 137 metres long and 37 metres wide. Just around the corner, but downstream, another 15 MTBs and two larger motor launches lay alongside the

---

[113] D Hist, undated interview with CPO Maurice Benoît.

[114] D Hist, RCN narrative, "RCN Operations in UK Waters after 20 September 1944: Coastal Forces."

[115] D Hist, "Board of Inquiry into Explosion at Ostend on 14th February 1945 — Narrative."

main Coastal Forces mobile unit. Not far away were several LSTs and minesweepers. In all, 32 vessels and the mobile unit were crowded into an area of just one third of a square kilometre.

Fanned by an offshore breeze, the fire spread rapidly. The 29th's boats, furthest up the crique, were the first to go. MTBs *465* and *462* blew up almost immediately, followed quickly by the British *438* and the Canadian *466*. Two behind them, *444* from an RN flotilla and the 29th's *459,* drifted before burning themselves out. Three Canadian boats at the head of the crique were saved by the quick response of *485's* coxswain, who started engines and moved the whole trot forward out of danger. The conflagration spread through the harbour, ultimately destroying 12 MTBs, including five from the 29th, and seriously damaging five others.

The inner basin was engulfed in flames. According to the base commander,

Heavy explosions were taking place, possibly from torpedo air vessels exploding, ammunition, including 6-pounders were exploding in all directions, rockets were exploding and depth charges were burning, and there was a sheet of flame covering the whole area, covered by a pall of black smoke. LSTs, minesweepers, and MTBs were trying to get away and there were numerous men in the water all around the scene of action. At the same time a large number of aircraft were going overhead at 1500 to 2000 feet, who immediately started to fire all their recognition lights, and one man even baled out in his alarm.[116]

The blast from the explosions shook walls throughout Ostend and broke windows five kilometres away.

The toll was tragic: 64 were killed and scores were wounded, including 29 killed and 20 wounded from the Canadian flotilla. There could have been more casualties but most of the crews were on "make and mend," and many sailors were ashore. Most rushed to the waterfront when they heard the explosions but were unable to get near their boats and were forced to take cover from shrapnel and other flying debris. The 29th's doctor, Surgeon Lieutenant W.L. Leslie, two sick bay attendants, and the chaplain saved many

lives despite powerful explosions nearby, and vessels from the outer harbour moved towards the crique to pull more than 40 sailors from the water.

The subsequent board of inquiry attributed the disaster to shoddy and lax practices within the mobile base and the 29th flotilla. *MTB-464's* motor mechanic, who had violated standing orders, was found primarily responsible for the outbreak of the fire, but evidence indicated that other MTBs may have contributed to the large amount of fuel in the harbour. Commander Brind was relieved of his command, and four Canadian officers, including the flotilla commander, his deputy, and the CO and First Lieutenant of *464,* received the Admiralty's "severe displeasure."

The 29th, which lost five of nine boats in the disaster, was disbanded. Both Canadian and British officers saw little purpose in working-up new boats and crews in what were obviously the closing stages of the war. Recommendations that the surviving boats and crews join another unit were similarly dismissed. Instead, the flotilla was withdrawn and its four boats were used as replacements for RN flotillas. The surviving sailors were asked to volunteer for the 65th's spare pool but none stepped forward, and they returned to Canada where they scattered amongst the various manning pools across the country. The 29th's leader, Lieutenant Commander Tony Law, sadly concluded in his final report, "*...it is to the extreme regret...that after many interesting months together the Flotilla must disband in such inauspicious circumstances.*"

The 65th flotilla continued the fight. Transferred to Ostend to fill the void left by the disaster, the flotilla fought five successful engagements against E-boats, either driving them off or, in one instance, sinking one. But the operational load came at a price. Since moving up the Channel in September 1944, Lieutenant Commander Kirkpatrick calculated, the 65th had put in *more sea time per boat than any other flotilla, boat for boat, refits excepted.*" This took a heavy toll on its sailors; leave was rare and at the beginning of April the flotilla medical officer reported an increase in operational fatigue.

---

[116] D Hist, naval records.

Fortunately, the end was at hand. On the night of 12/13 April, two of the 65th's boats forced two E-boats to abandon an attempt to sow mines along the North Sea convoy routes; although the sailors on board the MTBs could not know it, that was the final E-boat sortie of the war.

When peace finally came, Canadian warships were kept busy enforcing the surrender and opening up occupied ports. On 11 May, *Iroquois* took part in Operation Kingdom, the boisterously welcomed return of Crown Prince Olaf to Norway after five years in exile. A few days later the mood changed as the destroyer helped escort two German cruisers into bombed-out Kiel. Meanwhile, *Haida* and *Huron* landed relief supplies at various ports along the Norwegian coast, and at one *Haida* threw a party for more than 1500 happy children. After a hectic month, the three ships began their voyage home across the Atlantic. Sailors spent the days chipping away the layers of dull wartime paint and shining up the brass that emerged from underneath. At night, they watched ships steaming peacefully by, their lights burning brightly for the first time in five years.

(PA 145770)

CHAPTER V

<u>*RHINELAND*</u>

On a hill just on the outskirts of Groesbeek, there stands a windmill overlooking a valley through which the border line between Holland and Germany runs. And dotted across the valley are scattered farm buildings. On the other side can be seen the Reichswald and to the left and in the distance the rolling country with factory chimneys and churches marking towns and villages. Why the Germans left that windmill intact, will always be a mystery, for obviously it was the best observation post in the countryside. Certainly had they known what was going on there during the last weeks of January and the first week of February, it would not have been left standing. During that period it was filled with officers from Generals down to subalterns each day planning Germany's destruction.

The windmill had been used by regimental officers as an O.P. direct fire of the regiment on target for months, but during this period they found it hard to get enough room in the top story of the mill to observe the zone for visiting officers from British units literally queued up to get a look at the ground they were going to attack. At

first there were Generals who said little then came Brigadiers and Lt. Colonels who invariably asked, "Can you put me on the ground?", lastly came Majors and subalterns who discussed the details of their plans for hours studying each track, house and bush until the FOO's from the regiment knew as much about their plans as they did.[117]

The bustle of activity around 4th Field's observation post signalled the beginning of Field Marshal Montgomery's offensive to drive the Germans beyond the Rhine. Delayed by the German Ardennes offensive, earlier plans were now revised, refined, and timed for the second week of February. Montgomery's concept of operations called for a coordinated attack by First Canadian and Ninth US armies, the Canadians to drive a northern pincer from Nijmegen to meet an American southern one in the Rhine plains between Wesel and Cologne. With the west bank clear, Second British Army would cross the river and drive into the heart of Germany.

---

[117] D Hist, "History of 4th Field Regiment."

Along with Normandy and the Scheldt, the Rhineland battle was a Canadian watershed, but it differed from the others in two important respects. First, the operation aimed not to liberate occupied territory but to conquer German soil. Second, it was the climactic battle of the Canadian Army, the magnitude of which it was not to see again.

General Crerar had under his command II Canadian and XXX British Corps, with seven infantry and three armoured divisions, and three independent armoured brigades. Besides organic divisional field regiments, there were one super-heavy, five heavy, and 17 medium regiments, as well as the Canadian Rocket Battery, with a total of more than 1200 guns. They required 350 different ammunition types, the portion to be shot in the three days before D-Day being equivalent to 25,000 medium bomb loads. There were 3400 tanks, with 276,750 rounds for their main armament, along with Crocodiles, Weasels, Kangaroos, Wasps, and Flails, their movements screened by a 30-kilometre continuous belt of smoke. The Army's ration strength was more than 450,000, most of them not Canadian.

In preparing the battlefield, sappers constructed and widened about 150 kilometres of roads, using 18,000 logs, on which 35,000 vehicles drove an average of 200 kilometres daily using about five million litres of fuel. Sappers also had almost 2000 tons of equipment for five major bridges, including a Bailey span of 400 metres. From 13 railheads, 446 freight trains dumped supplies equal to 89,000 three-ton vehicle loads. One thousand soldiers deployed on traffic-control duties planted 9600 route signs; aerial photo technicians produced 500,000 prints and 15,000 enlargements; and the 819,000 map sheets that were distributed used 31 tons of paper.

Crerar had call on the resources of No 83 Group for air cover, No 84 Group for close support, and 1200 medium and heavy bombers for heavier destruction. Medical units planned to handle casualties at a rate of 1000 a day, with a peak of 5000 by the third day of the battle. In all, Crerar's resources for the operation were more than those at Vimy Ridge, and not much less than those the Allies deployed on D-Day.

The ground over which the battle was to be fought presented an extremely difficult tactical challenge. First Canadian Army's task was to clear Germans from the area bounded by the Meuse and the Rhine, which meant advancing southeastwards into a reverse funnel that expanded from a base 10 kilometres wide between Mook and Nijmegen in the north and tripled in width before reaching a line Xanten-Geldern 65 kilometres beyond. From 4th Field's observation point, viewers saw on the left, or north, a flooded 30-by-15-kilometre lake bordering the Rhine, from which a few villages protruded above water. Skirting the southern edge of the flooded land was the main road that ran from Nijmegen to Cleve, then on through Moyland and Calcar to Wesel. South, on the right flank, was a narrower flood plain along the Meuse. Between the two rivers, and blocking easy access from the west to Cleve, was the Reichswald Forest, a 13-kilometre-wide and seven-kilometre-deep tangle of woods cut by trails. At the far end of the wood, 15 kilometres due south of Cleve and connected to it by a main road, was the town of Goch. Both Cleve and Goch were important objectives because they controlled the few good roads in the area. Beyond the Reichswald was a 15-kilometre stretch of undulating farmland that ran to another wooded sector, Hochwald and Balberger Wald, which protected the approaches to Xanten and Wesel.

Although neglected from the time it was first laid out in the 1930s, the Siegfried Line, stretching from Cleve to the Swiss border, was a formidable obstacle. In this northern sector were three fortified zones. The outpost to the main defences, running across the western face of the Reichswald, had a double series of trenches and an antitank ditch in front of the forest, strengthened by farmhouses and villages that had been converted into strong points. Five kilometres further east, and throughout the Reichswald proper, was the main Siegfried Line with more antitank ditches, concrete emplacements for antitank and machine guns, minefields, and barbed wire entanglements. North of the forest the corridor leading to Cleve was protected by a succession of trench systems on the high, rugged Materborn. The third barrier, running in front of Hochwald and Balberger Wald, consisted of two and sometimes three lines of entrenchments 600 to 900 metres apart supplemented by antitank ditches, wire, and minefields.

German commanders differed in their assessments of the threat. The local commander correctly appreciated that the Allies would attack from Nijmegen where they already had a bridge over the Waal. His superiors disagreed, insisting that the offensive they knew was coming would be mounted further south, at Venlo or Roermond. Consequently they deployed only the 84th Division reinforced by three parachute battalions in the north, and kept their reserves well back.

Timing of the new offensive, first scheduled for early January when frozen ground eased vehicle movement, had to wait until the debris left by the German spoiling attack in the Ardennes was cleared away, and it was not until late January that Montgomery was able to set D-Day. General Crerar's army was to strike southeast from Nijmegen first, on 8 February, with Operation Veritable. Two days later the 12 divisions in Lieutenant General W.H. Simpson's Ninth Army were to launch Operation Grenade, to drive northeast from their positions around Aachen. Between them, they would force the Germans to spread their reserve divisions along a wide front, and trap them with their backs to the Rhine.

The schedule, however, soon came unstuck. Before they could strike, Simpson's forces had first to capture the dams over the Roer River that controlled the downward flow of water through the sector of their proposed attack. The Americans reached the dams just as Veritable began, but not before the Germans sabotaged their water release mechanism, not to cause an immediate heavy flood, but to ensure a steady continual flow of water over several days. With their way blocked by a newly formed lake, the Americans were forced to wait for two weeks until the water level dropped. The result was that instead of forcing the enemy to split his reserves to counter the two pincers, the Germans were able to concentrate all of them against Crerar's attack. Aided by bad weather that restricted Second TAF's interdiction missions, the Germans quickly committed elements of 10 divisions in the north. In time, once the flood receded, and with German reserves concentrated

in the north, the Americans were able to break out spectacularly, as they had done in Normandy the year before. Like Normandy, as well, Canadian and British units had to fight against concentrated German reserves in a succession of bitter attritional struggles in the most difficult circumstances imaginable.

General Crerar planned his attack in three phases. The first was to break through the narrow Siegfried corridor into Cleve and clear the Reichswald; the second was to secure the fortified villages in the open ground beyond the forest; the third would break through the Hochwald-Balberger layback position and advance to Geldern-Xanten. Lieutenant General Brian Horrocks' XXX British Corps was responsible for the first phase, and when his front was widened II Canadian Corps would move in alongside to take over the left flank. Horrocks had five divisions for his initial assault: from right to left in line were 51st Highland, 53rd Welsh, 15th Scottish, and 2nd and 3rd Canadian. In reserve were 43rd Wessex and Guards Armoured divisions.

When plans for Veritable had begun to take shape in the middle of December, General Crerar had not included any Canadian formations. Brigadier N.E. Rodger, the II Corps Chief of Staff, described in his diary that

General Crerar told Corps Commander of the plot for 21 Army Group's next battle — 30 Corps to do it through 2 Canadian Corps striking into Reichswald Forest and thence South between Waal and Maas — all to be timed to strike into top of German armoured reserves just when they are being committed against the Americans. General Simonds wrote General Crerar a note pointing out the repercussions and bad taste which would come out of this from our Canadian soldiers — to be left out of THE battle — probably the one that ends the war. General Crerar saw Monty the following day and apparently as a result 3 Canadian Division was included in the 30 Corps attacking divisions.

Canadian soldiers may not have been as offended to be left out of the forthcoming action as Simonds assumed. In any case, their role in Veritable's early stages was a supporting one, the main assault being delivered by Horrocks'

British divisions. Horrocks was an engaging, popular commander. Brigadier James Roberts, who was commanding 8 Canadian Brigade, received a message a few days before the battle began that Horrocks wished to have a closer look at the German positions from a forward outpost of one of Roberts' battalions. He duly arrived — *"his usual bubbling self"* — and they went forward to a Queen's Own Rifles' standing patrol, *"seated in a deep, well-dug hole, indulging in one of the soldier's favourite pastimes, brewing a pot of tea."* After gaining what information he could about the enemy from the corporal commanding the patrol, Horrocks asked him if he could borrow his dark-green beret before going further forward because it was less visible than his own red-badged general's forage cap. The astonished corporal obliged and wore the general's cap until he returned and said goodbye.[118]

Soldiers knew that an operation was pending, but they could only speculate about how and when it would include them. Brigades and battalions had trained hard over the winter months; they practised drills to fight through forests, guided, ironically, by a German Army pamphlet based on the experience of the Finnish Army in its war with the Soviet Union. A few days before the operation began the diarist for the Canadian Scottish wrote:

> The troops remain in the dark so far as the operation is concerned, but rumours of various types begin to seep through the "unusual channels." A "battlewise" Bn {battalion} cannot be cooped up in a Bde {brigade} Concentration Area with Tanks, Buffaloes, and Ducks milling about the roads without the men smelling an operation of some kind approaching.

The Regina Rifles emphasized its platoon and company battle procedures, especially in the dark, because *"the coming operation is expected to involve night work insofar as our part is concerned."* The commanding officer and his second in command were able to get up in light aircraft to reconnoitre the area they would be fighting in, and liaised with the 8th and 9th brigades to be brought up to date on latest enemy activity on their part of the front. As D-Day loomed closer, *"Roads are being made out of bounds to ordinary traffic after dark to all for*

heavy movement of armour and supplies up into the area." On 3 January, the commanding officer met with a unit of flail tanks, which were to clear lanes through minefields; AVREs (Armoured Vehicles Royal Engineers), whose task was to remove road obstacles and destroy pillboxes; and tanks, which would support the infantry's advance. Next day, officers took turns visiting a model room to get more detail about the plan and the ground. Continued flooding forced some last-minute changes in plan, and they traded their supply trucks for amphibious Buffaloes.[119]

The other assault and follow-on battalions of 3rd Canadian Infantry Division were no doubt thankful that amphibious vehicles were available, because the North Shore Regiment measured the water rising at a metre every three hours. Its role was to lead in Buffaloes, with Le Régiment de la Chaudière following in assault boats. Sappers were included in the first assault wave to build ramps for the unloading of jeeps and Bren gun carriers, while other engineers worked to keep open what few roads were not under water.

On 7 February, Montgomery had his final conference with his army commanders, which General Simpson recorded in his journal.

> *Tomorrow at 0630 a total of 1200 field guns start a two-hour heavy Artillery barrage, before elements of British XXX Corps of the 1st Canadian Army, on a narrow sector from the Maas River to the Rhine River, hitting at every known gun, field and foxhole emplacement. {It is assumed} that the Germans will open up with all their own arty, anticipating an attack. Therefore, there will be a one hour silence during which time, every known instrument for recording sound and flash and hearing aid available will listen in and plot all Jerry guns firing these return concentrations. At 0930 all British guns will open up again, and at 1030, XXX Corps will attack on an extremely narrow front. Monty's plan for mass and concentration. The Field Marshal is cocky in his confidence of success.[120]*

---

[118] J.A. Roberts, *The Canadian Summer* (Toronto: University of Toronto Bookroom, 1981), 108.

[119] NAC, RG24 Series, particularly unit war diaries.

[120] USAMHIL, Carlisle Barracks, William Simpson Papers.

The first German city was Cleve, with the flooded Rhine plain in the background. (PA 145756)

The ground north of Cleve was more suited to boats than jeeps. (PA 131221)

A few hours later, with plans, conferences, and recces completed, Veritable exploded when more than 400 heavy bombers, some from the RCAF's No 6 Group, obliterated Cleve and a good part of Goch, while mediums dropped 400 more tons of high explosives on Weeze, Udem, and Calcar. Then the guns began bombarding 268 selected positions of 84th Division, on each of which were deposited about nine tons of shells during the day. These were supplemented by "Pepper Pots" — groups of mortars, antitank, anti-aircraft, and medium machine guns — that periodically swept defended areas, while 12 projectors of the 1st Rocket Battery hit other specific targets. As General Simpson had written, a pause after this initial bombardment lured the Germans back into their trenches, and into firing their own defensive artillery, which was then promptly hit by counter battery fire and another huge barrage.

Second Canadian Division's principal role was to maintain the security of the start line, along which it was already deployed. Two battalions of 5 Brigade, the Calgary Highlanders and Régiment de Maisonneuve, had the additional task of securing the near section of the Nijmegen-Cleve road and capturing the town of Wyler. The artillery preparation had neutralized most of the defenders, but anti-personnel mines remained to inflict heavy casualties.

Third Division's mission was to secure the main attack's left flank by capturing the fortified villages and hillocks that remained above water in the almost completely flooded wide plain along the south bank of the Rhine. The sector could not have fit more aptly the nickname Water Rats that they had given themselves in the Scheldt, and General Spry deployed 7 Brigade on the right and 8 on the left with 9 Brigade initially in reserve. Units soon left dry land for the lake, with the river on their left and the Nijmegen-Cleve road on their right, and drove towards their objectives, small villages a few kilometres away. Spitfires and Typhoons strafed the town as the North Shore Regiment headed towards Zandpol, where the Queen's Own Rifles would take over and capture Millingen. Like the rest of the division that first day, the battalion faced little opposition, and for a time the operation was more of a technical than a tactical challenge. Communications problems, for example, forced them to establish a system of relay stations.

Supporting the 8th Brigade was 16th Field Company, whose mine-gapping tasks were made all the easier by rising flood waters — Buffaloes could swim without touching the ground. They tried to clear mines by setting off submerged charges, so follow-on troops would have a clear route forward when the area dried, but the results were inconclusive. At one point they had to use their assault boats to rescue a Buffalo carrying the equipment of 8 Brigade's tactical headquarters, after the latter had grounded itself and stalled.

Seven Brigade entered the battle in the early evening with German resistance stiffening, but soon after it moved out the Regina Rifles' D Company started to send back prisoners. The Canadian Scottish spent the day waiting, and as its companies moved up in late afternoon the unit diarist could not help but reflect:

We who watched these men go down the road and who exchanged cynical jokes with them as they passed thought back to former days when this Bn {battalion} marched into an attack. The faces have changed in the Rifle Coys since we were in France. Many of the old-timers have gone.

They were quickly engaged in a fight typical of 3rd Division's water-logged attack. The Canadian Scottish first moved eastwards, then swept north to take the village of Niel, near the centre of the flooded area between Millingen on the Rhine and Kranenbourg on the Nijmegen-Cleve road. Surrounded by the large moat, the battalion's objective was effectively a fortified island. Fifteen minutes after shoving off in Buffaloes, B Company called for artillery support, and Major Morrison, the gunner's representative, *"immediately turned on the full weight of the guns at his command."* Slight initial opposition soon increased and, facing heavy machine gun and mortar fire, the company commander sent one of his platoons around to outflank the strong point when *"Sgt Cummings distinguished himself by borrowing a Buffalo, and, with several other men blazing his way to the fore of the attack."* They took the position, remarkably with only two men wounded, and then began to clear mines and open roads to bring food and ammunition forward.

While the Canadians were securing their watery flank, the three British assault divisions mounted their main attack against the Reichswald. Taking into account flooding, topography, and German defences, General Horrocks had selected the Nijmegen-Cleve road north of the woods as his principal axis, and in mid-morning his array of supporting guns began to fire a barrage that advanced in measured steps of 300 metres every 12 minutes, each lift being signalled by rounds of yellow smoke. The massive gunfire neutralized and demoralized most of the defenders, and the assault troops rolled over them, the infantry carried in Kangaroos manned by Canadian troopers of the 1st Armoured Personnel Carrier Regiment. Horrocks described in his memoir the tangle of antitank ditches, minefields, concrete bunkers, and kilometres of barbed wire:

> *Not one single man was on his feet. The officers controlling the artillery fire were in tanks. The leading wave of the assault consisted of tanks with flails in front beating and exploding the mines to clear passages through the minefields. Then came tanks carrying bridges and fascines on their backs to form bridges over the anti-tank ditch. The next echelon was flame-throwing tanks to deal with the concrete pill-boxes, and finally infantry in cut-down tanks, i.e., with the top taken off, called kangaroos.*[121]

After a successful beginning, with leading troops advancing on Cleve, the battle itself seemed determined to demonstrate the truism that no plan survives first contact with the enemy. That evening the Germans breached the banks of the Rhine to raise water levels even further, and submerged much of Horrocks' main supply road. Then the baneful effects of the season took their toll. Because of the several weeks delay in beginning the operation, the ground had begun to thaw, and the movement of thousands of tracked and wheeled vehicles rapidly transformed soft turf into impenetrable mud. The extent of the problem was not immediately apparent, however, and with the rate of progress deceptively positive Horrocks made what he described in his memoir as *"one of the worst mistakes {I} made in the war,"* by

prematurely committing his reserve, the 43rd Wessex Division, that night. In front of them, one of the participants, Major General Hubert Essame, has written:

> *The 15(S) Division had just — but only just — gained the crest of Materborn. Their tanks, flails, crocodiles, carriers, and wheeled vehicles of all sorts lay inert in the mud all over the battlefield. Only one useable road led to Cleve, and this was jammed, nose to tail, with the transport, not only of 15(S) Division but also of quite a representative proportion of First Canadian Army. The floods north of this surviving axis were rapidly rising. It was raining and the weather forecast was bad.*[122]

As units of the division went up the backs of those in front, everything behind them telescoped into a large traffic jam. Forward movement slowed and the Germans gained time to bring in the first of their reserves. Then, when battalions fought their way into Cleve they found their way blocked by the massive amount of rubble caused by the preliminary bombing. To employ strategic heavy bombers in a tactical role like this was a long-standing controversy. As early as 1942, when the ill-fated raid on Dieppe was being planned, misgivings had been voiced that the positive effects of bombing had to be balanced by its negative effects of restricting mobility. For Cleve, commanders apparently concluded that the examples provided by the earlier bombing of the cities of Cassino and Caen would be outweighed by massive material destruction and its effect on morale; bad to them, good to us. As the war diarist of the Maisonneuves remarked, *"It was simply terrific."* However, General Essame described, with masterful understatement, all the unfortunate events that day, which had resulted in

> *a day of nightmare traffic congestion which made coherent troop movement almost impossible. In fact it had been proved — it is hoped for all time — that two divisions cannot operate satisfactorily on one axis — especially when the axis itself leads through a bog and is itself in*

---

[121] Brian Horrocks, *A Full Life* (London: Collins, 1960), 249-250.

[122] H. Essame, *The 43rd Wessex Division at War, 1944-1945* (London: William Clowes, 1952), 206.

131

places under water. In the circumstances it is not surprising that throughout the day the contacts of many of the commanders involved had been of a character which cannot justly be described as being noteworthy for their cordiality.

Weather permitting, Second TAF energetically supported Veritable, with No 83 Group flying combat air patrols while No 84 Group conducted close support missions like the one that preceded the North Shore attack. No 83 Group found few German aircraft to fight, and the five obsolete JU-87s that No 442 (RCAF) Squadron shot down on the first day were not much of a challenge. The Typhoons were more active, No 439's diarist recording that *"the air activity today was a treat for sore eyes, the pilots claimed that there was 10/10ths aircraft over the early morning target area."* Of the squadron's six operations, most were four-aircraft patrols, for a total of 32 sorties. Keeping the aircraft flying was a difficult and unsung task, the wing acknowledged:

Great credit is due to the ground crew for their part in today's attack as working conditions are far from ideal with water and mud everywhere. Some of the aircraft are parked in pools of water — bombing up and servicing of the kites is no picnic under such conditions. Out of 17 aircraft, 15 were on ops at one time today, which speaks well for the serviceability state.[123]

Several days of bad weather intervened, but improved conditions on 14 February allowed Second TAF to deliver an enormous effort of 9000 sorties — the most since the Normandy campaign. Among many successes that day, No 83 Group claimed its thousandth enemy aircraft, destroyed or damaged a record number of locomotives, and made more rail cuts than in any previous 24-hour period. No 126 (RCAF) Wing's Spitfires flew their greatest number of sorties to that date — 237 — with the two busiest squadrons managing 54 and 53 respectively. Among the Typhoons, No 440 established a squadron record of 55 sorties. *"This close coordination for the first time on such a scale between Canada's air and ground forces is historically significant,"* noted a report from Overseas Headquarters, because RCAF squadrons had now flown almost 1500 sorties in support of First Canadian Army.

At the end of Veritable's first day, II Corps staff, after surveying 50 prisoners of war from the German 84th Division and its supporting artillery, concluded that they had achieved tactical surprise, and *"there {was} little doubt that the speed with which attacking troops followed up the artillery barrage surprised the enemy very much."* One German NCO commanding a gun position of the 1062nd Grenadier Regiment had had no chance to fire it during the barrage and no time to destroy it afterwards. Ominously, however, another NCO commented:

it was common knowledge among them that, should they be overrun, the enemy could not get very far and that then paratroops would be brought in to restore the situation.

Surprise, tactical or otherwise, would be difficult to maintain and, as that NCO predicted, resistance in the forest stiffened as fresh enemy infantry and paratroops reached the position. The 15th Division clawed its way into Cleve, in which hardly a house had been left standing by the bombing. Germans in the town — through which ran the roads that Horrocks needed — held out for a time, but British troops near Bedburg demolished a major counterattack launched by the 116th Panzer and 15th Panzer Grenadier Divisions of 47th Panzer Corps, which had assumed command of the battle. Soon thereafter units of the 43rd Wessex Division got through the Reichswald and gained the high ground overlooking Goch. By then intelligence analysts had identified elements of five different German divisions, and it was evident their commanders were taking the attack seriously: should the British and Canadians break through the Reichswald quickly and gain Calcar and Goch, they might well be able to sustain their momentum right through to Wesel, the communications centre on the far bank of the Rhine that was crucial to the enemy's plans to either reinforce or withdraw.

With British and Canadian troops south of Cleve and the Reichswald, a German report concluded: *"By the night of 13 February there was no more talk of major counterattacks, but a*

---

[123] D Hist, squadron and wing Operational Record Books, and other RCAF records.

Roads could be found only by following lines of trees. (PA 143946)

Conditions were little better behind the lines where the RCAF's No 39 (Reconnaissance) Wing lived. (PL 42674)

defensive stalemate had been temporarily achieved." Had it been possible to follow Veritable's original premises, opposition could now be expected to lessen, because the Germans would have been forced to send divisions south to block the Americans. Instead, General Simpson could only wait until the floods facing him receded, and the Germans were free to send all their available reserves against First Canadian Army. The race for advantage gained momentum; the British and Canadians to break through, the Germans to reinforce and hold on — within days the enemy had deployed elements of 10 divisions with 1000 guns and 700 mortars. However much the Allies out-gunned the Germans, they could not bring the full weight of their materiel superiority to bear on the narrow front, through the atrocious terrain, and in the gloomy weather that grounded aircraft and bogged tanks and supporting weapons. What followed was a grim day-to-day struggle, metre by metre, to gain limited objectives, in the cold, mud, and rain.

After the first week of bitter fighting, General Crerar determined that he had gained sufficient room to bring General Simonds' II Corps in on General Horrocks' left flank. Taking command of 43rd Division, which was then near Bedburg, and a brigade of 15th Scottish that had been stopped just south in the Moyland Wood, Simonds' immediate task was to widen his frontage in order to commit more troops, first to secure the lateral Goch-Calcar road, then to break through the Hochwald layback defensive position. The only route he could use to deploy his 2nd and 3rd Infantry and 4th Armoured divisions for Blockbuster, as the Hochwald operation was nicknamed, was the road that ran southeast from Cleve to Calcar, and then skirted the Hochwald to Xanten, the Corps' eventual objective. Blocking the way to Calcar were Germans in the Moyland Wood.

On three successive days, 15th Scottish units had been stopped by fierce resistance from well-entrenched Germans in Moyland. As it denied forward movement along the main axis of advance, and consequently delayed the start of the attack's next phase, Operation Blockbuster, Simonds told Major General Spry to take the woods, in order to gain sufficient room to bring 2nd Division forward. Except for 9 Brigade,

which was still in the Rhine plain, Spry's division had pulled back to dry — or drier — land, and he now gave the Moyland task to 7 Brigade, which moved south from Cleve to relieve the Scots. In a well-executed assault, the Winnipeg Rifles, carried in Kangaroos, bypassed the woods to the south and took the village of Louisendorf. Simultaneously, the Reginas attacked Moyland but encountered not only a considerable number of heavy machine guns among the trees, but also heavy artillery firing from across the Rhine. B Company cleared a section of forest with the aid of Crocodile flame-throwers, one of which exploded, but the Germans counterattacked whenever anyone moved.

Casualties mounted to the point where A Company was unable to continue. The unit diary records that *"many men, although not actually casualties are suffering from exhaustion due to continual shelling and nature of the woods,"* and there was general agreement that

> *the shelling and fighting in these woods have been just as bad as anything encountered in Normandy. Few PW taken have been mainly paratroops, many of which have been moved into this sector in the past 24 to 48 hours from Northern Holland!*

Next day the Reginas gained half the forest, at a cost of 120 casualties, while the Canadian Scottish were able to reach a clump of farm buildings on a small knoll — "Slaughterhouse Hill" — just to the south, where they took a terrible beating as well, which left their three forward companies with fewer than 150 men. Once more, unrealistic estimates of German strength produced pressure from higher commanders to get moving: from Army Group to Army to Corps to Division to Brigade to Battalion to the PBI — "poor bloody infantry" — at the front. General Spry told Denis and Shelagh Whitaker, when they were researching their fine book, *Rhineland*:

> *The people upstairs... seemed to feel that the pace of the battle could be carried on regardless of the realities of the situation — regardless of the weather, of the reduced air support as a result of weather, of the flooding and the breakdown of the roads, tracks, and trails and of the ensuing supply problems. When troops are wet, cold,*

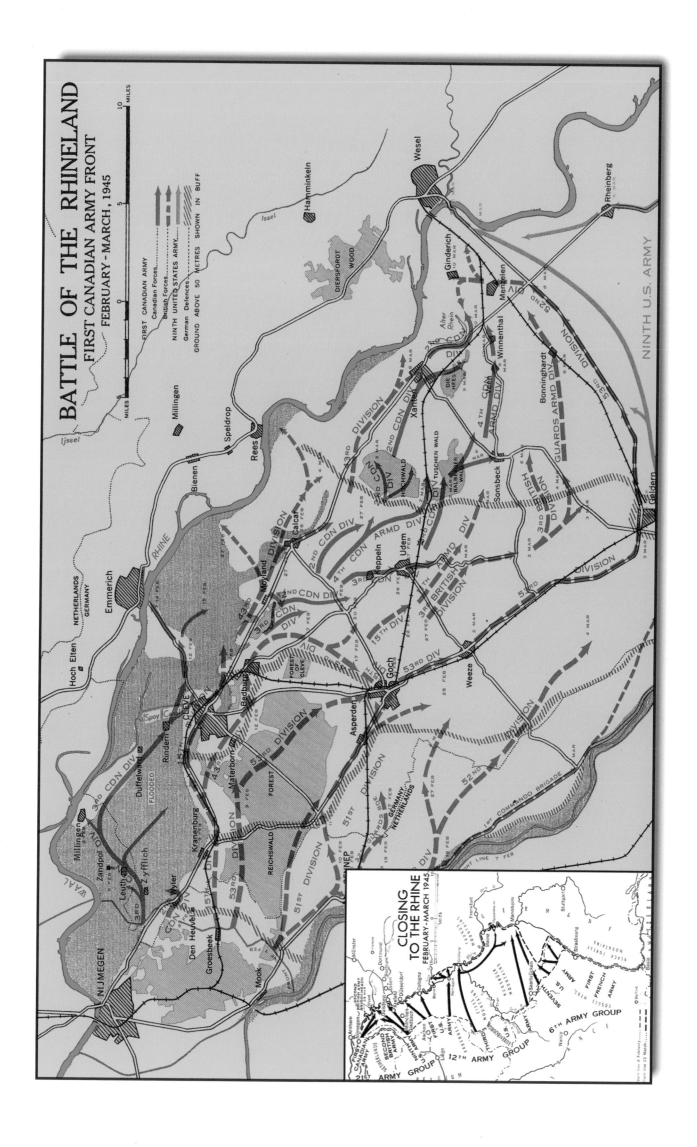

BATTLE OF THE RHINELAND
FIRST CANADIAN ARMY FRONT
FEBRUARY - MARCH, 1945

FIRST CANADIAN ARMY
Canadian Forces...........
British Forces...........
NINTH UNITED STATES ARMY...........
German Defences...........
GROUND ABOVE 50 METRES SHOWN IN BUFF

MILES

NINTH U.S. ARMY

NETHERLANDS
GERMANY

GERMANY
NETHERLANDS

CLOSING TO THE RHINE
FEBRUARY - MARCH 1945.

miserable, bloody-minded, scared, and tired, it takes time to move and assemble, re-assemble, and deploy them. Everything slows down.... These personnel, logistic, geographic, and weather problems were being partially ignored by the senior commanders. They really didn't understand the sharp end of battle. They had a mental block; they'd never been there. If we had taken a little more time, even another two or three hours of preparation, of reconnaissance, of plotting and planning at various levels (perhaps even my own), we would have done better, without the staggering and unnecessary losses. We rushed our fences.[124]

The result was an order to a half-strength company of the Canadian Scottish to assault across 800 metres of open ground to take the Moyland Wood defences that had already stopped several battalions. The 68 men duly moved out; an hour later five returned. Two days later, after beating off continuous counterattacks, the Canadian Scottish survivors marched to the rear, piped on the way by a single piper. However much pipers, bands, and regimental traditions may be derided by cost accountants, regimental spirit can work wonders. Here, the

shrill, triumphant sound of the pipes gave something to the men that nothing else could. Almost automatically the bone-weary soldiers began to march in step, until by the time they were close to "home" they were marching as if they were in Aldershot, with pride in every step.[125]

The battalion's young second-in-command, Major W.H.V. Matthews, who already wore two Military Crosses, told the Whitakers that he was standing with a seasoned pipe major in 15th Scottish Division as they marched in. *"He was a big, tough ex-Scottish guardsman,"* Matthews recalled.

I'll never forget him. He was standing there in the moonlight watching our companies come in, some of them with only ten or twenty men left. There were tears rolling down his cheeks, and he turned to me, "Makes you fucking think, don't it kid."

On 21 February the Winnipeg Rifles, supported by the 12th Field Regiment, whose gun positions were no more than 600 metres from the woods, as well as Typhoons, tanks, and flame-throwers, finally took the position, at a cost of 105 casualties.

While 7 Brigade was fighting in Moyland, 2nd Division began moving forward from Cleve. An officer in 4th Field, which supported them, was amused to be

now invading Germany reading maps printed on the back of German maps of Northumberland County, England, dated 1940, and captured by the British in Brussels in September 1944.

The milieu was different, he continued, as *German civilians, looking bewildered and unhappy, moved back along the roads carrying a few belongings or pushing them in a little cart, now and then looking back fearfully as shells crashed somewhere behind.*

Four Brigade led with the task of securing a section of high ground straddling the Goch-Calcar road, about three kilometres south of Louisendorf, which was to be the start line for another advance. Following a heavy barrage designed to roll back over German reserve positions, and with each battalion supported by a squadron of Fort Garry tanks, the Essex Scottish on the right and the Royal Hamilton Light Infantry on the left moved out from Louisendorf at noon on the 19th, their lead companies in Kangaroos and the others following on foot. Mud, mines, and antitank guns immediately intervened, but both battalions got to or near their objectives and dug in. They were immediately counterattacked, as they no doubt expected, but they could not know that it was merely the first of a continuous wave of assaults that continued through the night and over the next week. It was their misfortune that bad weather had prevented aircraft from finding what remained of Panzer Lehr Division while it was moving by rail from Krefeld to the Calcar ridge to reinforce 116th Panzer Division. Although both German divisions were much reduced in numbers, their battle groups were able to overrun some of the Essex's positions and seriously threatened the RHLI, which reported that

124 Denis and Shelagh Whitaker, *Rhineland: The Battle to End the War* (Toronto: Stoddart, 1989), 145.

125 R.H. Roy, *Ready for the Fray (Deas Gu Cath): The History of the Canadian Scottish Regiment (Princess Mary's), 1920-1955* (Vancouver: Evergreen Press, 1958), 389.

Moving through the Rhineland forests was a tedious process... (PA 138353)

... and once into open ground it was no better. (PA 113673)

at daylight this morning the enemy counter attacked with tanks and infantry.... Confidence in their attack was apparent as some enemy were brazen enough to approach our positions on bicycles. After four Panther tanks were knocked out by PIAT and other anti tank weapons the counter attack seemed lacking in spirit and the supporting infantry were easily dispersed with some casualties and a few of our own.

Over a period of 12 hours, 4th Field alone fired 3400 shells into a small target area. At one point,

The only comunication the company commander had was his "18-set" wireless but by the use of it, he called the battery commander at battalion headquarters and asked for artillery fire. The battery commander within three minutes had fire landing so close to the infantry slit trenches that the heat of their blasts could be felt. Back and forth, in and around the little red dots on his map, the battery commander fired, asking now and then, "How's that? Are those effective?" And the voice in his earphones would answer, "That's fine, can you keep them coming there?" After almost a thousand rounds had been poured over by the guns, the voice in the earphones had calmed down and his message had changed from "Send reinforcements before it's too late" to "They seem to be pulling out."

With support like that, and bolstered by the Royal Regiment, the Queen's Own Cameron Highlanders, and the self-propelled antitank guns of the 18th Canadian Anti-Tank Battery, as well as Typhoons when the weather cleared on the 21st, the brigade restored its positions and held on until the Germans withdrew to the Calcar ridge a few kilometres to the south.

Whenever persistently hostile weather allowed, Second TAF aircraft intervened to support Canadian and British troops who were advancing over Veritable's middle ground. Some flights were in close support, while others worked to keep more German reserves from the battlefield. While 4 Brigade was enduring below, No 439 (RCAF) Squadron's Typhoons reported their busiest days. On 22 February the squadron flew its greatest number of sorties ever, to make 28 railway cuts, crater a road, and destroy three flat cars, one armoured vehicle, and two tanks. Pilots had not only flak, weather, and mechanical

failure to concern them on these low-level attacks, No 442 Squadron reporting that

on one of the afternoon shows, S/L {M.E.} Jowsey had to bale out over Germany. It is believed that he was the victim of a freak accident, being hit by his own bullets ricocheting while strafing some MET {mechanized enemy transport}. He was seen to land and the Squadron feel he is OK.

The hunch was accurate, for Jowsey evaded capture and got away.

Previously, pilots had been careful to avoid attacking civilian targets in occupied territory, but now that they were virtually in Germany pilots treated the enemy unmercifully. Hedley Everard, who had served in several theatres, reported 40 years later:

Freedom to roam over Germany with a squadron or flight of eager pilots was like the gathering of vultures at a carcass. Everything below was a war-legitimate target. Hitler's War Machine, that I had vowed to help destroy years ago in Canada, had shrunk to its original German borders. There were no Burmese coolies below my wings now; no desert Arabs; no Italian peasants; no French farmers; no Dutch civilians — all were enemy.[126]

Typhoon squadrons found the German Air Force more active. *"The Luftwaffe in the past week has become particularly aggressive in attacks on small groups of aircraft,"* commented Group Captain A.D. Nesbitt, commanding 143 Wing. He explained that they adjusted their own tactics to meet them.

Our splurge of record breaking rail cuts and sorties was made possible by flying in small units of four and sometimes two aircraft. Luckily, the Hun was too slow in taking advantage of this and Intelligence reports indicate that our rail cutting has had the desired effect on front line problems of supply for the enemy. Therefore, there is no longer any need to expose the pilots to unfair disadvantage. All missions now are carried out by large formations.

On the ground, with the Goch-Calcar road secured, and Goch itself in British hands by the

---

[126] H. Everard, *A Mouse in My Pocket* (Picton, Ontario: Valley Floatplane Services, 1988), 380.

21st, Veritable was almost completed. At the beginning of the operation General Crerar had appreciated that if all conditions turned out favourably — weather, ground, air support, enemy reactions — XXX Corps tanks could be on the Xanten-Geldern line in a few days. None of the conditions broke favourably and, instead, between 8 and 21 February the Army had had to fight without respite to advance its front between 24 and 32 kilometres against defences manned by virtually all available German reserves. Now, with floods receding, General Simpson was about to begin Grenade, and start driving the 300,000 men of his Ninth Army through the 30,000 Germans defending the wide-open Rhine plain opposite Dusseldorf and Duisburg, to meet the Canadians. On 23 February, 2000 guns helped the Americans gain a bridgehead across the Roer, and two days later their tanks were driving hard for the Rhine against spotty opposition.

With the Americans swinging a hard hammer, General Crerar adjusted his anvil. His plan called for XXX Corps to move first, on 22 February, to advance south of Goch where they would be in position to protect the flank of II Corps, which would, four days later, launch the main attack. General Simonds' first objective was the banana-shaped ridge between Calcar and Udem that shielded the Hochwald; his second was the Hochwald itself; his last was Xanten. He pondered three possible approaches. The main Calcar-Xanten road on the left was the most obvious, and Simonds rejected it for that reason, as he did the approach on the right flank because it was too close to his boundary with XXX Corps and he feared that inevitable traffic congestion would slow him down. He chose instead the centre route, along the line of the Goch-Xanten railway, which ran through a gap between Hochwald and Balberger Wald and which sappers could convert into a roadway. All three divisions would assault on narrow fronts on 26 February, then once the infantry had rolled up the ridgeline from north to south tanks would drive forward to exploit; 4th Canadian Division to move through the gap and 11th Armoured around the right of Balberger.

While regrouping, moving gun positions, and dumping ammunition and supplies in preparation for the attack, II Corps intelligence noted that the enemy had no intention of withdrawing. Air photos showed new positions from which the Germans obviously intended to hold the Hochwald and maintain their bridgehead west of the Rhine. These last defences of the Siegfried Line, consisting of a forward line of infantry positions between Calcar and Udem, supported by a formidable antitank screen, were manned by the depleted but still effective 47th Panzer and 2nd Parachute Corps.

General Simonds' conduct of the two-week battle that followed has been controversial ever since, which is not surprising considering that daily casualties numbered around 300. Writing from the perspective of his subject, Simonds' biographer concluded that his "dominating idea for the battle was to keep the attack moving day and night at least until he had occupied the Hochwald feature and launched a force down the railway line to Xanten," and that, as such, it went essentially as planned.[127] The most comprehensive criticism of his approach, in Denis and Shelagh Whitaker's *Rhineland*, comes from those who had to implement the plan in conditions not unlike those their fathers and uncles had experienced at Passchendaele, not far away, in an earlier war. The authors themselves reckoned the plan to be "ill-conceived," because Simonds attacked at the Germans' strongest point rather than where they were most vulnerable. Besides, their comprehensive research among veterans revealed considerable bitterness over what was allowed to happen. One complaint, also hearkening back to the First World War, was that senior commanders and staffs were so detached from realities on the ground that they lost touch with the battle. One of the veterans commented:

At division level up they didn't know what the hell was going on. Instead of going forward to find out what was happening, the senior staff made their decisions from sitreps {situation reports}.[128]

---

[127] Dominick Graham, *The Price of Command: A Biography of General Guy Simonds* (Toronto: Stoddart, 1993), 192-210.

[128] Denis and Shelagh Whittaker, *Rhineland*, 227.

When control broke down after the first day, the result was

> *a real shambles. There was a definite lack of coordination. When some unit was supposed to capture an objective and failed to do so, other troops were not advised of the fact. This happened on any number of occasions.*

The cause was poor intelligence, an artillery observer from 12th Field Regiment remarked.

> *Intelligence was very poor and so many Divisions were trying to do so much that one never knew when an attack was apt to be mounted through your particular front.*[129]

Simonds' decision to send his tanks through the Hochwald gap has also been questioned. Squeezing into a narrow defile enabled the Germans to concentrate their antitank guns to cover not only the wide-open approaches to it, but both flanks of any force that tried to drive through. When the difficulties in moving through the gap became evident, commanders might have moved their main axis further south along the edge of the forest. That would have been extremely close to the inter-corps boundary, but the lamentable effects of boundaries were hardly greater than staying on that deadly course. Perhaps the most serious criticism was the way in which the commanders continued pressing the battle unrelentingly after the Americans had clearly broken through and were driving in behind the Germans. At that point the Canadians might well have simply hung on to their gains and gone on the defensive while Ninth Army outflanked the Wesel pocket.

That was not to be, however, and every unit that fought through the Hochwald and into the Wesel pocket had its own tales of horror and courage. As was always the case, the achievements of most went unsung, except by their comrades, because they were unrecorded. A few examples will perhaps serve to illustrate experiences that even the most vivid imagination finds difficult to comprehend. One such act of bravery was carried out by Sergeant Aubrey Cosens of the Queen's Own Rifles.

The Queen's Own was 8 Brigade's lead battalion when it attacked towards the town of Keppeln in the early morning of 26 February, as Blockbuster began, with the Chaudières and the North Shore Regiment following a few hours later. On the right, D Company followed closely behind a barrage to reach its objective, a hamlet called Mooshof. As was their custom, the Germans had withdrawn from the buildings to avoid shellfire and brought down their own mortars and artillery immediately the company arrived, before counterattacking and re-occupying the buildings. Cosens' No 16 Platoon was quickly reduced to himself and four others, but, undaunted, he took command, ordering the other four to cover him while he sprinted across an open field to a nearby tank and directed its fire against the main farmhouse. The tank moved forward to get closer and Cosens led his few men in their own counterattack. Having attracted the attention of German defenders, the Sherman crashed through one of the building's walls and Cosens went through the hole and re-captured the house before moving on to the other two, which he also took single-handedly. Cosens never had the opportunity to wear the Victoria Cross — the Commonwealth's highest decoration for bravery — that he was awarded; a sniper killed him as he was on his way to report to his company commander.

Major J.W. Powell of the First Hussars was also recommended for the VC, a result of his conduct in supporting the North Shore Regiment in this same action — in which his squadron was reduced from 19 tanks to four. The citation was duly approved through the necessary channels all the way up to Field Marshal Montgomery, who amended it to an immediate Distinguished Service Order.

Fourth Canadian Armoured Division entered the battle after the two infantry divisions completed their tasks, or appeared to be about to do so. For flexibility, the division was organized in integrated battle groups, each made up of armour, infantry, and support vehicles. One of the assault groups, for example, incorporated the Canadian Grenadier Guards, elements of the Argyll and Sutherland Highlanders, flame-throwers, and Flail tanks; and their experience exemplified the difficulties all had when operating over sodden ground in the face of shrewd defences that were arranged to draw the

---

129 T.J. Bell, *Into Action with the 12th Field, 1940-1945* (Holland: The Regiment, 1945), 119.

(PA 160830)

The price.

(PA 192007)

(PA 153188)

tanks past forward outposts onto an antitank screen. Squadrons had gone only a short distance when two tanks were disabled by mines and several others were mired in mud. The rest continued on until a Tiger tank and an 88mm gun, hidden in one of the small farms that dotted the open countryside, opened up simultaneously and knocked out four more of the Canadian tanks. Throwing smoke to mask their movement, the survivors quickly reversed and found another route, but the 88 opened fire again, destroying the regimental commander's tank and three others. Again, the troopers withdrew, relying on infantry to take out the guns, and, with their help, the Guards finally captured the farms. Leaving the infantry to consolidate, the tanks then withdrew to replenish.

The attack into the gap by another battle group, the South Albertas and the Algonquins, provides another example of horror and courage. Mud bogged down a dozen of their tanks and slowed their approach drive to a speed of about a kilometre an hour, and as they got closer to the front they could see fire coming and going in both directions, as well as pyres of smoke from burning tanks. The battle group's objective was high ground, south of the railway and just west of the Balberger Wald, that controlled access to the defile separating Hochwald from Balberger Wald. During the night of the 27th some B Squadron tanks and infantry got down into the valley in front of the objective, but others were delayed and had to make the run in daylight. One crew member described how they

raced down the side of the valley following the tracks of the tanks that had gone before. I have no idea how long it took us to get to the bottom, it seemed like hours. We passed abandoned tanks and carriers, destroyed by enemy fire. We were now in the open, in broad daylight, in sight of the enemy's guns. He opened up on us, we could see shells dropping all around and I never prayed so fervently in my life. This was the only time I thought I would not make it.... Just after crossing the first ditch we came under direct anti-tank fire and found ourselves pinned behind some houses. Every time we moved the German anti-tank guns who had our range fired on us, so we stayed, in the rain, in the

mud, unable to go forward or to go back. Meanwhile the battle to throw the enemy out of the woods and off the hill was raging in front and on both sides of us.

A Squadron and the Algonquins' Carrier Platoon tried to outflank the position on the right. They expected that 11th British Armoured Division, moving south of the railway, would have forced Germans to withdraw, but it had been slowed down as well, and the enemy had 88mm guns in place that poured deadly fire upon the Canadian tanks and carriers. The Germans

knocked out the front tank and the rear tank, and when we had no place to go we were left with no alternative but to abandon the tank and run like hell."[130]

Eight tanks and a dozen carriers went up in flames in a few minutes, and all morning long the Germans swept the area with fire, while the Algonquins beat back seven counterattacks.

At II Canadian Corps Headquarters, intelligence officers were reporting that 6th Parachute Division had taken the full impact of Blockbuster, and

The impression of the paratroops, who have made up the bulk of the prisoner take so far, was that there was very little behind them in the way of lay-back troops.

That may have been so, but the Germans had concentrated their weapons, including most of their 88s, to defend the narrow defile that 4th Armoured's battle groups were trying to force. In the gap, David Marshall recalled,

all hell broke loose. The most concentrated artillery barrage any of us had endured came down on us. The noise was indescribable. We could see through the periscopes, trees shattering all around us and could feel the tank rock with explosions.... With the lifting of the shelling came the enemy tanks. Over the rise in front of us came the snouts of two tanks, a Tiger and a Panther, heading our way. When our gunners had them in their sights, and before the German tanks could level out to bring their 88's down on us, our three tanks opened fire with all guns blazing and stopped the attack, destroying the Panther and forcing the Tiger to retreat.

---

[130] D Hist, Marshall, "Me and George."

By the beginning of March, the fighting along the Calcar ridge and the Hochwald had drawn in all parts of General Crerar's command. II Canadian Corps was deployed along a 17-kilometre front. On the left, 43rd (Wessex) Division moved down the Calcar-Xanten road, skirting the Hochwald along its northern edge. To its right, 2nd Canadian Infantry Division was advancing slowly through the forest itself. A little to the south, 4th Armoured continued in its attempt to force the gap between Hochwald and Balberger Wald. On the Corps' right, 3rd Division was approaching Balberger Wald. Across the inter-corps boundary, XXX British Corps was similarly spread along a 19-kilometre front, 11th Armoured Division on the left, 3rd Infantry and 53rd (Welsh) on the right, the last moving on Geldern. All were attacking, holding, regrouping. In 2nd Division's sector on the left, Major Frederick Tilston was fighting his first attack as a company commander when his battalion, the Essex Scottish, attempted to get into the Hochwald. Behind a creeping barrage, he led his men across 500 metres of open ground, and was wounded in the head at about the time that his left platoon came under heavy fire from a machine-gun post. Running forward, Tilston managed to toss a grenade into the latter, silencing it. Approaching the wood, he was again wounded, this time in the hip, and, falling, he waved his men on before struggling to his feet to catch up. Managing to lead his company through hand-to-hand fighting, he remained with the survivors as they consolidated and defeated several counterattacks. Ammunition having run low, Tilston, though under fire, made his way to the company on the left to replenish his supply of grenades and bullets. He survived, though had both legs amputated, and was awarded the Victoria Cross.

A little south, and with Ninth Army's leading tanks only 30 kilometres from Canadian positions, the Lincoln and Wellands, along with the Argylls, had gained a hold on the western end of the Hochwald gap, and the Lake Superiors and a squadron of the Grenadier Guards were ordered to widen it. The Lake Superiors had been fighting since 26 February and each of its companies was no more than a skeleton; A Company had 34 men, B Company 27, and C Company 44 — there was no D Company. Together they were short of a full-strength rifle company, all of them were exhausted and hungry, and their commanders had little information about the Germans. Moving into the maelstrom, all 10 of the Guards' tanks were either bogged down in mud or shot away by Tigers and 88s. Somehow, these enduring men got to their objective where they were immediately counterattacked. Two Algonquin platoons riding on the tanks of the Foot Guards tried to reach them but were stopped within sight just a few hundred metres short. Eight Lake Superior survivors got back, and burial parties next morning found the grisly scene where the others lay. The unit war diarist described it.

The mouth of the Gap bore the signs of intense shell-fire; the ground pitted, scarred, and torn by fire of all kinds. The trees in the gully ... were cut to ribbons. The houses were heaps of rubble, and were still smoldering. There was unforgettable courage recorded here... Pte Yanchuk, G, was within a few yards of an enemy posn, lying on his back with a grenade clutched in his hand: killed as he charged. At his side... Pte Middlemiss, W.R., was sitting in a shell-hole in a life-like posn. He had been with Yanchuk when a burst of small-arms fire in the abdomen stopped him. He crawled into a shell-hole, sat there, and died. An Unknown Canadian made the enemy posn. With arms locked around a German he was burned to a crisp by a mound of hay which caught fire alongside the slit-trench in which he fought hand-to-hand... Sgt Lehman, T.M., was lying a few yards away, struck down as he brought in the pl. Stretched out in line, lying as they fell were... Cpl Gray, J.W.... Pte MacDonald, D.J.... Pte Couture, G.F.... Pte McRobbie, W.

The burial parties were able to do their melancholy work because the Germans, with their main route over the Rhine now seriously threatened by Ninth Army's rapid advance, had withdrawn from the Hochwald to concentrate on the defence of Wesel. On 6 March the Germans began moving back across the river, protected by others dug in around a defensive pocket 15 kilometres deep and 22 kilometres wide. Now squeezing it were First Canadian Army in the west, Second British Army to the southwest, and

Ninth US Army in the south. With his troops already on the Rhine, General Simpson was confident that they could seize crossings south of Wesel but was unable to persuade Montgomery to allow him to do so.

While all three Allied armies pressed closer, General Simonds assigned his divisions three main tasks. In the north, along the Rhine, 43rd (Wessex) and 2nd Canadian were to advance on Xanten, five kilometres eastwards from their positions on the western edge of the Hochwald. Further south, 4th Armoured was to move through Veen and Winnenthal, an eight-kilometre march east from the southern tip of Balberger Wald, while 3rd Division cleared Germans from the right flank. Neither of the latter came easily, as German paratroopers fought on hopelessly but tenaciously to protect the crossing sites; nor did the set-piece attack that was arranged to take the Corps' principal objective of Xanten on 8 March. General Simonds' plan called for 43rd Division's 129 Brigade to attack from the northwest along the road from Marienbaum, while on its right 4 Canadian Brigade assaulted from the west. Supported by Sherbrooke Fusilier tanks and Crocodiles, and behind a smokescreen to mask their movements, the Essex Scottish deployed on the left and the Royal Hamilton Light Infantry on the right. The Essex got along reasonably well, but the RHLI ran into trouble when the Germans allowed the companies to pass by before opening fire on them from the rear. It was a deadly and effective tactic that killed or wounded 134 men, half the division's toll but not enough to halt the Canadian assault, when the Royals moved up through the Essex. On 9 March, 5 Brigade relieved them and moved through the town to high ground beyond. By that night, 2nd Division had taken more than 900 prisoners.

By then in full retreat, the Germans completed their evacuation by the 10th, and blew the bridges the following day. While Second British Army prepared to cross the Rhine, the Canadians could add up their accomplishments and their losses. In a month of fighting as bitter as Normandy and the Scheldt, First Canadian Army faced an enemy that grew in size from one division to 10 before Operation Grenade siphoned off some German troops to the American front. From 8 February to 10 March the army lost 1049 officers and 14,585 other ranks, of whom 379 and 4925 were Canadian. They captured 22,239 prisoners, and, in all, the Germans are estimated to have lost some 90,000 men in the Rhineland. It was a serious blow, but the Reich still had sufficient, though dwindling, resources to keep fighting. The war had two more months to go.

CHAPTER VI

FINALE

I remember standing there, looking down the road which they would use to enter The Hague. On the third day, I saw a tank in the distance, with one soldier's head above it, and the blood drained out of my body, and I thought: Here comes liberation. And as the tank came nearer and nearer, I had no breath left, and the soldier stood up, and he was like a saint. There was a big hush over all the people, and it was suddenly broken by a big scream, as if it was out of the earth. And the people climbed on the tank, and took the soldier out, and they were crying. And we were running with the tanks and the jeeps, all the way into the city.[131]

Early in February, while Canadians were preparing themselves for the Reichswald and Hochwald, Lieutenant General Charles Foulkes was informed that his I Canadian Corps, then fighting in Italy, was to join the First Canadian Army in northwest Europe.

The decision to reunite Canadians in their own army for the final weeks of the war had a long history. With the precedent of the Canadian Corps in the First World War well in mind, when Canadians first went overseas to Britain it had been the firm intention of the government and the

eventual commander of First Canadian Army, Lieutenant General A.G.L. McNaughton, that Canadians would fight together as a united formation. In time, McNaughton's army was designated as the spearhead for the forthcoming invasion of France, but events intervened and pressure mounted to get Canadians into active operations. An operational task, it was argued, would not only boost morale, but also provide both soldiers and their commanders with invaluable operational experience that they could only partially simulate in training. When Allied planning was under way in the spring of 1943 to extend the Mediterranean campaign from North Africa to Sicily, the Canadian government asked that its troops be included. Consequently, on 10 July, 1st Canadian Infantry Division and 1 Canadian Armoured Brigade joined six British and American divisions in the largest amphibious assault landing ever mounted.

---

[131] Maria Haayen, quoted in David Kaufman and Michiel Horn, *A Liberation Album: Canadians in the Netherlands, 1944-1945* (Toronto: McGraw-Hill Ryerson, 1980), 117.

145

General McNaughton's plan to return the Canadians to Britain, where they would pass on their operational experience to untried units before Operation Overlord took place the following year, was overtaken by events. After the month-long Sicilian campaign, 1st Division and 1 Brigade led the British Eighth Army's assault on the Italian mainland at Reggio Calabria in September. There they began a long march north, not along a soft underbelly but over the crocodile's back, and learning in the process, as the distinguished British historian Michael Howard has remarked, that "if one wants to conquer Italy, the southern end of the peninsula is not the best place to begin."[132] Crossing one defended river line after another as they moved through the difficult mountainous terrain of central Italy, the Canadians were stopped at Christmas-time 1943 just beyond the Moro River south of the innocuous Adriatic port of Ortona where the character of their war changed: *"Everything before this {had} been a nursery tale,"* 1st Division's commander, Major General Christopher Vokes, told the divisional historical officer. His battalions' rifle companies lost half their men, and leaders, as casualties at Ortona. At the same time, instead of returning to Britain, Vokes' division was joined by 5th Canadian Armoured Division and the Headquarters of I Canadian Corps. First commanded by Lieutenant General Crerar, then Lieutenant General E.L.M. Burns, the Corps became operational on 1 February 1944, taking up the legacy left by the Canadian Corps in 1918.

After a winter in static lines on the Adriatic, the Canadians moved across the Apennines in May to take part in Operation Diadem, the Allied offensive to liberate Rome. At the beginning of that attack, 1 Canadian Armoured Brigade supported 8th Indian Division in its successful assault on the Gustav Line at the base of Monte Cassino. I Canadian Corps then took over the advance through the vaunted Hitler Line, and then along the Liri Valley that led to Rome. On 4 June, two days before the invasion of Normandy, some "D-Day Dodgers" in the integrated Canadian-American 1st Special Service Force were among the first to enter Rome. After advancing to Florence, 1st Division moved back to the Adriatic with 5th Armoured for what was hoped would be the final battle of the Italian campaign, against the Gothic Line south of Rimini.

At the end of August the Canadians cleared the outposts of the defences and brilliantly broke through the main German positions before the enemy knew that he was being seriously threatened. But then, for want of ready reserves, Eighth Army was unable to exploit the opportunity, and the Germans regrouped on successive blocking positions to stall the offensive until rains came, grounding aircraft and bogging down tanks. Instead of "debouching in the Valley of the Po," and going "onward to Vienna," as they had been led to expect, the Canadians crawled from one river line to the next canal in October, gained a respite in reserve in November, and were back in winter lines in December and January.

Rather than ending, the campaign became drearily familiar to survivors of the first Italian winter and equally distasteful to newcomers. Only now, instead of mountains, troops had to negotiate the canals, rivers, and sodden ground near Ravenna and the Valli di Comacchio, countryside that was not unlike the Dutch polders in which the 2nd and 3rd divisions were then plodding.

By this time, the reasons for dying in Italy seemed more obscure than ever. The original purpose of the campaign had been to free the Mediterranean for shipping; then it was to knock Italy from the war, and secure airfields in the south from which heavy bombers could hit targets in Central Europe that were beyond the range of British-based airplanes. In 1944, the rationale of the campaign had evolved further — into a gigantic holding operation to keep German divisions in Italy and away from either the eastern or the northwest European fronts. It was not a role to inspire soldiers, particularly since the operational objective of keeping Germans in Italy contradicted the more immediate tactical objectives of driving them out, and made it difficult to sustain morale and motivation. As had happened the year before, rising numbers of battle-exhaustion cases suggested that the combat effectiveness of infantry battalions was being stretched to the breaking point. For example, while the overall number of battle casualties in 1st Division declined at the end of December, the ratio of exhaustion cases to wounded in the last week rose to more than 60 per cent. The numbers concerned the Corps' senior doctor sufficiently for him to inform the Commander that *"indications suggested the troops were about at their limit as an efficient fighting force."*

---

[132] M. Howard, *The Lessons of History* (New Haven: Yale University Press, 1991), 10.

Bridging the Rhine. (PA 113687)

Moreover, the shortage of trained infantrymen was, if anything, an even more serious problem in Italy than it was in Holland. An example will illustrate. When the Gothic Line fighting culminated on San Fortunato Ridge on 22 September (the day Boulogne fell) General Burns signalled Canadian Military Headquarters in London that he urgently needed infantry reinforcements because of unexpectedly heavy casualties. CMHQ responded by combing Royal Canadian Ordnance Depots and other support units for 500 men, who were then put on a reinforcement draft. On arrival in Italy, they were informed that they were now infantrymen. These men had to be retrained and, meanwhile, shortages meant that wounded men were returned routinely to combat, in some cases prematurely. General Foulkes visited one soldier in hospital in Ravenna on Christmas Day — he had been wounded, returned to his unit, and wounded again, all in the month of December. On Boxing Day the commanding officer of a reinforcement battalion told Foulkes' senior Medical Officer that he was receiving men from convalescent depots *"with open wounds, limitation of movement and unfit for duty."* Increased absentee and desertion rates compounded infantry shortages and, in an attempt to stem the manpower bleeding, commanders applied a disciplinary tourniquet. Between five and 10 courts martial sat daily during the last months of 1944 and the early months of 1945, to award exemplary punishments of between two and five years' penal servitude for a variety of offences. As usual, a soldier-poet caught the essence of these difficulties in commendably few words:

> *Oh, what with the wounded*
> *And what with the dead.*
> *And what with the boys*
> *Who are swinging the lead.*
> *If this war isn't over,*
> *And that goddamn soon,*
> *There'll be nobody left*
> *In this bloody platoon.*

Almost a third of the 90,000 Canadians who served in Italy became casualties, 5399 killed, and no one wanted to be the last in this neglected and forgotten campaign. Canadians were never quite sure whether, in Italy, they were liberators or conquerors, and it is not surprising that most of those serving in February 1945 seem to have embraced the announcement of Operation Goldflake, the move to Belgium, with undisguised delight. They had little idea of what they were getting into — but they knew what they were leaving.

I Corps planning staffs left immediately to prepare the way, followed shortly thereafter by the rest of the Headquarters, which became operational at Nijmegen on 15 March. Units followed, their route from Italy leading from Naples and Leghorn, through Marseilles, along the Rhône River valley, past Lyon, Dijon, Mâcon, Melun, and Paris to Belgium. Convoys drove during the day and stopped every evening in prepared staging camps. For 5th Armoured Division, Goldflake meant moving 20,000 troops, 5600 wheeled vehicles, 450 tanks, and 320 carriers, by rail, road, and sea. The first convoy left Leghorn on 15 February and was at Dixmude in Belgium 12 days later. One Armoured Brigade embarked on 8 March and followed the same route. First Canadian Infantry Division, which remained operational in the line until late February, began embarking on 7 March and a month later was concentrated in the Reichswald. By the end of March more than 58,000 soldiers had moved north.

> *No one was sorry to be leaving. There were no false regrets or sentimentalities. Italy was dirty. Italy was battered. Italy was wet and cold in the winter and Italy in the summer was a melange of heat, flies and dysentery. We were glad to see the last of it.*[133]

The experience of the Governor General's Horse Guards, 5th Division's armoured reconnaissance regiment, can serve as an example of the mood among the men. The Horse Guards spent much of January, which was *"bitterly cold and raw, with alternating rain and snowstorms,"* as infantry along the dykes of the Reno River, until relieved by the Italian Cremona Division in mid-month. While they were recuperating, rumours began circulating that they had to practise getting on and off boats, possibly to land in Greece. Very early on the morning of 11 February they began moving south for parts unknown: along the familiar Via Adriatica through Rimini, Pesaro, and Ancona to Porto Civitanova, where they turned inland and spent the night near Foligno. Next day, *"after a beautiful drive through the mountains"* in pleasant weather, they staged for

---

133 D Hist, "The Governor General's Horse Guards."

Casualties remained high after entering Germany. Here, a jeep ambulance loads up, receiving a wounded soldier from stretcher-bearers. (PA 113872)

Nurses worked just behind the front in medical and surgical units. (PA 128234)

the night at Pontassieve outside Florence. On the 13th, *"Our arrival at Leghorn, the main military port of Northern Italy, had settled any doubts in most people's minds"* that they were heading for France.

Following their advance parties, the first contingents set out from Leghorn in mid-February on crowded landing craft and Liberty ships for the 36-hour voyage, on a perfectly calm sea, to Marseilles, where they drove to a staging camp 30 kilometres north of the city. Next morning the first convoy left, lunching on "mystery meat" sandwiches on the road and driving past Avignon, Montelimar, and Valence, to a second staging camp. There they had dinner — too often rations *"containing a high proportion of M and V, that sadistic mixture of canned meat and vegetables that was the bane of our existence"* — watched a movie provided by the ubiquitous Auxiliary Services, and slept under the stars. After breakfast next morning the tour through southern France continued to the great enjoyment of most:

After long months in battered, war scarred Italy, the drive through France was a very great pleasure. The good roads, the undamaged towns and villages, the well tended countryside and clean intelligent looking populace, convinced us that we were back in civilization and it was very very good. Civilian cars came sailing down the highway, with their charcoal burners at the rear, young maidens on bicycles drew a chorus of frustrated whistles and the warmth of the welcomes seemed the genuine article. The people had obviously never been liberated in quite the Italian fashion.

Belgium was even better.

When the men arrived, they were paraded and informed that they would be billeted in civilian houses, sleeping between white sheets, and there was a delighted and incoherent cheer. With the assistance of Monsieur L'Inspecteur de Police, hundreds of billets had been arranged and the men were led to their houses, in each of which one or two were quartered, and in no time at all they were part of the family. We loved Belgium and we loved the Belgians. They were genuinely friendly and anxious to help, and they could not do enough for us. The men arrived without local money, and for the first couple of days, many a Canadian soldier enjoyed the four hundred pubs of Iseghem at the expense of his allies. The beer of Flanders was weak, but it was certainly plentiful and hordes of Canadians swarmed the friendly little pubs, with their pianos and accordions and their air of good cheer. There was surprisingly little drunkenness. The whole business was rather like a dream and as it was almost too good to be true, we behaved like a group of small children, who were very, very good, lest the dream be snatched away from us.... Never, since we had left Canada, had the Regiment been in such a civilian atmosphere. Spring was on the way with the days turning warmer, the trees and hedges bursting into leaf and the first spring flowers struggling through the earth, in the neat little gardens. It was peace and it was wonderful.

* * *

Leaves to Britain, Paris, Brussels, Bruges, Ghent, and Vimy were possible, and

the facilities for entertainment were so much greater than anything we had previously encountered, that we at last began to realize how the other half had been living.

The comparative lavishness of the new theatre also applied to military resources and equipment. All were amazed at the now commonplace zoo of Kangaroos, Crocodiles, Alligators, Buffaloes and other specialized armoured vehicles. Rocket-firing Typhoons were several cuts above Hurricane-bombers. General Montgomery visited, driving past the men lining the street in a jeep driven by their dynamic and highly respected divisional commander, Major General B.M. Hoffmeister, a militia soldier who had risen from battalion commander in Sicily to the command of their division in the remarkably short period of eight months, all of it in action at the front. Montgomery, *"in his inimitably dogmatic, but entertaining manner,"* spoke to all the division's officers in nearby Ypres, and they had to familiarize themselves with not only new equipment, organizations, and methods, but also the strange campaign that other Canadians had been fighting in France, Belgium, and Holland. To brief them, the Historical Officer visited his counterpart for

information for the writing of a general report on Canadian activities in NW Europe since "D" Day for distribution down to all units of I Canadian Corps to put them in the picture so far as this campaign is concerned.

As part of their reorganization, 5th Division disbanded its 12 Infantry Brigade — composed of

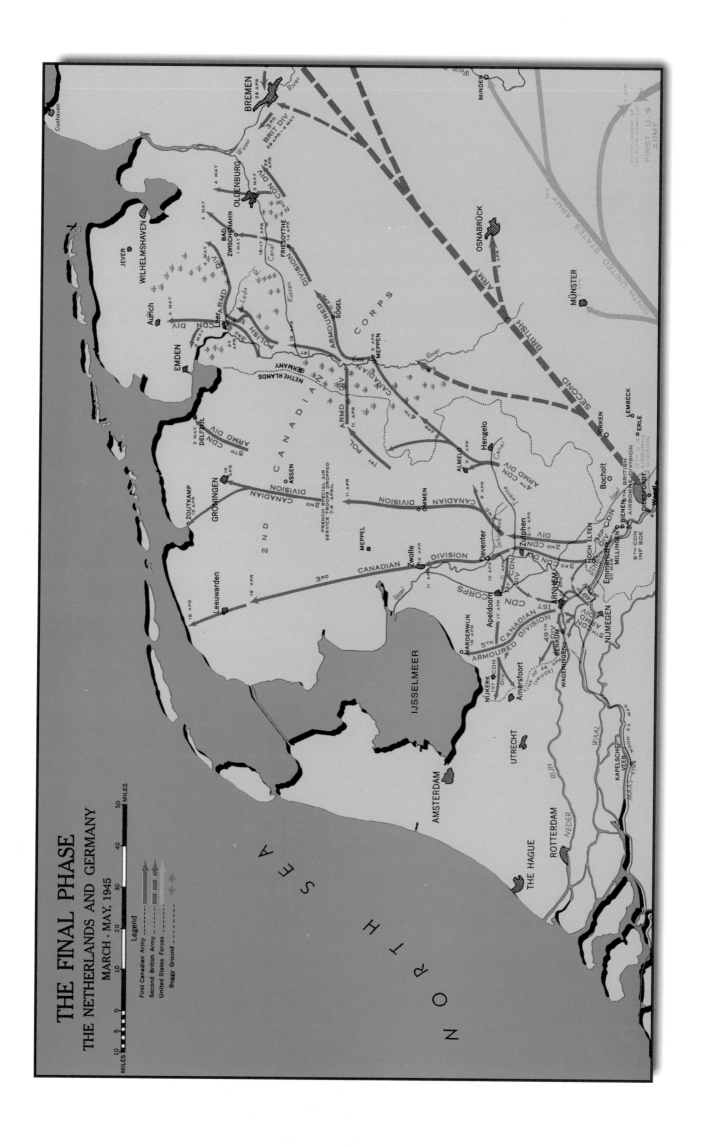

THE FINAL PHASE
THE NETHERLANDS AND GERMANY
MARCH - MAY, 1945

Legend

First Canadian Army
Second British Army
United States Forces
Boggy Ground

MILES 10 5 0 10 20 30 40 50 MILES

the Princess Louise Dragoon Guards, the Westminster Regiment, and the Lanark and Renfrew Scottish Regiment — which they had formed in Italy to have more infantry to fight in mountains. The GGHG re-equipped as a regular armoured regiment with the principal role of supporting the Irish Regiment of Canada, the Perth Regiment, and the Cape Breton Highlanders of 11 Infantry Brigade, and they received new tanks. Each squadron headquarters had two regular Shermans and two mounting 105mm guns, while each of four troops of tanks had two Shermans with the usual 75mm guns and two with 17-pounders. The three regiments of 4 Armoured Brigade — Lord Strathcona's Horse (Royal Canadians), the 8th Princess Louise's (New Brunswick) Hussars, and the British Columbia Dragoons — also drew new equipment.

Great events were unfolding while I Corps was moving. Except for small sectors in the Saar, the west bank of the Rhine was cleared of Germans; and before then, while the Canadians were finishing Blockbuster, Second British and Ninth US armies were preparing to assault across the river as the main Allied thrust into Germany. The offensive comprised two parts: an assault river crossing (Operation Plunder), followed by an airborne assault by XVIII Airborne Corps composed of the 6th British and 17th US Airborne Divisions (Operation Varsity). By the time that Veritable, Blockbuster, and Grenade had finished, however, the British attack was no longer the sole Rhine crossing, nor even the principal one. Several opportunities were being actively exploited along the length of the river. The US First Army reached Cologne at the beginning of March, brilliantly seized an intact bridge further south at Remagen a week later, and took Koblenz and Mainz soon after. Even further upstream, Third Army crossed at Oppenheim the night before Montgomery's attack on the 24th, and Seventh Army was preparing to do the same.

After crossing the Rhine, 21st Army Group's task was to drive for the Elbe between Magdeburg and Hamburg, with Ninth US Army on the right and Second British Army on the left. First Canadian Army's mission was to bridge the Rhine at Emmerich and drive north to clear Holland and the German coastal sector of the North Sea to the Elbe. When the US Ninth and First armies successfully encircled the Ruhr at the beginning of April, however, General Eisenhower decided to go towards Leipzig rather than Berlin and directed Ninth Army to revert to General Bradley's 12th Army Group.

Canadians had a minor role in Plunder and Varsity. The 1st Canadian Parachute Battalion parachuted into Germany as part of 6th Division, and 9 Brigade assaulted across the river under command of 51st Highland Division to take Emmerich and the Hoch Elten ridge, which, five kilometres northwest of the city, dominated the river. The rest of 3rd Division, then all of II Canadian Corps, then concentrated in the bridgehead before breaking out and advancing north and east on the left flank of Second Army. For the last phases of these operations, I Corps was to clear the western half of Holland and II Corps the eastern. Overall, facing the combined might of First Canadian, Second British, and Ninth US armies, possessing about 2500 guns and almost unlimited numbers of tanks and aircraft, the Germans had about 30,000 men in two depleted Corps with fewer than 50 tanks. Those in the immediate Canadian sector were from 2nd Parachute Corps. The Germans had, however, an assortment of anti-aircraft guns still in place, and these exacted a huge toll of Dakotas and their training gliders when the airborne divisions flew in on the morning of the 24th. Some of them carried 1st Canadian Parachute Battalion, whose task was to secure a woods behind the river crossing sites. They quickly overcame strong opposition, and it was during this firefight that one of their medical orderlies, Corporal F.G. Topham, earned the Victoria Cross: despite being badly wounded himself, and ignoring his own safety, Topham continually exposed himself to German fire to rescue wounded comrades. After the bridgehead battle, the unit moved rapidly northeast, going further into Germany than any other Canadians, and reached the Baltic port of Wismar just before the first Red Army troops arrived.

The first Canadians to cross the Rhine, in the early hours of 24 March, were riflemen of the Highland Light Infantry who went over in Buffaloes, and by the end of the day they were joined by the rest of 9 Brigade and the attached North Shore Regiment. Their job was to open up an exit from the confined bridgehead, which was ringed by several fortified villages, then swing left to clear the right bank of the Rhine to Emmerich. Once the latter was secured, 3rd Division, then

II Corps and First Canadian Army, could construct the bridges they needed to sustain their operations beyond the river. The HLI had a hard fight to clear German paratroopers from the first town, Speldrop, and the North Novas an even more difficult one when they were unfortunate enough to draw the key road junction of Bienen, which shielded large guns in range of bridge crossing sites and which was defended by highly rated panzer grenadiers now fighting on their own soil. In his memoir, *Journal of a War,* Donald Pearce has left a gripping account of that small, possibly typical battle that cost his battalion 114 casualties, 43 of them killed, just weeks before the end of the war.

Around Bienen the ground was flooded, the only approaches to it running along dykes that were completely covered by self-propelled guns, interlocking machine guns, and registered mortar fire. Several British attacks had been unsuccessful when the North Novas were told to take the town because its resistance was delaying the advance from the bridgehead. Their objective was the main Emmerich-Rees road that could be reached only from the front across completely open ground. A and B companies attacked in the morning but were driven to ground. When C and D company commanders were called to battalion headquarters they found not only their Commanding Officer, Lieutenant Colonel Donald Forbes, but also Brigadier Rockingham and General Horrocks, the Corps Commander, who made it emphatically clear that Bienen had to be taken without delay.

After being briefed by his company commander — three companies would assault from three different directions at 1430 — Pearce returned and briefed his platoon *and distributed an extra rum ration to the boys.* His own plan was simple. After the two leading platoons took the first group of houses 30 metres in front, they would go over the last dyke in extended line and each section would take a specific house in the village. Three regiments of artillery began firing 15 minutes before H-hour, and British tanks blasted every house they could reach. At H-hour, when the two lead platooons crossed the dyke, *an elaborate cross-fire from three directions cut them down like grass as they ran,* but survivors got to two of the farm buildings. Pearce continued:

My platoon assaulted in a single extended wave over the dyke-top and down the other side. Ten tumbled down, nailed on the instant by fire from two or maybe three machine-guns; we had gone broadside into their central defences. The rest of us rolled or dropped into a shallow ditch, hardly more than a trough, six inches deep, at the bottom of the dyke. The Bren gunners put their weapons to their shoulders, but never got a shot away. (I saw them after the battle, both dead, one still holding the aiming position.) I called out to my corporal only a few feet away, "We've got to make a dash for it. We've got to get to that house." He raised his head to answer and dropped flat. A rifleman on my left took aim at a German weapon pit, and with a spasm collapsed on my arm. His face turned almost instantly a faint green, and bore a simple smile.

Defenders concentrated their fire on the small group until one man, incredibly, stood up, walked forward, and tossed grenades into two of the weapon pits, before he himself was shot. With the defence loosened, Pearce called to his men to follow him to link up with the other platoons: *"Only one man was left to follow me. The rest we buried later that day, or dispatched to hospital."* With his commander wounded, Pearce took charge of the survivors, and reported to his Commanding Officer:

I hadn't any idea, apparently, of how far gone I was emotionally. Instead of furnishing a coherent account, I simply stood in front of him weeping inarticulately, unable to construct a sentence, even to force a single word out of my mouth. He approved my release from front-line platoon-leading, which I had requested of him two or three weeks before, when it had really begun to break me.[134]

While Typhoons from No 143 Wing bombed gun positions behind the objectives, the battalion made some progress and the HLI cleared Bienen the next morning, 26 March, allowing other 3rd Division units to move through the bridgehead to Emmerich. When they passed through that city later, its destruction by bombing and continual shelling reminded 1st Division veterans of Cassino. The position itself was vital because, along with the Hoch Elten ridge, it controlled the bridge sites that First Canadian Army required for maintenance beyond the Rhine. Seven Brigade reached its outskirts on the night of 27/28 March, receiving support from 4th Armoured Division

---

[134] Donald Pearce, *Journal of a War* (Toronto: Macmillan, 1954), 162-165.

tanks firing from south of the river. The Canadian Scottish, Regina Rifles, Winnipeg Rifles, and Sherbrooke Fusiliers had a difficult time getting across the canal that barred its eastern approaches. Then they had to clear the city in vicious street fighting, but they had it by the 30th and that night 8 Brigade took the Hoch Elten ridge with little opposition. It had been so heavily bombarded for several days that when the North Shore padre, Father Raymond Hickey, reached it he doubted that

a mole could have been found alive in that forest.... It just looked as though a giant had gulped it into his mouth, chewed it a couple of times and then spat it out.[135]

After 3rd Division secured bridge sites, 2nd and 4th divisions poured into the packed bridgehead. Crossing the Rhine was a memorable occasion, Prime Minister Churchill marking it with one of the more famous pees in recent history when he disdainfully emptied his bladder into the river. He would have agreed with a trooper of the 8th Recconnaissance Regiment who wrote:

As we look back on the campaign as a whole, it is the opinion of most of us, that crossing the Rhine was the greatest thrill we experienced and seemed to stir us more than any other single event. This was the same Rhine of which we dreamed and which seemed so far away as we grimly held our toe hold in Normandy against the then mighty Wehrmacht, now fleeing into their own hinterlands in confusion.[136]

It was particularly poignant for an NCO of the British Columbia Regiment who crossed on Easter Sunday, 1 April: 28 years previously he had spent his Easter Sunday attacking Vimy Ridge.[137]

After sappers completed Blackfriars Bridge — at 600 metres the longest Bailey span of the war — in the British sector at Rees, they put three more across the Rhine near Emmerich, allowing First Canadian Army to assume command of II Corps, and 2nd and 4th divisions to break out. The concentration of forces in the confined space beyond the river was overwhelming, wrote a unit diarist:

In that bridgehead as far as one could see were men, vehicles, guns, tanks and supply lines. Immense strength waiting, as we were, for the command to move forward.

When his force was ready, General Crerar ordered II Corps to advance north and to clear eastern Holland and the North Sea coast of Germany —

not to trap and destroy the Germans in that sector, but to drive them north towards their last escape hatch by sea. The task of I Corps was to clear Germans from Arnhem Island between the Waal and the Lower Rhine, capture Arnhem, and then liberate western Holland.

II Corps' advance began with 2nd Division in the centre headed for Groningen, 3rd Division on the left directed on Leeuwarden, and 4th Armoured on the right headed for the German North Sea ports. In due course 1st Polish Division joined the chase, coming in between 2nd and 4th divisions. Communiqués invariably described the situation as fluid, and that it was, as each platoon, each battalion, each brigade, and each division had its unique experiences in these final weeks, which, for some, resembled the earlier pursuit across France. Once more, scout cars led, with engineers close behind to bridge canals, rivers, and cratered roads. On the left, after 3rd Division battalions cleared Zutphen and Deventer in costly fights, resistance faltered and they advanced rapidly over the 120 kilometres to Leeuwarden, which their scout cars reached on 15 April. The division had moved 185 kilometres in 26 days, constructing 36 bridges and taking almost 5000 POWs along the way. In the centre, 2nd Division got smartly over the Twente Canal and continued on one main axis north to Groningen, its front screened by the 8th Recce and its left flank by cars of the Royal Canadian Dragoons. Brigades, leap-frogging behind, moved the 140 kilometres from the Twente Canal to the North Sea in two weeks. They were helped by the exploits of two regiments, about 700 men, of the French Special Air Service who were dropped on the night of 7/8 April to take bridges, harass Germans, and make contact with the Dutch underground. On the 11th the 8th Recce saved one detachment that had been trapped in the town of Spier. The most difficult fight was in clearing the streets and houses of Groningen, which was taken on the 16th, the day after the RCD entered Leeuwarden and reached the North Sea just beyond Dokkum and Zoutkamp. In 16 days the division had advanced 180 kilometres, built bridges whose

[135] R. Hickey, *The scarlet Dawn* (Campbellton, New Brunswick: Tribune Publishers, 1947), 253.

[136] D Hist, unit records.

[137] Douglas Harker, *The Dukes* (Vancouver: The Regiment, 1974), 285.

Lieutenant David Bryce Wilson RCNVR. Sent into Germany to liberate Canadian sailors from POW camps, Wilson discarded his dark naval uniform and adopted army battle dress after some Germans mistook him for a Gestapo officer. (PMR 9432322)

length totalled 320 metres, and taken more than 5000 POWs. En route the now-liberated citizens of towns and villages showered them with spontaneous joy.

Fourth Division's axis took it to Almelo, where 1st Polish Division came alongside and took the left axis to Winschoten and the sector west of the Ems River, while 4th went northeast into Germany towards Meppen, Sogel, Friesoythe, the Kusten Canal, and Oldenburg. *"Funny thing,"* wrote Trooper David Marshall, *"when we passed the border into Germany, all the waving and the smiling and the laughing stopped. Our greetings were sombre, hateful looks. Well, we didn't like them much either."*

From then on, however, he found it unlike the pursuit from the Seine, more of *"a methodical retreat, where we had to fight all the way"* and where small battle groups on the flanks fought their own private wars. Even the adolescents and old men who manned many of the German defensive positions in the vain hope of salvaging something of their war could kill when behind a machine gun or an 88mm antitank gun, which is why, Marshall recorded, *"As we moved through the country we did not leave a haystack or barn unburnt, and if the house did not have a white flag, then it went too."* Vehicles were roadbound and these were strewn with mines, cratered, and blocked with felled trees, forcing units to telescope and making them easy targets for mortars and artillery. When fire forced them to stop, wet fields and peat bogs restricted tank movement but gave the defenders lucrative fields of fire, as Marshall discovered when his own tank was shot out from him by an unseen weapon.

Soldiers moving into Germany saw things they could scarcely believe when they overran concentration and forced labour camps. The scope of the overall medical and social problem revealed at this stage of the war is difficult to conceive. In II Corps area alone there were 42 prisoner or displaced persons camps containing Russian, Polish, Czechoslovak, Yugoslav, Italian, and other inmates, in which the most appalling conditions were typical. In the largest camp 18,500 people were temporarily housed in the hangars and buildings of a German air field. There, a visiting doctor reported,

The Canadian Army had established a small field hospital which had been set up by No 21 FDS {Field Dressing Station} and consisted of tented wards for men and women, an obstetrical ward, case room, operating room and babies ward. Four Nursing Sisters were attached. This unit had patients and were very happy to be working on something which they described as nearer to civilian practice than anything they had seen in the army. A mobile bath unit was also in the camp, consisting of 8 sections and within 36 hours some 18,500 people had been bathed.

In one smaller but not atypical camp there were 1600 Russians, of whom half were sick and a third had advanced tuberculosis. In addition, 45 were blind, 33 were psychotic, and there were 450 amputees. Six Russian doctors were trying to look after them. They had, of course, no X-ray equipment, and *"were using wooden stethoscopes of monaural type which they had contrived themselves."*[138]

* * *

On call above the soldiers on the ground were free-wheeling RCAF Typhoons and Spitfires. The final pursuit was a swashbuckling time for tactical air force pilots, the essence of which was preserved in a report written at the time by Flying Officer Carl Reinke.[139] He described how wings rather than squadrons were the main functional unit, and to maintain continuous air support they had to be mobile and able to operate from either developed airfields or rough farmyards. Pilots still had to contend with German fighters — including the new jets — from time to time, but interdiction and ground support missions remained their main tasks, making fighting a more individualistic and personal experience. Rather than shooting at fleeting, indirect targets, the pilots could clearly see the men and vehicles they were attacking on the ground. Reinke thought:

All of that, the individual daring and initiative, the rough field life, the day-long concentration on the job, the comparative lack of diversions, added up to something distinctive. You sensed a difference as soon as you walked into a Fighter mess. Whether it was under canvas or in some abandoned farmhouse or an ex-German mess, the picture was the same; Aircrew strutting or lolling about in outfits which could best be accounted for as utilitarian. They would consist

138 D Hist, unit records.
139 D Hist, "Fighter Wings on the Continent."

"Wilson soon came face-to-face with the horrors of Nazi Germany." After a mass grave was discovered outside their town, these villagers were made to build coffins and give the victims a proper burial.

of British khaki battle-dress, flying boots topped by high white socks, a blue or khaki shirt open at the neck (collar outside the tunic), or a rollneck sweater in white or blue or gray, a bright bit of silk as a scarf (perhaps a piece of parachute silk), maybe a leather Irvine jacket surmounting the whole. For variation, parts of khaki and blue battledress might be combined, such as a khaki top and blue trousers, or vice versa, or including a civilian windbreaker. There was, invariably, a revolver carried over the hip, in its grey webbing holster and belt. The flying boots were often a study in themselves, their loose tops revealing as varied a bunch of items stuck down inside, as one traditionally expects in a small boy's pockets — navigation maps, a couple of emergency ration packages, one or two Penguin books, a Digest of some sort, cigarettes, a knife or two, chocolate, and perhaps other incidentals.

They were young, vigorous, and confident professionals whose casualness, however posed it may have seemed, had a purpose. Collars were opened because Spitfire cockpits became very hot in the sun; boots were filled with necessities because pilots always had to be ready to fly. While clearly preferring to fight it out with German aircraft, even when outnumbered or against the new faster jets, they resigned themselves to the Luftwaffe's absence. Shooting up trains and bombing bridges gave some satisfaction because it allowed pilots to see that they were impeding German movement, but that style of warfare also made them uneasy, because

not having had the army's conditioning to front-line slaughter and mutilation, many had to force themselves to fire their guns when an enemy column of men or horse-drawn carts was in their sights. Some didn't. Many of the others had to assume a pose and "talk tough" to maintain their own conditioning for the job at hand, rather than trying to impress any incidental by-standers. A normal Canadian lad of 19 or 22 had to consciously harden himself to the kind of assignments the Fighters were called on to carry out; so he was likely to act the role consistently, on duty and off... half a dozen aircrew were standing around outside in the balmy spring evening sunshine. One pseudo-tough pilot began "giving off" about the "sport" he had had that afternoon firing at Gerries as they dived off their trucks as their M.T. {motor transport} column was shot-up. There wasn't any sport to compare

with shooting Gerries as they dived for a ditch, he insisted, with a kind of chuckle. But none of the others made a syllable of comment or picked up the theme in any way. The topic died, in a void.

Trains and vehicle transport were lucrative, if dangerous, targets because of heavy and unpredictable flak, and there were other hazards, recounted one Spitfire squadron commander, Bill Olmstead. Diving to strafe a truck convoy, Olmstead did not realize that his 500-pound belly bomb had not released from an earlier attack.

Attacking the first lorry I opened fire at three hundred yards in a medium dive. The vibration of my guns shook the bomb free, so that it struck the truck when I was less than fifty feet above the vehicle. It blew the truck to smithereens, knocked me unconscious, and blasted my aircraft several hundred feet upward. My Spit slowly rolled onto its back, and when I regained consciousness, two or three seconds later, I was heading for the ground upside down. Death was only seconds away, although I was too dazed to think clearly. I moved the control column hard and the aircraft righted itself, pulling out of the dive just above the tops of the trees.[140]

Olmstead's almost completely disabled airplane lurched him back over friendly lines where he bailed out and survived to fly again next day.

The RCAF formation that worked most closely with the army was No 39 (Reconnaissance) Wing, whose squadrons took the aerial photographs on which the army's intelligence assessments depended. As Reinke explained, they had four tasks: high-level photography, low-level oblique photography, visual tactical reconnaissance, and artillery and contact recce. High-level photography was a very specialized task, well within the RCAF's legacy in mapping the Canadian North in the 1920s and 1930s. Spitfires were adapted for the high-level missions, which averaged around 20 a day. With their aircraft stripped of armament — to save weight and to keep them from straying into combats — and loaded with enough extra fuel to extend their flying range to four or five hours, pilots took photos of everything from airfields to minefields, from gun emplacements to basic topographical data for overprinted maps. They

---

[140] Bill Olmstead, *Blue Skies* (Toronto: Stoddart, 1987), 228.

carried two cameras, with either a 20-inch or 36-inch lens, set to overlap horizontally and vertically, and 500 exposures of film. Pilots would fly level sweeps at an altitude of around 9000 metres and trigger their cameras to click automatically.

When they landed, the film rolls went to the Mobile Field Photographic Section (MFPS) for processing, and from there prints went to an army Air Photographic Interpretation Section (APIS) where interpreters plotted them on a map before closely studying them with stereoscopic instruments. The photos provided immediate tactical intelligence about defensive positions, gun emplacements, and the like, which was used to update overprinted maps. Housed in just four vans, the few men in the MFPS could produce almost unlimited numbers of prints. In the five days before the Rhine crossing they turned out 286,500 prints from 32,091 exposures, using 60 kilometres of printing paper, 8000 litres of chemicals, and almost 200,000 litres of water, which was trucked from a canal a few kilometres away. They also moved quickly. Photos taken on the morning before the Rhine crossing were processed and flown to England in time to brief paratroopers that evening.

* * *

While II Corps was advancing north and east under the air force's aluminium umbrella, General Foulkes' I Corps came into action from its positions at Nijmegen. In order to cross the innumerable rivers and canals that surround western Holland, Foulkes set two separate operations in motion early in April. In the first, 1st Canadian Infantry Division was placed under II Corps to attack west across the Ijssel River around Deventer to capture Apeldoorn. The second required 5th Armoured Division to clear the south bank of the Neder Rhine, while 49th British Division crossed the Rhine and the Ijssel and took Arnhem. Once it had been secured, 5th Division began to drive north through Arnhem to the Ijsselmeer, in the process outflanking and isolating the German garrison in Apeldoorn. General Hoffmeister's rapid advance forced the Germans out of that city, prompting one of the strangest battles his division had experienced. Two groups of withdrawing Germans avoided the Canadians, but in the early morning of 17 April a third stumbled

directly into the village of Otterloo where not only the 17th Field Regiment had set up its gun positions but where also the divisional headquarters was located. Intending to escape, the Germans stumbled into the Canadian positions in the dark and a nasty firefight developed. The gunners fired over open sights at Germans less than 100 metres away, and GGHG tanks tried to pick out targets in the confused darkness while themselves avoiding antitank weapons. The situation was not eased until daylight when Irish Regiment flame-throwers arrived to scorch the ditches.

Fifth Division reached the Ijsselmeer soon after, and in the first weeks of April I Corps drove the Germans 70 kilometres west of the Ijssel River, taking more than 7000 of them as prisoners. Although it was becoming abundantly clear to both sides that the war was almost over, the manner of its ending was not. The enemy still had about 120,000 troops west of the Grebbe Line that ran southeast from Amersfoort to the Neder Rhine and, having sent 5th Armoured to northern Holland, General Foulkes was left with just 1st Canadian and 49th British divisions to handle them. With too few troops to attack this large German garrison entrenched in strong defensive positions, the Corps halted on 19 April when negotiations began with the purpose of relieving the large civilian population caught between the two sides.

The Holland Pocket contained the country's major cities — Amsterdam, Rotterdam, The Hague, Utrecht — containing 40 per cent of the population. Estimates of tens of thousands of citizens facing imminent acute starvation had prompted Queen Wilhelmina in January to send a warning to King George VI, Prime Minister Churchill, and President Roosevelt:

Conditions...have at present become so desperate, that it is abundantly clear that, if a major catastrophe, the like of which has not been seen in western Europe since the Middle Ages, is to be avoided in Holland, something drastic has to be done now, that is to say before and not after the liberation of the rest of the country.

Their plight in the following months deterioriated from alarming to appalling, but a combination of political and military factors inhibited a resolution of the unfolding tragedy. Arranging a political accommodation with the German occupiers to feed the civilian population required the highest-level political sanction because the Allies had mutually agreed not to treat with the enemy other than on the basis of unconditional surrender. Moreover, military commanders were persuaded that they could free Holland more quickly by defeating Germany's armies than by making individual and isolated deals with them, however strong the humanitarian demands.

All the while, the Dutch people in the urban centres were trapped with little food and dimishing hope as conditions steadily worsened. In 1946 Mr. J. Nikerk, Secretary of the Netherlands-Canadian Committee, gave a compelling account of how the tragedy had evolved within the rhythm of the course of the campaign, and Dutch reaction to it.[141] Spirits rose and fell to BBC reports that filtered in over clandestine radios. Hopes soared when the Allies landed in Normandy but then, when stalemate followed early success, it was, Nikerk wrote, *"difficult not to give way to feelings of impatience."* Hope rose once more when Allied troops breached the Seine, liberated Paris, and crossed the Belgian border. Dutch civilians watched as

> *Panic over{came} the German occupation troops and the minority who... cast in their lot with the enemy. Almost as satisfying as the Allied advance {was} the spectacle of fear striking into the hearts of the Dutch Nazis and their masters.... The climax {was} reached on Tuesday the 5th of September. All roads leading to the east of the country {were} jammed with German military cars loaded down with hastily packed luggage and pilfered goods. Holland {was} convinced that liberation {would come in} only a matter of days.*

Spirits ebbed again, proportionally, as the Germans recovered with the Allies kilometres near but light-years away. A dangerous false lift accompanied the arrival of parachutists who dropped into Grave, Nijmegen, and Arnhem, when *"Every hidden radio {became} a news distribution centre. Housewives, school children, grocers, milkmen, every loyal Dutchman {helped} to pass on the news."* Anticipating quick results, Dutch railway workers went out on strike and paralyzed the country's transportation system. The Germans responded harshly, flooding polders, stopping fuel supplies, restricting food distribution, blowing up port facilities in Rotterdam and Amsterdam, and looting industrial machinery and equipment. *"Now the mask {fell}*

off completely and the enemy {gave} up the last attempt at hypocrisy." Without fuel and power, cooking even the little food that was available became difficult and, as important for morale, radios could not function. The daily caloric level fell incrementally from a pre-war level of 3000 to 400 or less. Beetroot replaced potatoes as a dietary staple.

> *On the streets women, old men and children {could} be seen begging for a slice of bread or for one potato. Skipping school {was} common now. In an ice cold room, with an empty stomach, what child {could} sit and study? Moreover they {were} needed to relieve their mothers in the endless food queues.*

The Red Cross delivered some food, but not enough. One of their officials reported that people were eating flower bulbs. Supplies of food and fuel in nearby Belgium could reach Holland in hours by trucks and barges, but the way was blocked and minesweeping the Dutch coast would take several weeks. Death rates doubled over the previous year, and the Germans continued to flood land while threatening to blow up even more vital dykes. Other reprisals tightened the noose: 10 or 20 or more political prisoners shot for each underground killing. Men from 17 to 60 were rounded up for deportation to German labour camps, 50,000 in Rotterdam alone in that unforgiving winter:

> *A village is surrounded. Military commands shrill forth from loudspeakers. Whoever does not stand in front of his home packed with his blanket on his back and spoon and plate in his hand ready to go into slavery, will be summarily executed.*

As became abundantly clear in spring, military command is an unenviable process of choosing between equally unpalatable options. The only way to stop the slaughter and relieve Dutch starvation was to defeat Germany, but the question was whether Holland would be liberated sooner by defeating the German army or by reaching an immediate accommodation to relieve the civilian population. In April the Allies could not tell what the Germans intended to do in western Holland: defend it to the last, evacuate it, and leave garrisons, as they had in the Pas-de-Calais and the Scheldt; or apply their frightening threat of even

[141] Norman Philips and J. Nikerk, *Holland and the Canadians* (Amsterdam: Contact Publishing, 1946), 19-28. See also Walter B. Maaas, *The Netherlands at War: 1940-1945* (London: Abelard-Schuman, 1970).

Marlag und Milag Nord shortly after being liberated. Fighting continued around the camp for a number of days. (PMR 94319)

more dangerous flooding, particularly by destroying the newer dykes that protected the recently reclaimed area of the Ijsselmeer. If the Germans chose to defend strong points in the flooded area, the prospect of fighting dwarfed even the magnitude of the Scheldt. Moreover, the Allies would have little choice but to unleash their massive firepower on defended urban centres, and that would almost certainly kill more civilians than German soldiers. Field commanders warned their superiors about the inevitable price of massive destruction, and advised that they not proceed west of Utrecht. Taken for the best of motives, the decision to stop, however, was puzzling if not unfathomable to the Dutch:

In the western towns millions {were} longingly looking for the liberators. The air {was} thick with rumours — people ask each other, where are the liberators? Everybody agrees that if the liberators {wanted} to save the crowded towns from the murderous fight, they {could} do so. People cynically ask{ed} each other, "Is it better to die of hunger in undamaged towns?"

Held on the Grebbe Line, I Corps had virtually stopped fighting by 19 April, and ceased fire on the 28th. Over the next few days General Foulkes met with German representatives at Achterveld to discuss relief measures, and the Germans finally agreed to permit Allied convoys through their lines. While the talking continued, bomber aircraft began a daily air-drop of 2200 tons of food, the first planes arriving on 29 April to drop 500,000 rations near Rotterdam and The Hague. In a week they delivered more than 11 million rations. A pilot with the RAF's 150 Squadron described the experience of flying over at 300 metres, at an agreed speed and course, while watching German AA gunners track them as they went and seeing messages sketched on the roofs of barns saying: *"Thank you, Canadians."*[142] Mr. Nikerk described the scene.

In the streets, on the roofs, in the gutters, before the windows, any place from which one can see...all Holland {was} dreaming.... Waving sheets, blankets, towels, tea-cloths and what not. Many {got} lumps in their throats, tears in their eyes. This {was} one of the boldest dreams that have come true. Few {said} it frankly but many {felt} it — that {was} the unexpected, unheroic, strange end of the war in West Holland.

It was a relief for pilots to fly missions that were not meant to destroy, and Army Service Corps

drivers felt the same when, on 2 May, their 30-vehicle convoys from eight Canadian and four British transport platoons began leaving Canadian lines every half hour carrying a daily 1000-ton supply of food and fuel to depots set up by the Dutch. They continued for a week, and together such interventions saved countless lives. A Dutch doctor told a senior Canadian medical officer he *considered that if the liberation of Holland had been delayed another month, the results would have been quite catastrophic. As it was, it was estimated that the average weight loss in the large cities in adults was about 20 pounds.*[143] These were averages and, of course, some were far worse off. The most infirm at first went undetected because, too weak to stand, they were unable to leave their houses to join the food-lines. Especially affected were the poor and unwanted infants. Canadian medical officers estimated the following distribution of cases of starvation showing oedema: in Amsterdam, up to 20,000; in Rotterdam and The Hague, each 10,000; and in Utrecht, 1500.

* * *

An urgent humanitarian task as the war wound down was evacuation of prisoners of war who were liberated when the Allies overran German camps. It was essential that POWs, including 4156 Canadians, be removed from the war zone as expeditiously as possible, not only because of the obvious danger but also because of the immense difficulties associated with feeding and accommodating them in occupied Germany.

The job of supervising the evacuation of POWs was assigned to American, British, and Canadian Contact Liaison Officers (CLOs) from all three services who followed just behind the advance troops so that they could enter camps immediately after they were liberated. Initially, they were to look after their "own kind" — an RCAF CLO would be responsible only for captured Canadian aircrew, not British or American — but this proved difficult since the German system of dividing prisoners from different services into separate camps had broken down as they moved

---

[142] D. Kaufman and M. Horn, *A Liberation Album: Canadians in the Netherlands, 1944-1945* (Toronto: McGraw-Hill Ryerson, 1980), 104-105.

[143] D Hist, unit records.

Lieutenant Wilson with some liberated naval POWs.
(PMR 94323)

Time out after a hard day at the office. (PA1 16730)

them around behind their crumbling front lines. As a result, CLOs tried to help their own but not at the cost of not assisting other POWs.

The RCN's CLO was Lieutenant David Bryce Wilson, formerly the navigator of the 65th flotilla's *MTB-748*. Selected for the duty because he spoke some German, Wilson departed England for the Continent on 31 March, equipped with a three-ton lorry, complete with Royal Marine driver, a radio set that he did not know how to operate, bedding, and emergency food rations. One of some seven CLOs assigned to 21st Army Group, Wilson's specific task was to find and evacuate 174 Canadian naval and merchant POWs known to be held in a cluster of camps around Bremen (the Germans had selected this area because the sandy soil frustrated tunnelling). As he passed through devastated Le Havre on his way to the front, Wilson saw

> *hundreds upon hundreds of German prisoners of war actually labouring in long lines carrying rubble and things, clearing up all the mess...the sight of all those young Germans of labouring age, of military age, working away with their bare hands gladdened my heart.*[144]

When he arrived in Germany, Wilson came face to face with the stark horrors of Nazism. As German resistance crumbled, civilian and military prisoners were moved away from the front lines, both east and west.

> *What started happening was that train loads of boxcars filled with humanity, or marching columns of prisoners moving in reciprocal directions, started meeting all over the North German Plain. And whenever the Germans in charge of these desperate cargoes began encountering similarly freighted trains or columns coming from the opposite direction, they realized that the game was up, and that there was not the slightest point in going any further in either direction. So they just started abandoning those people wherever they were, and going under cover themselves. This is what happened on April 8, apparently a train from Hamburg with three box cars pulled into our village, onto the siding, and the engine took off leaving the three box cars behind.... According to what we learned on April 27, these pathetic creatures were just left there imprisoned in these box cars.*

Showing *"no charitable intentions or human instincts"* towards those trapped in the boxcars, the citizens of the village left them to starve, and then buried them in a pit just before the Allies overran the site. Soon after, a small boy asked a British soldier if he would like to see the grave, and the full horror was revealed.

The German villagers were put to work digging up the bodies and placing them in coffins. Wilson, who was in the area anxiously waiting for the naval camps to be liberated, was nearly sick to his stomach as he supervised this work.

> *One of the first things I did was to nip back to the Quartermaster stores and buy a pipe and some tobacco, the first pipe I ever bought in my life and the first time I ever smoked one, but by holding this pipe under my nose as I smoked it I was able to force myself to witness the ghastly, grizzly {sic} proceedings as the villagers were obliged to take these bodies out one by one and put them in coffins.*

With this completed, the dead — Wilson thought them Poles or Russians from a concentration camp — were given a proper burial:

> *But God! The soldiers were bloody-minded — as we all were. Well, everybody gathered around the fresh graves, and "Off caps"...bare heads bowed. The Burgermeister said a few prayers and then {I} made a little speech saying who these people were, how they'd come to be there, and why this could never happen again, and so on. And then the earth was shovelled in over these same poor anonymous innocents, but this time they were in boxes at least. A little bit of respect had been shown. But it was really all too late; it was all so horrible to think that just on the eve of the German surrender 109 humans had their lives snuffed out a mere few weeks before help could reach them.*

But Wilson *could* help the POWs. On 28 April, the day after the gruesome burial plot had been discovered, Marlag und Milag Nord, the camp holding the captive sailors Wilson was seeking, was finally overrun. At 1100, Wilson drove into camp in a jeep flying a Canadian red ensign, to find the men quietly assembled. Leading Writer Stuart Kettles, who had been taken prisoner exactly one year earlier when HMCS *Athabaskan* had been sunk, and Gordon Olmstead, a merchant ship officer captured when his ship had gone down in March 1941, were on the other side of the wire

---

[144] D Hist, RCAF records, and the David Bryce Wilson biographical file.

that morning. For days, they had heard the sounds of battle raging around the camp but no Allied soldiers appeared until the morning of the 28th when Kettles *"saw the first of our liberators, a tank driver of the Scots Guards. Boy he looked good."* But Kettles recalled no sense of exhilaration.

> *Strange as it may seem, there was no celebration, no shouting, no nothing. That was probably due to the fact that it was difficult to realize, and to top it all off, we had been expecting them for about three weeks, and more or less took the view that "it was just about time they got here." We learned later, that the Scots Guards had been given orders that morning to take the camp that day, no matter how they did it, at the same time not to use any big guns. This was for fear of dropping a shell into the camp and killing some of the P.O.W.'s.[145]*

Fighting continued around the camp for three more days, with the occasional shell falling within the camp itself. Wilson noted that

> *the effect of this was to increase the nervousness and restlessness of the ex-prisoners of war, who were most anxious to avoid being recaptured and so found it very difficult to stay put during the early days.*

He did what he could, distributing Red Cross parcels and arranging for fresh white bread to be brought into the camp daily from a field bakery. In the meantime he searched for more RCN POWs, and produced a long nominal list of the names, using Leading Writer Kettles as his clerk and three German "censorettes," who had previously vetted prisoners' mail, as typists. The original plan called for 1000 personnel to be evacuated each day, but poor weather and transportation slowed the process. Many, including Wilson, were still there when the war ended.

I Corps had stopped firing on 28 April and sporadic fighting in northern Germany against II Corps was interspersed with local surrenders. As it happened, the Lincoln and Welland historian wrote, *"The war did not end in any spectacular sweep or climactic battle.... It merely petered out."*[146] While it was grinding down, Brigadier Rodger noticed

> *a strange feeling of restlessness and wonder getting about. The long awaited end is at hand and instead of a celebrating and exciting atmosphere developing it is almost the reverse. The battle becomes slower, less fighting but lots of craters and blown bridges. The tanks become more careful; rumours of demobilization start, officers wonder to what job they will go on return and when. Who is going to do occupation — Corps or Army? What divisions are to stay or go to Burma?*

On 1 May, Rodger noted in his diary that he heard *"Red flag over Reichstag...beginning to expect surrender in a matter of days now... {then at} 2230 hours — Radio announces 'HITLER is dead. Doenitz takes over'."* Italian forces in Italy surrendered the next day and, at noon on 4 May, 21st Army Group informed General Crerar that Montgomery was negotiating unconditional surrender with representatives of Admiral Doenitz. Crerar immediately instructed II Corps not to proceed with the attacks that 1st Polish and 3rd Canadian divisions were about to launch; nonetheless 20 Canadians died that day and three more died on the 5th. In the evening Crerar heard simultaneously from the BBC and Montgomery's Headquarters that hostilities in 21st Army Group's sector were to cease officially at 0800 on 5 May. Soon after, General Foulkes received the surrender of Fortress Holland from the immediate German commander in a battle-scarred hotel in Wageningen. Two days later, at Rheims, the German General Alfred Jodl formally surrendered all German military forces to General Eisenhower, an action that was subsequently ratified by Russian Headquarters in Berlin.

Private Bradley's war ended with little drama.

> *This morning at 0800 o'clock {5 May} our part of Germany surrendered; in other words we've seen the last of our fighting. I've often wondered how I'd feel when it came about; well, I don't feel a bit different. When I first heard about it last night after having had a move of about 25 miles, and on the way our carrier threw a track, so we spent 2 hours in the rain fixing it. We got back and the boys told us it was all over. I was so damn tired I just thanked God and went to bed.*

In Marlag und Milag Nord, David Bryce Wilson remembered.

> *That night all around us the Army people, camping in tents, were celebrating in a way you*

[145] D Hist, Stuart Kettles, "A Wartime Log: A Personal Account of Life in HMCS *Athabaskan* and as a Prisoner of War."

[146] R.L. Rogers, *History of the Lincoln and Welland Regiment* (St. Catharines, Ontario: The Regiment, 1954), 270.

would have expected of them — carousing — after all, they'd earned the right to celebrate, but I fell into a very deep depression that night. It was the first time after years of war and worry that one could actually let one's nerves go, and sit back and try to think about the whole experience, and it was in fact a very depressing time. I didn't really sleep that night.

* * *

At the end, the 200,000 men and women of this citizen army were strung out over northern Europe from Bremen to Dunkirk. II Corps formations filled an occupier's role in Germany, while I Corps units had the delicious experience of moving into Holland's major cities. All were represented on 21 May when 16 pipe bands and five brass bands led composite units of First Canadian Army through The Hague in a spectacular victory parade.

Returning the troops to Canada was as complex a task, if a much happier one, as getting them to Europe had been. Repatriation was complicated by a need to help occupy Germany, and to recruit a division for service in the war against Japan. The Canadian Army Occupation Force, initially built up from volunteers, and soldiers recently arrived in Europe, assumed control of much of Land Oldenburg in early July, where they remained until the following summer. Command of 6th Canadian Infantry Division, which was to fight in the Pacific, went to Major General B.M. Hoffmeister, the army's most outstanding operational field commander, and by July more than 22,000 volunteers had left for Canada.

Stuart Kettles, Gordon Olmstead, and Charlie Bradley went home. On 7 May, Kettles was finally evacuated from Marlag und Milag Nord:

We were put into army trucks and driven 110 miles to an airport at Diepholtz. On our way down we saw plenty of Germany that had really been damaged, or should I say flattened. It was really great to see. On our arrival at Diepholtz, which was a clearing base for Prisoners of War under the authority of the British 2nd Army.... We were checked in, given our billets in tents, and then on to the mess hall, where we received the first decent meal in nearly a year. After a meal we were issued with chocolate, cigarettes and a Red Cross ditty bag.

Bad weather delayed departure for three days but Kettles' group finally flew to Brussels, where he encountered *"the first honest to God woman I had seen in a year"*:

She was working with the Canadian Red Cross and it was quite a surprise. The treatment we received here was far beyond our wildest imaginings. We left the airport for St. Anne's barracks, where we ran into everyone Canadian.... We were given a short medical inspection for lice, bugs, crabs, etc. We then filled out various forms after which we received 10 shillings in English currency and 4 pound, 10 shillings in Belgium francs. We were then taken and given any clean clothing we required and from there to the first real hot shower in over a year. After the shower, we hopped into our clean clothing, and then went to be sprayed with a white powder to kill any possible bugs, lice, etc. we may still have with us. At 11:30 PM we were taken into the mess hall and received the best meal to date. After we had finished we went down to a small store and enjoyed a couple of cool whiskeys and a couple of beers, and then back to barracks and turned in.

The next day Kettles was flown to England in a Lancaster bomber, and after spending a week there, with thousands of other Canadians, boarded the huge passenger liner *Aquitania* for New York. From there, a train took him north to Montreal where a wild reception awaited:

They had the Navy band from Montreal to greet us. We stood on the platform for about 30 minutes while the band serenaded us, and then they finally decided it was time to whisk us off to barracks for breakfast. The band left and we thought it was all over, but little did we know it was only beginning. We picked up our little bits of luggage and began to wend our way out of the station. However the band pulled a fast one and had gone just outside the station entrance where they had fallen in on the street, and as we came to the entrance were greeted with more music. There were also about 3,000 civilians standing around, cheering, why, God only knows. You would think something had really happened. About the most touching thing of it all was when Stoker Polson, who had been a prisoner of war with us, was finally spotted by his wife. It is hard to say whether they both laughed or cried, but you can depend it was as happy a welcome as you would

Finale. Germans walking home under watchful eyes, while a Dutch family returns to more normal life. (PA 134287)

ever wish to see. In fact it was so good, that we almost lost Polson, but he finally showed up about 30 minutes late, but boy was he happy. Strange thing this married life.

The next night, Kettles boarded a train for the final leg to his home town, Ottawa. Expecting another warm welcome, he and four other sailors from Ottawa decided *"what to do when we finally got off the train."* His family had their own ideas.

Jim, Ernie, Kirk were right at the train door waiting for me, and to be quite truthful, from there on it is all very, very hazy. Kisses here, shouts there, hand shakes somewhere else. Well, the fun and noise finally subsided and we hopped into Jack's car and made our way to Jim's where they had everything all set, just waiting for the match to start it going, and believe me it certainly took off.

Everyone I wanted, friends I had never seen or heard of before, were there, but boy what a time. I'd really like to do it all over again. It was really worth a year in Germany to find that they thought that much of the "black sheep of the family." How I can ever repay them is something that will have to work itself out through time.

What does it take to work out. Right now, all I can say is it's a feeling I have never had the opportunity of experiencing before. What it will all bring, I don't know.[147]

Merchant seamen, the true heroes of the Battle of the Atlantic, according to one leading RCN officer, did not share the enthusiastic homecoming that Kettles and other service veterans received. *"We were a little disappointed,"* recalled Gordon Olmstead, when, along with 24 others, he arrived in London on V-E Day to find Canada House closed. Its staff had gone to join in the celebrations that erupted that day, and Olmstead and the others were left to scrounge accommodation for themselves. A week later they boarded the small "banana boat" SS *Bayano* for passage back to Canada. There was no dockside greeting when they arrived in Halifax, but Imperial Oil held a low-key dinner for merchant sailors: *"nothing fancy but good hospitality."* Next day, they boarded trains for home.

Charlie Bradley, who a few months before had been so eager to get out of uniform and find a job, any job, was now less certain. He explained to his mother:

I don't know how to begin this letter. You see I've signed up to go to the far east. I know you won't like that at all, but you must look at my side of it. I feel I'm too young to settle down; I'm only 21, and besides I don't like the idea of starting into some trade when everybody is doing the same. I'll just end up getting a rotten job that I won't like at all.... I will be home for 30 days leave.... I hope you can get your holidays when I'm there and we can spend them together wherever you want to go. You don't have to worry about money; I'll have over $300 cash.... What you can do is get me the stuff I'll need when I'm there: an average size suitcase, 1 set of pyjamas, 3 sets of summer shorts and tops, 2 dozen handkerchiefs, 4 towels, 6 pairs of cotton socks (black), 1 pair black shoes size 7, swimming trunks (26 waist), 2 khaki shirts size 14. Use my money from the cheques for that, only if you don't need the money yourself.

Bradley's troopship arrived in Halifax harbour on the day Japan surrendered, V-J Day, where it anchored offshore all day for fear of landing troops in the midst of riots similar to those that had occurred on V-E Day a few months earlier. He was then 21 years of age.

* * *

It is not surprising that some soldiers, sailors, and airmen found themselves at loose ends when the war ended and it was time to pick up the threads of their lives. Some of them had left their families as teenagers in autumn 1939, a lifetime back, and had undergone an unusual late adolescence in Britain, Italy, France, Belgium, Holland, and Germany. They had seen and experienced things that caused some to grow, others to wither and never recover. Normal lives had been put in limbo for the duration, one of them wrote:

The war has been fought on an island, suspended in time and space, that has little relation to the life we left or to which we are now returning. That after all, is true of any war. Those who have taken part belong to a fraternity that is forever closed. Years from now, those who are left, no matter how ancient or decrepit, will still get a vicarious pleasure rehashing old times and laughing at jokes that only those who "speak the language" will be able to understand.[148]

---

[147] Kettles, "A Wartime Log"

[148] D Hist, "Governor General's Horse Guards."

SELECT BIBLIOGRAPHY

GENERAL WORKS

Admiralty. *Arctic Convoys, 1941-1945*. London: HMSO, 1954.

Barnett, Corelli. *Engage the Enemy More Closely*. London: Norton, 1991.

Bennett, R. *Ultra in the West: The Normandy Campaign of 1944-45*. NewYork: Charles Scribner's Sons, 1979.

Berger, M., and B.J. Street. *Invasions Without Tears*. Toronto: Random House, 1994.

Copp, T. *The Brigade*. Stoney Creek, Ontario: Fortress Publications, 1992.

Copp, T., and R. Vogel. *Maple Leaf Route: Antwerp*. Alma, Ontario: Maple Leaf Route, 1984.

____. *Maple Leaf Route: Scheldt*. Alma, Ontario: Maple Leaf Route, 1985.

____. *Maple Leaf Route: Victory*. Alma, Ontario: Maple Leaf Route, 1988.

Copp, T., and B. McAndrew. *Battle Exhaustion: Soldiers and Psychiatrists in the Canadian Army, 1939-1945*. Montreal: McGill-Queen's University Press, 1990.

D'Este, C. *Decision in Normandy*. London: Collins, 1983.

Elliott, S.R. *Scarlet and Green*. Toronto: Canadian Intelligence and Security Association, 1981.

Essame, H. *The 43rd Wessex Division at War, 1944-1945*. London: William Clowes, 1952.

Everard, H. *A Mouse in My Pocket*. Picton, Ontario: Valley Floatplane Services, 1988.

Forbes, C. *Fantassin*. Sillery, Quebec: Septentrion, 1994.

Foster, T. *Meeting of Generals*. Toronto: Methuen, 1986.

Graham, D. *The Price of Command: A Biography of General Guy Simonds*. Toronto: Stoddart, 1993.

Greenhous, B., et al. *The Crucible of War: The Official History of the RCAF*, III. Toronto: University of Toronto Press, 1994.

Gray, J.M. *Fun Tomorrow*. Toronto: Macmillan, 1978.

Halliday, H.A. *Typhoon and Tempest*. Toronto: Canav Books, 1992.

Hamilton, N. *Monty: Master of the Battlefield, 1942-1944*. London: Hamish Hamilton, 1983.

____. *Monty: The Field Marshal*. London: Hamish Hamilton, 1986.

Hickey, R. *The Scarlet Dawn*. Campbellton, New Brunswick: Tribune Publishing, 1947.

Hillsman, J.B. *Eleven Men and a Scalpel*. Winnipeg: Columbia Press, 1948.

Hinsley, F.H., et al. *British Intelligence in the Second World War*, III, Part 2. London: HMSO, 1988.

Horrocks, B. *A Full Life*. London: Collins, 1960.

Howard, M. *The Lessons of History*. New Haven: Yale University Press, 1991.

Kaufman, D., and M. Horn. *A Liberation Album: Canadians in the Netherlands, 1944-45*. Toronto: McGraw-Hill Ryerson, 1980.

Lamb, R. *Montgomery in Europe, 1943-45*. London: Buchan and Enright, 1983.

Larrabee, E. *Commander in Chief: Franklin Delano Roosevelt, His Lieutenants and Their War* (New York: Harper and Row, 1987.

Law, C.A. *White Plumes Astern*. Halifax: Nimbus, 1989.

Lawrence, H.E. *A Bloody War*. Toronto: Macmillan, 1979.

____. *Tales of the North Atlantic*. Toronto: McClelland and Stewart, 1985.

Maass, W.B. *The Netherlands at War, 1940-1945*. London: Abelard-Schuman, 1970.

Milberry, L., and H. Halliday. *The Royal Canadian Air Force at War, 1939-1945*. Toronto: Canav Books, 1990.

Ministry of Defence, *U-Boat War in the Atlantic*. London: HMSO, 1989.

Moulton, J.L. *Battle for Antwerp*. London: Ian Allan, 1978.

Nicholson, G.W.L. *Canada Nursing Sisters*. Toronto: Samuel Stevens, Hakkert, 1975.

____. *The Canadians in Italy, 1943-1945*. Ottawa: Queen's Printer, 1957.

Olmstead, B. *Blue Skies*. Toronto: Stoddart, 1987.

Pearce, D. *Journal of a War*. Toronto: Macmillan, 1965.

Phillips, N., and J. Nikerk. *Holland and the Canadians*. Amsterdam: Contact Publishing, 1946.

Roberts, J.A. *The Canadian Summer*. Toronto: University of Toronto Bookroom, 1981.

Roskill, S.W. *The War at Sea*, III, Part 2. London: HMSO, 1961.

Sclater, W. *Haida*. Toronto: Paperjacks, 1980.

Scott, P. *The Battle of the Narrow Seas*. London: Country Life, 1945.

Shores, C. *2nd Tactical Air Force*. Reading: Osprey, 1970.

Schull, J. *The Far Distant Ships*. Ottawa: King's Printer, 1950.

Stacey, C.P. *Six Years of War*. Ottawa: Queen's Printer, 1955.

____. *The Victory Campaign*. Ottawa: Queen's Printer, 1960.

Strong, K. *Intelligence at the Top*. London: Cassell, 1968.

Weigley, R. *Eisenhower's Lieutenants*. Bloomington: Indiana University Press, 1981.

Wemyss, D.E.G. *Walker's Hunting Groups in the Western Approaches*. Liverpool: Liverpool Daily Post and Echo, 1948.

Whitaker, D. and Shelagh. *Tug of War*. Toronto: Stoddart, 1984.

____. *Rhineland*. Toronto. Stoddart, 1989.

Williams, J. *The Long Left Flank*. Toronto: Stoddart, 1988.

REGIMENTAL AND UNIT HISTORIES

A History of the First Hussars Regiment, 1856-1980. The Regiment, 1981.

Barnard, W.T. *The Queen's Own Rifles of Canada,1860-1960*. Toronto: Ontario Publishing, 1960.

Barrett, W.W. *The History of the 13th Canadian Field Regiment*. Holland: The Regiment, 1945.

Bell, T.J. *Into Action with the 12th Field, 1940-1945*. Holland: The Regiment, 1945.

Baylay, G.T. *The Regimental History of the Governor General's Foot Guards*. Ottawa: The Regiment, 1948.

Bird, Will. *No Retreating Footsteps: The Story of the North Nova Scotia Highlanders*. Kentville, Nova Scotia: Kentville Publishing, n.d.

____. *North Shore (New Brunswick) Regiment*. Fredericton: Brunswick Press, 1963.

Boss, W.H. *The Stormont, Dundas and Glengarry Highlanders, 1783-1951*. Ottawa: Runge Press, 1952.

Brown, K., and B. Greenhous. *Semper Paratus: The History of the Royal Hamilton Light Infantry*. Hamilton, Ontario: RHLI Historical Association, 1977.

Buchanan, G.B. *The March of the Prairie Men: A Story of the South Saskatchewan Regiment*. Weyburn, Saskatchewan: The Regiment, 1957.

Cassidy, G.L. *Warpath: The Story of the Algonquin Regiment, 1939-1945*. Toronto: Ryerson, 1948.

Castonguay, J., and A. Ross. *Le Régiment de la Chaudière*. Levis, Quebec: The Regiment, 1983.

Cent ans d'histoire d'un régiment canadien français: Les Fusiliers Mont-Royal, 1869-1969. Montreal: Éditions du Jour, 1969.

Duguid, F. *History of the Canadian Grenadier Guards, 1760-1964*. Montreal: Gazette Printing, 1965.

Fetherstonhaugh, R.C. *The Royal Montreal Regiment*. Westmount, Quebec: Gazette Publishing, 1949.

First Batttalion: The Essex Scottish Regiment, 1939-1945. Aldershot: Gale and Polden, 1946.

First Battalion: The Regina Rifle Regiment, 1939-1946. Regina: The Regiment, 1946.

Goodspeed, D.J. *Battle Royal: A History of the Royal Regiment of Canada, 1862-1962*. Toronto: The Regiment, 1962.

Gouin, J. *Bon Coeur et Bon Bras: Histoire du Régiment de Maisonneuve, 1880-1980*. Montreal: The Regiment, 1980.

Harker, D. *The Story of the British Columbia Regiment, 1939-1945*. Vancouver: privately printed, 1950.

Hayes, G. *The Lincs: A History of the Lincoln and Welland Regiment at War*. Alma, Ontario: Maple Leaf Route, 1986.

Jackson, H.M., ed. *The Argyll and Sutherland Highlanders of Canada (Princess Louise's), 1928-1953*. Montreal: The Regiment, 1953.

Morton, R. *The Fort Garry Horse in the Second World War*. Holland: The Regiment, 1945.

Rogers, R.L. *History of the Lincoln and Welland Regiment*. St. Catharines, Ontario: The Regiment, 1954.

Ross, R.M. *The History of the 1st Battalion Cameron Highlanders of Ottawa (MG)*. Ottawa: The Regiment, 1946.

Roy, R. *Ready for the Fray (Deas Gu Cath): The History of the Canadian Scottish Regiment (Princess Mary's), 1920-1955*. Vancouver: The Regiment, 1958.

Stanley, G. *In the Face of Danger: The History of the Lake Superior Regiment*. Port Arthur, Ontario: The Regiment, 1960.

Tascona, B. *The Little Black Devils: A History of the Royal Winnipeg Rifles*. Winnipeg: Frye Publishing, 1983.

Warren, A. *Wait for the Waggon: The Story of the Royal Canadian Army Service Corps*. Toronto: McClelland and Stewart, 1961.

Willes, J.A. *Out of the Clouds: The History of the 1st Canadian Parachute Battalion*. Port Perry, Ontario: privately printed, 1981.